Biog
G

W9-ADZ-133

JAMES GILLIS, PAULIST

JAMES GILLIS, PAULIST

a biography by

James F. Finley, C. S. P.

HANOVER HOUSE   GARDEN CITY, NEW YORK

Nihil obstat: JUSTIN O'BRIEN, C.S.P., *Censor Deputatus*

Imprimi potest: WILLIAM A. MICHELL, C.S.P., *Superior Generalis*

Nihil obstat: REV. EDWARD J. MONTANO, S.T.D., *Censor Librorum*

Imprimatur: ✠ FRANCIS CARDINAL SPELLMAN, *Archbishop of New York, August 7, 1958*

The nihil obstat and imprimatur are official declarations
that a book or pamphlet is free of doctrinal or moral error.
No implication is contained therein that those who have
granted the nihil obstat and imprimatur agree with the
contents, opinions or statements expressed.

Library of Congress Catalog Card Number 58-12042
Copyright © 1958 by Doubleday & Company, Inc.
Printed in the United States of America
First Edition

TO
WISDOM,
TO
WISDOM'S SPOUSE

PREFACE

If you pick up the average popular book that tells the history of the nineteen-twenties, you won't find the name of James Gillis. Granted, most of the pieces written about the period are frequently out of perspective, being maudlinly nostalgic or wantonly gaudy, but even the fairly sober, faintly scholarly reminiscences seldom include in their reference the item, "Gillis, Rev. James Martin."

You could start in the index at *A* and move past Amos and Andy; Anderson, Sherwood; Arbuckle, Roscoe (Fatty)—skip to the *B*'s and let your finger trace past Berlin, Irving; Browning, Frances (Peaches)—go over the *C*'s, the *D*'s, the *E*'s—move through the whole alphabet and finish at the *Z*'s with names like Ziegfeld, Florenz; Zwillman, Longy—and you will not find the name of James Gillis on the roster.

The bizarre, the outlandish, the inconsequential are listed. For example, you'll find Emile Coué written about in books. In 1923 the dapper, professorially geared Frenchman dropped in on America and sold us a bill of autosuggestion with his catch phrase, "Day by day in every way I am getting better and better." With astonishing eagerness Americans bought the idea of repeating the formula, certain that if they firmly suggested to themselves happiness or affluence or fame these elusives could be achieved. There is no record that anyone except Coué was made happy, rich, or famous by using his theory—yet he is a well-known and well-documented figure of the age.

Along with Coué, Freud is inscribed in the period histories; so also are Al Capone and "Legs" Diamond, Clara Bow and "Cockeye" Mulligan, Mary Pickford and "Black Jack" Pershing—it seems that anybody who was anybody is listed in the annals of this age—but not Father James Gillis. This is a strange fact, because popularity of any sort was so easily gained in this fidgety age of off-with-the-old, on-with-the-new in the matter of novelties and fads, philosophies and personalities.

The overlooking—or ignoring—of Father Gillis in the secular memoirs of the decade is more to be remarked upon when it is realized that in these very years this man was considered in the Catholic Church to be an outstanding orator, lecturer, writer, and editor. It was in this span of time—the glorious, riotous, golden, uninhibited, roaring twenties—that James Gillis reached maturity in his priesthood. If you want to put a date on the point of this maturation, write down October 21, 1923. It was a Sunday, and on the evening of this lovely fall day James Gillis can be said to have arrived at a peak in his Paulist missionary priesthood that was to set him far above his contemporaries in letters and thought.

It was a peak that he would sustain for the next thirty years. He was to cross the country time and again to lecture in metropolitan centers before thousands; as an editor he would be among the first to castigate the deceits of Hitler and Mussolini to the point where these men placed him high on their personal grudge lists. In these thirty years James Gillis would write and preach strongly against labor racketeers and Communist sympathizers and be threatened with violence by both groups. He would become the foremost radio speaker of his day and yet be unceremoniously dropped from a major network. He would earn the displeasure of a President whom he labeled "unfit" and he would face the hatred and rebuke of the people who elected that President to an unprecedented third term. These are a mere scattering of incidents in a life filled with great events for fifty-six priestly years.

James Gillis was one of the most trenchant writers of a quarter century, an orator judged by professionals as a nonpareil, an American fervently and articulately dedicated to his country, her welfare and her ideals, a scholar of vast interests and wide knowledge, a champion of all the oppressed—he was described as "one of the greatest American priests of the twentieth century"—yet he doesn't rate a line in the histories of the decade that saw him burst into the full bloom of that greatness.

A look into his life proves James Gillis deserves better treatment from the world he served so well.

Many of the pages that follow telling of the Gillises—mother, father, brother, and sisters—and the lives they all shared belong justly to Mary and John Gillis. Theirs is the atmosphere that no stranger can capture and theirs are the memories that no outsider can treat tenderly enough to convey the atmosphere. I am grateful for their sharing of these memories.

If you visited Mary and John in their neat, old-fashioned home in Jamaica Plain, outside Boston, you'd be welcomed graciously. Their home has had a long tradition of being open to strangers. The trait of hospitality, inherited from their mother, continues even today despite the inconveniences of advanced old age. Entertaining guests can be a formidable chore when you are over eighty—but Mary and John Gillis push aside those years and allow concern for the visitor to be their only consideration.

Naturally their talk runs to the past, because that is where their fondest recollections lie. "Affectionate Remembrances" could almost be the title of a conversation with them, because affectionateness pervades their speech and manner as they retell the story of their lives. Their speech is gentle, their gestures moderate and controlled, their tone and action indicating the serenity and surety of love that must have been the essence of the Gillis family life.

The greater part of the conversation would go to discussing "Jim"—"Father James"—"Father." The different denominations they gave their priest-brother fall oddly in a pattern that reflects the different aspects under which they recalled him: as brother, inside the family circle with no strangers about, he was "Jim"; as a very special brother with company present and more formality needed, he was "Father James"; as removed, aloof, the famous Paulist involved in worlds beyond their world, he was "Father." Yet the conversation would not extol James Gillis as someone different from the rest of them. To Mary and John he was not developed out beyond the family circle—he was merely part of it—a more famous Gillis than the rest, to be sure, but cradled, schooled, shaped in and by the family influence.

Mary and John Gillis are the kind of boon for which any biographer would give a fortune. They present a picture of their brother James that is as true and real as anyone could want. The story they tell is out of vivid experience and depends not at all on faded photographs or wrinkled documents or crumbling letters. The description of Father Gillis's background, birth, and boyhood rests on no one's fuzzy guess or biased interpretation. This is the story as the Gillis family lived it.

I am equally thankful to the Right Reverend Monsignor Joseph Gibbons of Providence, Rhode Island. His generosity and co-operation in preparing this portrait were most encouraging. As Mary and John Gillis are the living voices of what their brother was in boyhood, Monsignor Gibbons is the living voice of what James Gillis was for all the succeeding years of his life. Monsignor Gibbons spans the whole period of Gillisana from the day James Gillis stepped on St. Charles campus to the day he was interred in the Paulist Church's South Tower Cemetery in New York.

The perspective, the insights, the considerations on Father James Gillis are quite accurately drawn because they are interpreted in the light of a sixty-two-year bosom friendship. Monsignor Gibbons sees James Gillis close up, but the look is candid and honest. There was mutual admiration between these men, but there was never any pretense or sham about their relationship.

I am indebted to all the Paulists for their interest and to the men who suggested details for this portrait of Father Gillis that helped to develop and balance it. Special thanks go to Father Justin O'Brien, C.S.P., who graciously agreed to review the manuscript at its completion.

Last, but so important, my thanks go to the unselfish and faithful assistants who volunteered time after working hours to aid in readying the manuscript—to Helen Fleming for her tireless research, to Louise Wehman, Virginia Theis, and Annette Moglia for their patience in typing and retyping the manuscript.

CONTENTS

JAMES GILLIS, PAULIST

FALSE PROPHETS

chapter 1

James Gillis was an exciting preacher throughout his life. In all his long years, however, he was never any more electrifying than on that fall evening in the early twenties when he began his famous "False Prophets" series at St. Paul the Apostle Church in New York City. The day was Sunday, the date was October 21, 1923, the time was 8 P.M.—James Gillis met and won the acclaim of a church audience that was accustomed only to the very best in preaching. Within a week of his opening service he was rated as "the best of the very best."

The enthusiasm attending this "False Prophets" series was unusual enough to be remembered and remarked on even to the present day. The memories of those who attended the week's lectures are yet vivid with the pictures of the throngs that converged eagerly, animatedly, upon the Paulist Fathers' Fifty-ninth Street parish. From the far reaches of upper Manhattan and the Bronx they came, cross-town from the East Side, up from the Village, over from New Jersey; singly, in clusters, in groups they streamed toward the Ninth Avenue church. Decorously but definitely, as they saw the swelling crowd already jamming the steps ahead of them, they bustled and pushed their way forward, resolving all the while to come an hour earlier the next night just to be sure they'd get a seat.

It was not James Gillis who had initially attracted the majority of these people. St. Paul the Apostle Church had its own reputation solidly established through the years by all the Paulists who had lived and worked at Fifty-ninth Street from the first days of the foundation of the parish.

Even today old parishioners of St. Paul's get a misty look of memory in their eyes when they chat about the early years of their parish. These people remember their West Side of New York when it was not choked with truck traffic, stagnated with warehouses, or run down at the heels by property deterioration. They remember it as a neighborhood of solid, respectable poor and middle-class people sprinkled with a touch of well-to-do and fashionable families. The block or street, as in so many urban centers of the period, was the limit of one's total activities—you lived and played, loved and raised your family, grew old and died all on the block. Life centered around the home and the church and the grouping of such blocks as made your neighborhood.

On the West Side, great parishes like Sacred Heart, St. Matthew's, and St. Paul's were the dominant centers of their respective neighborhoods. Athletic and social rivalries were keen, and pride in one's parish was a not uncommon aspect of the life of the neighborhood. The Paulist parishioners had this pride of parish to a high, and sometimes mighty, degree because they knew the "something special" that surrounded their church.

After all, this was the cradle of the Paulist Community. The spirit of Isaac Thomas Hecker, the zealous founder of the Paulists, permeated the walls, the floors, the columns and arcades of the great church. Touched by the same flame as Father Hecker were George Deshon, Francis Baker, Augustine Hewit, Walter Elliott—in fact, the whole early band of first Paulists who suffered through the beginning years of the Community. The pentecostal zeal of these men made them not just great missionaries—it made them great priests of the people, and the people could not help knowing the interest, the care, the love of these men for them and their families.

The Paulist parishioners took pride in the further knowledge that their huge fort-like church on Ninth Avenue was New York City's focus for Catholic religious services of a special or extraordinary nature. Here the High Mass, the Vespers, the various liturgical functions were conducted with the same precision, grace, and pomp that mark them now. But, even beyond these liturgical attractions, the parishioners knew that their priests had established St. Paul's as a center of good preaching. The oft-repeated phrase of the day summed up the situation—"You always hear a good sermon at the Paulist church."

Preaching was yet a leading interest in the twenties, and a good orator of the decade could muster as great an audience as any other attraction. St. Paul the Apostle Church, the Paulist parish on New York's West Side, made preaching a paramount interest, and to step into the pulpit of this church was to stand in "the pulpit of the day."

Even in the decade that followed, the Paulist pulpit was to maintain a place of prominence in New York. As the thirties approached, interest in preaching waned and religious services were losing ground in their contest with other activities for people's attention, but the church on Ninth Avenue still attracted its crowd.

As late as 1928 the Paulist Fathers introduced a young priest, Fulton J. Sheen from Catholic University, to their New York congregation. The pulpit of the Paulist church was to prove powerful enough to provide a lively springboard that launched a glorious career for the young cleric from Washington, D.C. After two successive seasons of preaching under the Paulist aegis, Father Sheen was to become a New York favorite and in a short time take his place beside Father Gillis as the one-two punch of the NCWC's *Catholic Hour* radio series.

The Paulist church is constructed for great preaching. As one old Paulist Father said, "Every aspect of the building, exterior and interior, allows for no mumbled *fervorino* or casual homily." The church in itself seems to be imperiously demanding eloquence of any man who mounts its pulpit. Its over-all vastness dwarfs you as you step in the great center door and peer down to the apse. The great arched ceiling seems to sweep out of sight as you gaze upward, and awe increases as you move down the aisle and note the unbelievable width of the span that rests on titan-size granite pillars.

With the bright lights thrown on for an evening service, all the spaciousness is exaggerated as shadows deepen the arches and accentuate the width of the aisles that reach to the side walls. And now, as if all this sea of space were not enough to defy a preacher with its demand to be filled, imagine this one last note—the pulpit in the Paulist church is set high above the pews, in the center of the church along the right-side aisle. The preacher standing in that pulpit is struck with the instant realization that the building challenges him to fill its seeming boundlessness.

Pack four thousand people into the pews and aisles below the preacher and you have a faint idea of the reason behind the statement the old Paulist made that St. Paul's allows for no mumbled *fervorino* or casual homily. Such a scene cries for a hero to play it.

On first sight Father Gillis may not have seemed that hero to some of the congregation who came to the first evening of "False Prophets." Sitting in the great church, listening to the organ prelude, those who did not know James Gillis may have speculated on the looks or manner, the weight, the height, the wit or disposition of the preacher who was to appear.

When the warning bell rang and the organ broke off its song

and the throng rumbled noisily to its feet, it is not unthinkable that some felt a stab of disappointment as the preacher of the evening crossed the sanctuary. James Gillis was not a big man physically; he did not possess in his forty-seventh year the profile of a Hollywood juvenile; he could not be said to appear a stirring, exciting speaker.

The front pewholders could see that James Gillis was short and balding. He had a small frame and seemed to be sharp-featured. As he genuflected, turned, and started out of the sanctuary to make his march down the long aisle to the pulpit, the people in the pews near his passage could turn and stare and see him closely. The baldness was not yet complete, but it was obvious time would take care of that. The face was not truly chiseled or hewed to the sharpness of the classic style—rather the sharpness came from an appearance of seriousness and severity that were in the over-all cast of the face.

Nevertheless, the watchers would feel something compelling in the short priest striding to the pulpit. It was in his manner, not his look, and if curiosity forced anyone to turn and stare at the figure moving toward the platform, the viewer would have caught what it was that intrigued. This was a big man's stride—not giant steps, but a giant's step—firm, straight, confident, deliberate. The back was erect, the head almost posed on the shoulders in the manner of a commander, the whole form radiated a sense of power and authority.

Once in the pulpit, James Gillis would seem dominantly tall and the note of authority would spread out from him to the remotest corners of the church. Then, as always, James Gillis would be recognized as having great presence in public. He would stand silently, gazing calmly around at his audience; he would wait until the last cough had been coughed, the last throat cleared; he would delay until silence crept across the immense throng and then—only then—he would begin.

In a clear, strong voice, articulating every syllable, James

Gillis would take command of the evening. With two or three sentences he was in charge of the proceedings and he made that position definite beyond any shadow of vagueness. His voice was not the kind the listener shrugged off or drifted from in distraction. A borrowing from Francis Thompson's *Hound of Heaven* aptly describes Father Gillis's preaching manner. The Paulist spoke:

> *. . . with unhurrying chase,*
> *And unperturbèd pace,*
> *Deliberate speed, majestic instancy . . .*

Each of these poetic lines is an aspect of the delivery that was to make him so outstanding through the years following "False Prophets." There was no haste, no slovenliness as he preached each well-chosen word that built his arguments. And the majestic importance of what he said carried over to his manner. He uttered the powerful and glorious truth in a richly endowed voice and in a singularly noble manner. He was all orator and admittedly—at this moment of 1923—soon to be without a peer among the preachers of the generation.

It is no wonder that by midweek the Paulist Fathers' great church was overflowing. Seats were at a premium. You came early or you remained standing, jammed in, person upon person, clogging the massive aisles that mark off the outlines of the building. Night after night four thousand people packed the great edifice.

As one old tad tells it: "There was never anything like it. I was comin' out o' the house for the third evenin's service. My sister had been after me to go over and hear the man Gillis who was doin' the great preachin'. I got down the street a bit and I wondered what had happened on the El as I watched the mob o' people pilin' down the stairs. The Ninth Avenue elevated train ran by the church front in those days, y' know, and we had a station right here at Fifty-ninth Street.

"Well, I sees this mob and I figured the electric power was dead or somethin' and the conductor had chased the people off the train. But I sees the train start up and rattle on its way uptown and I knew there was nothin' wrong with that train.

"I'm comin' down Ninth myself at the time, and then it hits me. They're goin' to church! It looked like the whole train had emptied out, the mob was that thick, movin' slowly along and toward the front steps. I put on the speed then, because I figured it would be every man for himself once the crowd got inside the church. I could have saved myself the trouble of hurryin'—there wasn't a seat to be had inside. Sure, we always had crowds in those days, y' know, but you could always find a seat here or there in that monstrous big church. This time there was nary a chair to be had and I had to stand for the full piece the man Gillis delivered.

"Ah, but it was a great bit o' preachin' and worth the standin' for. The man Gillis never swallowed a word that had to be said, and that night he was givin' it to them good. He was a great talker always, and that first night I heard him he was at his best.

"I got back to hear him later in the week—the last night, I think it was—and the people were out in abundance—more than I'd ever seen before. As I said, we always had a good crowd for everything in those days, but I think the man Gillis's turnout was the greatest.

"Ah well, now, I think it should have been because the man was the greatest himself in his day. There were few preachers could hold his hat—an odd one here or there, y' know, could put the fear o' God in us—but this man Gillis was always a treat to us, and that time he talked on Shaw and the rest of them blatherers he was at his best."

The first lecture was on George Bernard Shaw, whose preeminence in the 1920's and after was unchallenged. Shaw was so much the leader of the years before and after World War I that advertisements of his books could allege, "When Shaw speaks, all the world listens." Not all the people in the world who listened believed what they heard, but enough believed to make Shaw popular and well to do and imitated.

Father Gillis was one of the strong disbelievers as he commented on Shaw:

> His method is that of a mountebank, or a jester. His symbol is the cap and bells, his prototype the court fool. The fool was privileged to cut capers before the very face of the king. He might insult the king, mock him, mimic him, laugh uproariously at him. . . . And, to use a clownish phrase, he could "get away with it." . . . So, Shaw's trick is to insult those by whose favor he lives. He snaps his fingers in the face of his audience or his readers. He hits them on the head, sometimes with an airy bladder, more often with a knotted club. He tickles them with a rapier, and while they laugh, he sticks it between their ribs. For he is a murderous joker.

The words must have thrilled many people who had been confounded by the jibes and swipes of Shaw. To hear the debunker debunked was solace to those who had begun to wonder if they were out of step with the world because they could not assimilate Shaw's horribly profane but very popular utterances.

Father Gillis gave Shaw no more mercy than the author had allowed others. He continued:

> I dare not deny that he is brilliant. But if one asks me to confess that Shaw is an original thinker, I demur. For it seems to me that any fairly attentive reader of Shaw must quickly detect the fact that Shavian "originality" is in reality ready-made. He follows a formula. The formula is to ridicule what the human race reverences, and to extol what the human race abominates.

Then followed a neat scalpeling job on Shaw's writings. Example after example was peeled from the formula until it was revealed in its stark fleshless structure. The irreverence, the sham, and the danger of George B. Shaw were just as unsparingly tackled by Father Gillis.

Finally he concluded—and the church must have vibrated when his great voice pounded out the last sentences:

> As for us, we consider Shaw a misanthrope, a satirist without a heart, a pessimist, an immoralist, and an atheist. . . . Our hope for the salvation of society is bolstered up by a belief that Shaw's importance is enormously overestimated. If it be true that "when he speaks, all the world listens," we hope it is also true that the larger and saner part of that world not only listens but condemns.

These words are not what made "False Prophets" a success from the first evening. They aided in stirring the audience to interest and enthusiasm, but the power behind the words was the delivery of a master preacher slowly schooled in Paulist mission experience, finished and polished by years of public sermons and lectures.

What was giving impact to the subject matter is described by Father John C. Selner, S.S.:

> As a preacher and lecturer he was irresistible. His manner was perfectly consonant with his thoughts. He could put new meanings into words by the way he pronounced them. His whole body strained with his message, calm or vigorous or limp or cautious. He could declaim in a high-pitched, strident voice or recite on a low, foreboding tone or whisper with perfect distinctness; he could change suddenly from an impassioned orator to a man who had some inconsequential remarks to make to an acquaintance on the street. He had perfect control: slowness, speed, emphasis, melody, mock dramatics, sarcasm, holiness, awe, disgust, joy, wistfulness—whatever the message required! His style as a speaker was utterly unique. Anyone who would try to copy him would make a freak of himself. But when he spoke, he used every elocutionary device at the right moment and with fascinating effect.

The Shaw lecture whetted the appetite of those who attended the Sunday opening, and their enthusiasm was contagious. Word-of-mouth advertising packed St. Paul's for the Monday evening lecture on H. G. Wells.

James Martin Gillis lived up to every enthusiastic rave he'd received. He was the quintessence of urbanity and wit as he discussed Wells. Reading his talk, you can sense the delicate half-smile that must have played on his lips, the humor that must have lighted his eyes as he spoke:

> The worlds that Wells creates are, of course, incomparably better than the one created by God. The populations of Wells's worlds are as superior to the scrubby human beings who infest this earth, as we, in turn, are superior to the Cromagnon man or the Neanderthaler. His wars also are greater than ours. Our biggest was the World War. His is the *War of the Worlds*—not nations against nations, but planets against planets. Wells always "thinks big." He knows no boundaries. He is at home in the "great open spaces"—between the stars. How inept, therefore, and woefully inadequate is such a compliment as that of Anatole France, who says, "Wells is the greatest intellectual force in the English-speaking world." The "English-speaking world!" What a sphere of influence for a man whose vision comprises universes! A bungling compliment, indeed, to one whose *bête noire* is nationalism; whose immediate goal is internationalism; whose ultimate or, at least, penultimate ambition is interplanetarianism.

This was one of the opening paragraphs of the lecture. From this high point Father Gillis built his satiric analysis of H. G. Wells. Titters, laughs, an unrestrained guffaw or two greeted each reduction of Wellsian thought to its absurd conclusion. The crowd, enjoying the sharp puncturing thrusts, was in high spirits, yet never beyond the masterful control for which James Gillis was to become famous as a speaker. As always, he wanted

the smiles and laughs, used them to drive home his argument
that Wells was too ridiculous to take seriously.

On Tuesday, the third evening in the series, even the most
carping of critics agreed that James Gillis was here to stay as
an orator. He spoke on Sigmund Freud and tackled a subject
that was growing as controversial as any the age had seen.
Freud had been almost a quarter century on the scene at this
time, but the Freud furor was only breaking on the surface of
our society. It was the old story of a scientific theory taking a
generation to filter down from professors to people. In 1923
there was a lot of talk but not much accurate information concerning the Freudian concepts. Confused—more often mud-
dled—applications and discussions of the psychoanalysis theory
had brought a peculiar disorder to the era's thinking on moral
issues, especially those of a sexual nature.

The Freud lecture was not given in a humorous vein, because
Freud was not a man to take lightly. James Gillis was serious,
perhaps best described as grim, as he went at his task of considering Sigmund Freud's theory. He overlooked none of its
pitfalls and did not side-step any of its embarrassing aspects.
With eminent fairness he admitted its possibilities for the future
and granted the benefit that might come if a more correct approach to mental analysis were developed.

His summary is a cool, balanced appraisal of the basic
Freudian teaching, of the rabid cult it had been turned to, and
of the boon it could become. In 1923 James Gillis was twenty
years ahead of his age when he said:

> There is generally some truth and some wisdom even in
> the most perverse philosophies. Underlying the theory and
> practice of psychoanalysis is some of the virtue of the
> Catholic Confessional. As far back as the third century of
> our era, Origen advocated confession because it "external-
> izes the rottenness." The *Following of Christ* advises sin-
> ners to "spit the poison out." And all the world is aware that

"Open confession is good for the soul." . . . If it were possible to provide a class of practitioners of psychoanalysis, well trained, discreet, accustomed to mental and spiritual discipline, and sincerely interested in morality, the new art and science, if such it be, might be a boon to the human race, second only to the immeasurable boon of the use of the Sacrament of Penance.

But the literature of psychoanalysis and our experience of so-called "psychologists" give us little reason to hope for the existence of such a body of trained and virtuous psychoanalysts. . . . Until the psychoanalysts tone down their doctrines and purify their notions of ethics, until they expurgate the animalistic theories that so permeate and vitiate their systems, we shall be wary of them.

Sir Arthur Conan Doyle, Friedrich Nietzsche, and Ernst Haeckel were the subjects of the evenings from Wednesday through Friday. These talks are equal to the others for the humor, satire, logic, and style that fill each discourse and raise it far above average.

The crowds, as noted, increased with each succeeding evening. Yet it is unfair to stress the size of the congregation without indicating that this is not the only remarkable quality about the people who attended. They manifested an extraordinary variety of age, occupation, intellectual grasp, spiritual depth, and religious interest. Each throng held its solid core of the educated and uneducated, the young and the old, Catholics and non-Catholics—and, James Gillis might interrupt if he read that statement, "the sane and the insane."

He delighted in telling the story concerning himself and the accolade passed on his "False Prophets" series by a fugitive from a mental hospital. The patient had skipped from an upstate asylum and had come to New York City. He was harmless, and tractable on all occasions except one—when listening to a sermon.

Complaints from a number of churches led the authorities

to know he was in the area. The police were eager to pick him up, and this eagerness was shared understandably by the preachers who had been victims of his open and on-the-spot critique of their oratorical efforts. After a week of covering the critic's favorite churches the police tagged him and entrusted him to Bellevue. The doctors found the case simple enough but were fascinated by the man's mania regarding sermons.

"What is there about sermons that attracts you?" asked one of the examiners.

"It's not the sermons," replied the man, "it's the preaching of them. I can't stand bad preaching—that's why I tell these fellows what I think of their talks."

"You think you know good preaching when you hear it?"

The critic smiled tolerantly. "Of course I do. I'm an expert on speaking. I know a good preacher when I hear one."

The doctor riffled the cards before him. "These complaints seem to indicate you haven't found one preacher in New York who satisfies your standard."

"That's not true," the patient shouted, eyes lighting brightly. "There's one I could listen to forever—he's the best I've ever heard."

The doctor restrained the enthusiast and asked quietly, almost casually, "And who would that be?"

"Father James Gillis," was the fervent reply of the maniac. "He's the very best—he's *my* kind of preacher."

In a more serious vein, a modest and brief record that Father Gillis made in his preaching journal indicates how exceptional were some of the types in his audiences. Under the heading of October 21–28 he made this notation:

> Nine Lectures—False Prophets
> Great interest—more than ever. Specially large number —notable predominance of men—of young people (20 to

30) and those who seem addicted to some intellectual life.

They formed a group afterward—called Paulist Lecture Committee for purpose of continuing interest in similar future lectures. I am booked to lecture once a month.

These two short paragraphs of jottings tell us rather concisely how true and how towering was the peak at which James Gillis had arrived. The congregation was notable for its predominance of men, young people, and intellectuals.

To conquer the disinterest that men have in church services was as much a problem in the America of the twenties as it was (and is) in any country of any time. A poor preacher has trouble getting anyone inside the church, an averagely equipped man can attract women, a good preacher will manage to draw a fair sprinkling of men among a preponderantly female audience—only a truly great preacher attracts a congregation that shows a predominance of men.

The remarked-on presence of so many people in the twenty- and thirty-year brackets shows that Father Gillis was offering leadership in thought to those who were at a crucial period of their lives. These young people were aware, consciously or unconsciously, that the future was their great responsibility. Their elders by twenty or thirty years had led them into war; their world was a shambles where graciousness and good manners, decency and high morals were shattered and fractured things; their hope for a tomorrow of peace and serenity was looking wanner and paler with each passing day. They needed direction in a rudderless existence, and their faithful pursuance of Father Gillis's talks indicated they thought that he would settle their course.

The seekers after the intellectual life—the third group noted as a surprise element in the attendance—tip off the climaxing argument to prove that James Gillis had "arrived." In 1923 intellectualism had taken a strange turn. Like hydrochloric acid splashed on cloth, cynicism was eating huge holes in the mental pattern of the nation. Nothing was sacred to the scoffers who led the parade—and the scoffers were becoming the admired and the imitated. Shocking people became almost a game, and part of the shock treatment was the debunking of all things sacred, human, or divine.

God could not escape the debunkers. They lugged out their new-found and cockily spouting champion, Modern Science, and had him blast God away. They drafted their darling irreverents, the littérateurs and wits, and had them poeticize or laugh God away. They wheeled up their philosophers and sophisticates of logic and had them explain God away. It was a loud and repetitious and long-drawn-out argument, this postwar vetoing of God.

Those who rejected the debunkers needed a leader, a counterpunching champion. For these intellectuals who thought the mind deserved a greater use than making it a storage place for junk and rationalistic garbage, James Gillis took on that role. He was the sign that pointed to a deeper, finer source of wisdom; but most of all, he was the symbol of valorous refusal to drift with the crowd. He was what the Christian intellectuals needed so badly—a courageous voice that was not afraid to shout out that the world was wrong in denying God a place in its plan.

One last facet of this series of lectures that should be stressed is that the talks presaged the whole future of James Gillis's life. His challenge to the false prophets of the nineteen-twenties aptly describes the remainder of his years in the priesthood.

The series of talks shows us a man reaching out mightily to shoulder whatever staggering burden Truth could bring. In 1923 the acceptance, the quoting, the preaching, the championing of men like George Bernard Shaw, Sigmund Freud, Arthur Conan Doyle, H. G. Wells, Friedrich Nietzsche, Ernst

Haeckel was *the thing* to do. There were many more pundits and leaders of thought than these men, but these were the leaders of the popular phases of the new intellectual revolt that was sparking forward in the twenties.

James Gillis picked these men as the subjects of his great series of lectures. They were the giants, and Father Gillis had the courage of heart and conviction of mind that made him think the giants should be tackled first. And in more than stature, the short, agile, zealous preacher played the David to these modern Goliaths. He risked the consequences that all the Davids must face when they tackle the giants—whether they be the Goliaths of Social Complacency or Irreligion or False Philosophy or Popular Opinion or any of the other behemoth-like factors that challenge God and His Truth. He was too sharp, too wise not to know what he faced when he determined to buck the trend.

The expression, "he determined to buck the trend," does not mean that Father Gillis set out on a plan of opposition or contrariness for its own sake. He is not the clerical counterpart of the man who joined a political club and when asked what it stood for replied, "Sure, it's a grand outfit. It stands for bein' *agin* everything!"

Father Gillis did not buck the trend because it was the sensational thing to do and guaranteed to create interest in himself. His first search was for truth—and therefore, necessarily, he opposed evil under any guise or disguise. All of the evil that was due to popular misconception or that came from the chicanery of leaders, he faced courageously and he opposed that evil no matter how expensive the choice might prove ultimately. This is demonstrated in the future years of his life under the severest conditions. In fact, this dedication to tell the whole truth no matter what the cost was a thing of growing conviction. The vocation deepened through the years, and each succeeding issue of those years fixed James Gillis more firmly in his zealousness.

Father Gillis must have known a little of what lay ahead. He had many examples to consider, many biographies and auto-biographies that pointed up the penalty of such a career. If he looked no farther than his own Community's patron, St. Paul, he had a vivid example of where the road upon which he had set himself could end.

Any day he chose, Father Gillis could walk out into St. Paul's Church and gaze at the stirring mural depicting the death of the Great Apostle to the Gentiles. Old, bald, a little wizened, weary-looking—and alone—St. Paul kneels, ringed by enemies. A hulking executioner stands ready to sweep a sword through the hushed morning air and sever the tired head from the stooping shoulders. In this scene James Gillis had his answer to the question: How much does it cost to preach truth in season and out of season?

A more telling note on St. Paul can be found in Father Gillis's own words, and it might be a hint of the kind of martyrdom that the priest foresaw for himself. As you read the passage you wonder if James Gillis suspected the words could be written concerning his own future. Interestingly enough, the selection comes from the very series under discussion, "False Prophets."

In one of the early talks of the week, under the title "The Revival of Paganism," Father Gillis spoke about St. Paul and his preaching to the pagans of the first century. He said:

> If he had recited . . . metaphysical nonsense slowly, solemnly, and with a mystic chant; if he had rolled his eyes and softly modulated his voice; if he had spoken his message to the accompaniment of excellent music, his hearers might have cried out, "Hail, wiser than Socrates; hail, profounder than Plato; hail, prince of philosophers!"
>
> But no, he talked only of sin and repentance and judgment, of the recompense of good and of evil; so they told him he was mad. They dismissed him with a polite lie, as

men speak to be rid of the insane, "We will hear thee
again"; and when he was gone, they chuckled and laughed
and said, "The fool!"

James Gillis could have gained much more fame than the
histories of the past half century allot him had he wanted to
woo the world's favor by nonsense-talking and quack writing.
As we have seen, he couldn't get his name in the annals of the
twenties, yet he could have had reams of copy in the decade's
record if he had wanted to boob the sincere and cozen the
earnest in their desperate quest of truth.

He chose the more difficult path and surely knew that, like
Paul, he stood the chance of being called "the fool." The appellation could come in many ways—openly, subtly, in overt
flattery or open neglect, in mock attention or silent disapproval. You need not shout, "You fool!" in a man's face for him
to know you think him one. There are techniques the world
employs for rendering its decision that a man is a fool, and
Father Gillis must have weighed the possibility that he would
be the victim of such techniques.

He was the victim—all his life.

All the suspicions about his future that he might have had in
1923, when the serious, the interested, the virtuous minority
took him for their champion, came true. He was to see his
burdensome vocation become saggingly heavy; he was to know
the depth of rejection and the sting of defeat; he was to be
criticized, jeered, and rebuked for his ideas, but he was never
to quit his course—telling the truth against whatever big lie
was being told the world.

All the circumstances of James Gillis's life shaped around
him to frame this dedication he made toward Truth. His meri-
torious part in the picture is the evident talents he cultivated so
that he would be equipped to accomplish the charge—the
courageous will he strengthened to be able to continue the role

—the breadth and depth of spirit he developed to enable him to sustain the burden.

These are the triple sides that bounded his world. Within this triangle he lived his life, fashioned his priesthood, and faced his God. Out of its details, his story is told.

THE WELLSPRING

chapter II

There is an old Irish expression concerning children and their behavior which states succinctly, "Whatever they have and whatever they are, they don't get from the wind."

This old wives' dictum might seem to be an oversimplification of the modern psychological debate concerning environment vs. heredity; actually the maxim neatly covers the argument and accurately sums its conclusions. Children do not inherit size, temperament, personality, or character from the breeze that blows by a home. They are born, participators in example factors (good or bad) their parents manifest before them.

James Gillis was blessed on both sides of the formula "heredity × environment = the individual." The wellspring of his progenitors ran from a deep and clear source, and the parents to whom he was born provided saintly example to imitate. With such balance in his beginning, it is no wonder he grew up to the stature that marked his years in the priesthood.

James Gillis was born in Boston, Massachusetts, on November 12, 1876. His birthplace was within a stone's throw of the very spot where eighty years later he would stand and watch Archbishop Richard Cushing dedicate a Catholic Information Center in his name.

The ancestry of both his parents, James Gillis and Catherine Roche, was Irish. Neither parent came from Europe, both being first-generation Irish born on the American continent. The distinction of birth on the American continent as against birth in the United States is made by the family, since James Gillis senior saw the light of day in Montreal, Canada.

Father Gillis's paternal grandparents were residents of Enniskillen, County Fermanagh, Northern Ireland. They married there and decided on a honeymoon journey that would include a look at the fabulous world they had heard about in America. Their itinerary called for them to visit Canada, continue to the United States and settle—or return—depending upon their reaction to what they saw. The honeymooners never got to the United States. Montreal fascinated them with its Old World charm and piety, and they made their decision to look no farther. James Gillis senior and two other children were born in the ten years the couple had together. Death separated the young wife from the family at the end of this time.

All stories have within themselves other stories that intrigue and attract. This short-lived bride offers one of those charming side roads of investigation. We have time only for the briefest of glances down the road. The young woman—Mary and John Gillis heard her talked about as Grandmother Greene—was the daughter of a schoolteacher in Ireland. The father was tutor to the family of the Duke of Enniskillen and schoolmaster for the local boys. The man believed in education for all—girls as well as boys—and he braved the dislike of his neighbors by tutoring his own girl along with the children of the Duke. As a result the young lady was different from all the other ladies and lassies of her village—too different—she was the only one who could read a paper or book, figure a sum, write a note or a letter.

How true it is that one small change in our lives can affect the world of people who come after us. The young Miss

Greene loved reading history, absorbed the stories of peoples, their movements, their marches, their settlements and discoveries. She had been educated to a discontent with the small village that bound her. Fortunately she found a young man who had the same deep want of more space in which to grow, and their marriage began symbolically in a trip to a new world.

James Gillis senior had nine years with this mother. He indicated often to his own children that this woman was the greatest single influence of his life. As Mary Gillis recollects her father's remarks about Grandmother Greene she says: "Pa claimed he took everything from his mother. . . . She must have been a wonderful woman. He worshiped her and never got over her death. . . . She was only twenty-nine. . . . He said anything his mother told him, that's what he lived up to all his life."

Of all that James Gillis senior took from his mother, one thing was the desire to see more than the spot where he was born. When he reached his majority he decided to head for the United States. He had studied to be a machinist and he used the trade to work his way from Montreal down through New England and finally to Boston.

The senior Gillis had not come to look anything over; he had come to stay. Within a year of his arrival in 1870, he became a naturalized citizen. Such a definite drive toward permanency might have been given a nudge by the fact that in that same year he had met Catherine Roche of Cambridge.

Catherine was deeply in love with the young Canadian machinist, but with strange female reservations. Her vanity was wounded when she was teased by family and girl friends about the "boy" with whom she was "keeping company." Catherine Roche was beginning to find herself taking long, hard looks at her fiancé and she was having to admit he *did* look like a boy. It was an uneasy evening in the family parlor when she decided to broach the subject, but James Gillis took it well.

"I can't help my looks," he said quietly. "I work a man's job and earn a man's salary—I vote and my birth certificate says I'm over twenty-one. What more can I do to prove I'm a man?"

"There is something," Catherine replied, "but I'm afraid to mention it."

"What is it? Tell me and I'm for doing it."

Catherine Roche took a deep breath and then lost courage as she contemplated her suggestion. When she finally spoke her voice was small and hardly audible. "You could grow a beard." Her face was flaming and she didn't think she would blame this man if he ran out the door and never came back.

The bridal picture shows who won the evening. A lovely girl stands proudly beside a dignified, serious, handsomely mustached and bearded man. The decoration that made for maturity remained for the rest of the elder James Gillis's life. None of his children ever saw their father without the pale reddish beard that had won him a bride.

Boyishness did not mark the man as husband and father. He was completely in charge of his home and family. Within a few years of marriage the family numbered four children around its table. Mary came first, then James, followed by John and Katherine. A fifth child, a boy, survived only ten days.

Apparently James Gillis senior was the focus of training in the family. John Gillis said, "We were always trained by Pa. Since the day we could learn, he took care of us. Not that Ma didn't do it too, but when Pa was in the house he was in charge of us."

Mary Gillis elaborated on this by adding, "He always heard our prayers, every morning and night, and they had to be just so—but he was wonderful with us and never had a hard word if we missed."

The father was not a disciplinarian or martinet. His deep, abiding affection was the secret of his success with his family. This and the sterling example of his own solid character were the great forces that persuaded his household to follow him in his leadership.

James Gillis junior took after his father. He looked like him and acted like him. Mary Gillis says, "Jim was just like Pa. He was fair and had the deepest blue eyes, and he had the same way of holding himself—straight up and down even when a little fellow. In so many ways I could see Pa in him—in the studying and learning of his lessons, especially the catechism—they were so much alike."

Jim was like Pa, but with the great difference of all Jims who resemble their Pa—he was going to have chances Pa never dreamed of. James Gillis junior was to be afforded all the vast scope of education that his father had had to forgo. Not only had the boy indicated an appetite for learning, but he had demonstrated a capacity for it far beyond the average. Both appetite and capacity would be given the greatest of opportunity.

The principal of the public grade school was among the first to spot the possibilities that lay ahead for young Jim Gillis. All the Gillis children attended the local school—there was no parochial school at that time—but it was about James that the headmaster came to see the father. "Keep that boy at school," the man advised. "Keep him at it as long as you can afford it. He's got a good head on him and should be permitted to make the most of it."

James Gillis senior had already made up his mind to that. As a machinist his salary was not making the family rich, but they were comfortable, and a little could be put aside regularly for the boy's education. The father had long suspected that his namesake was unusually gifted—he had learned that fact to his own confusion on one occasion when proctoring the children's homework.

One evening all the children had been set to studying their lesson and readying their assignments for the next day at school.

The father and mother went off to the living room to talk about their respective days and chat over the problems and plans that concerned the raising of a family.

After a short time young Jim got up from the study group and walked inside to join his parents.

Mr. Gillis looked challengingly at his son. "Aren't you supposed to be getting your lesson? I thought you complained earlier that you had an especially hard one for tomorrow."

"I have it, Pa," answered Jim.

"In so short a time? I don't believe it."

"Honest, Pa, I can prove it," asserted the youngster.

Mr. Gillis rose from his chair. "You'll have to prove it," he stated firmly, leading the boy outside. "Where's the book?"

Jim handed his assignment over to his father.

"Go ahead," commanded Mr. Gillis, "and you'd better have it perfect."

When the young man finished he glanced around at his brother and sisters, savoring their admiring looks.

The elder Gillis was as much in admiration as the others, but he carried off the moment with true parental grace. "That's fine," he commented, handing back the book, "but better look over it once more. There's nothing like being doubly sure about having it down."

Upon the completion of grade school James Gillis was entered in Boston English, the high school nearest his home. At the end of his freshman year he transferred to Boston Latin School. The request to be allowed to transfer was his own; the family concurred in the transfer with their prayers that he could fulfill the requirements.

In James Gillis's boyhood days the Latin School, even as today, was one of the outstanding high schools in the East. Its rating was so high and its requirements so demanding that only top-grade students could hope to maintain its pace. To be graduated from Boston Latin School was like having a head start in life's race. There was a noticeable impression made by any family that could speak of their boy as "from Boston Latin." Listeners would nod their heads sagely, as if indicating that this family had little to worry about except where and how soon to retire and live off their successful son.

Young Jim Gillis was to have all this taken-for-granted glory —*if* he made the grades—especially *the* grade. The steep levy put on his possible future graduation from Boston Latin was that he must finish the four years in three. He had completed his freshman year in another high school, but the new authorities felt some adjustment should be made to insure the fact that he would be a totally Boston-Latin-educated man. Couldn't he repeat his first year along with his other courses?

He could and he did. Jim finished the four years on schedule, graduating in the same year as did his old chums whom he had left at Boston English. There is much more to this than the simple fact of graduating indicates. Young Gillis didn't just squeak through, panicked and frayed from the effort of covering the four-year course in the shorter time.

He collected scholastic prizes in the three years despite the pressure he was under. At the end of his course James Gillis climaxed his spectacular high school career by being chosen class valedictorian. The young orator's stirring speech was applauded enthusiastically. The rich young voice, the earnest manner, the spirited delivery captured the feelings of the assembly. The applause had hardly died when James Gillis was again called to stand before the crowded hall. The announcement vibrated through the hall that the talented senior had won the coveted Franklin History Medal, one of the outstanding awards of the school year. This time the applause was vigorous, warm, prolonged.

The Gillises were bursting with mixed feelings that had them alternating between smiles and tears. They wanted to get outside and breathe or they'd explode with the joy and pride that swelled inside them as they heard the handclapping that greeted their Jim's second appearance. And as they looked around at some of their seat-neighbors they knew they were not alone in the feelings that swept them. The glowing faces and broad smiles of many nearby meant that others also appreciated the young student's accomplishments.

James Gillis was Irish and Catholic and had topped the competition in the toughest course any student could face. He stood pre-eminent in an atmosphere where superiority meant surpassing the best. Like the youngster who makes the Notre Dame first squad, he had had to compete against the cream of the other schools, and he had competed the hard way—being allowed less time to accomplish more. And, again, he was Irish, he was Catholic.

In the late eighteen hundreds, Boston could not be described accurately as an Irish Catholic city. Certainly there were Irish Catholics there and in some abundance, but they were not the factor in Boston's life that they were later to become. To be Irish and Catholic in those days was still to mean living under a handicap—you were type-cast as poor, ignorant, slum-reared, and second-rate. Only the penumbral reaches of the future prestige and power of the Irish Catholics had been touched in 1895, the year Jim Gillis graduated from the Latin School.

That "one of their own" soared high above all the better-familied fledglings in his school was a sweet victory for the Irish Catholics. It was a justifiable pride that they manifested. After all, they desperately needed all these occasions to prove to their neighbors that they were capable of a scope of life far greater than the wretched homes and ghetto to which so many had been confined since the 1850's.

Jim Gillis was not conscious of all these currents and crosswinds that swirled around him. He was not making issues out of his lineage nor fomenting crises over his school report card. The issues in such instances are made by history; Jim Gillis's small part in this emergence of the Irish Catholic factor in Boston is mentioned in passing as a tiny ripple in the rising tide.

Jim himself at this time seemed to be as interested in baseball as he was in studies. He took the scholastic side seriously when studies were due, but he relished the play side when studies were over.

He had proved an adept scholar, but he was as proud of having made the Boston Latin baseball squad as he was over his Franklin Medal. After his first year at Latin, he went out for the school's team. There were a few smiles as "the little guy" trotted out with the big fellows, and maybe the grins were justified until proved otherwise. Jim Gillis had a bantam build and as a boy could easily have been nicknamed "Shorty" or "Tiny" or "Junior." He certainly didn't look like an outfielder despite his strong-voiced announcement to the coach that that was where he played. The coach hesitated, wondering perhaps if the boy could reach second base with a throw, let alone home plate—or, worse, would he get lost in the tall grass of some un-mowed park in which they played?

Jim didn't get lost, and he reached the plate with many a throw—he made the Boston Latin first squad solidly. The following year when he came out for the team there were no tolerant smiles or grins. There were votes to elect the new cap-tain of the team—Jim Gillis. That year he transferred to third base, a position better suited to his size and nimbleness. Young Gillis more than vindicated his teammates' choice of him to lead the squad. When the all-state team was selected at the end of the season James Gillis rested solidly at his new posi-tion. He topped the list in balloting for the best schoolboy third baseman throughout Massachusetts.

James Gillis gave no indications all through these years that the priesthood was in his thoughts. "Jim was not a pious boy in the way you'd think a future priest would be," says Mary. "Maybe we had crazy notions about these things. I guess we think a boy should be a mollycoddle, but Jim was none of that. . . . Oh, he was a good boy, real good—never a profanity or answering back to Pa—but there seemed nothing special, y'know."

Jim kept whatever thinking he was doing on the subject of a vocation strictly to himself. He might have been deeply involved in his interior soul, but he did not "pull a long face" in the family circle. There is evidence that he was acting in exactly the opposite manner than might be expected in such a situation. Acquaintances of a later day regarded him as very serious, close to being grim, when weighing important decisions. None of this mood was on him during this most important time of choosing his career.

Mary Gillis reveals that "he was full of fun." John corroborates this in his remarks that "Jim was not a wild joker, but he liked lots of humor. He'd have everybody in stitches with his mimicry and speeches. We used to go every Christmas Eve to visit friends of ours, and on those times I can recall the girls laughing so loudly at Jim's jokes that Ma had to tell him to stop for fear of the neighbors' being disturbed."

Jim Gillis was not the court-jester type at any time in his life, despite the seeming hilarity commented on in the Christmas Eve incidents. John Gillis is trying to convey some idea of the keen sense of humor and good high spirits that were trade-marks of Father Gillis all his priestly life. John is harmonizing the lights and darks of his brother's boyhood portrait. We are being shown the bright bands of youthful zest that are in the picture along with the somber tones of scholarliness. Simply, Jim Gillis was as balanced and integrated a young man in his personal and social life as could be demanded for his years.

Out of such balance and integration and a great desire to bring these characteristics to perfection came James Gillis's drive to become a priest. He made the announcement to his family after he had finished his freshman year at old St. Charles College in Ellicott City, Maryland. His intention had not been made clear to his mother and father when he'd entered St. Charles. They knew vaguely as he departed for the Maryland college that he was pondering a choice of careers. The parents knew that Jim had not fixed on any definite goal, although there had been suggestions from relatives and friends on all sides that he follow law or medicine or politics or teaching.

One old friend of the family had his own idea about Jim's future, but he had talked about the idea to no one but Jim himself. Father James O'Brien, assistant priest at St. James during the time the Gillises lived in the parish, had marked the boy for big things in God's service.

Father O'Brien taught Sunday school at St. James, and Jim Gillis was in his class. He had noted the sharp and prodding questions of the fair-haired tot who came faithfully each Sunday after Mass to learn the catechism. When the priest had tested the child with queries a little beyond the lesson for the day, he was delighted with the attempts that the boy made to answer.

When Jim Gillis passed to the higher grades, Father O'Brien followed his progress, called him in for counsel, directed his reading, and ultimately told Jim that he thought he should consider the priesthood.

The boy's response was not enthusiastic, not because of any repugnance to the idea, rather because the suggestion had surprised him. His own thoughts had skirted around, dashed in upon, ran from and back to the possibility that he had a vocation to Holy Orders. He had been thrilled by the contemplation of the priesthood, but he had honestly wondered if he belonged in so high an estate.

The reaction was as normal as having a taste for ice cream. Millions of Catholic boys gaze upward on a priest at Mass and feel that surge of desire to be a part of the awesome dignity of Christ's priesthood. In an instant the same million boys are plunged downward in sincere youthful abashment that they have considered themselves worthy of such a pinnacle. Some never permit the thought to rise again, prevented (or preventing themselves) by one cause or another from assaying the great dream again. Some turn to prayer and the seeking of counsel, begging God and competent men to help them decide whether that first movement toward the altar is a vocation or a passing fancy.

James Gillis was among the second group and he cherished the advice and confidence of Father O'Brien. He knew, however, that he must make his own decision. Father O'Brien could do no more than point to the altar—Jim Gillis must open the gate and mount the steps for himself.

Seven diaries of James Gillis were found after his death. The first entry of the earliest of the septet is dated October 20, 1895, and the last entry of the seventh book is headed December 21, 1900. In five years, two months, and one day, James Gillis took great strides forward to the priesthood, but the path down which he strode shifted, veered sharply, disappeared, and came to view again on an entirely different road in an entirely different terrain. Once upon the new way, he never faltered, but the time spent in reaching that way was torturously frustrating and discouraging.

The diaries are filled with entries faithfully made from the first month at St. Charles to the reception of subdiaconate for the Paulist priesthood. What prompted the keeping of these journals is not indicated. James Gillis states only the resolution "to write something every day, whether it be important or not," as his explanation for recording his life.

Did he think his thoughts so important that they should be preserved for posterity? Such a question arises always when journals and notebooks are found among the effects of public figures. Truly enough, only the author of the diaries could answer us.

There is no doubt that any intelligent, seriously thoughtful person must realize when he makes notes on his moods and changes, records his thoughts and activities, that all these words may someday be read or published. Library shelves are filled with thousands of biographies that any earnest boy may read. It shouldn't take him long to learn that much of the biography is the subject's own notes, letters, and assorted writings. When the boy daydreams of his personal future and envisions success in his hoped-for career, he cannot help including the possibility that someone may even write *his* life. That lurks in his mind (no matter how hard he tries to push it aside) and it does affect his diary. Even if he never alludes to this daydream, his entries are influenced and they become more self-conscious account-ings of his living than those an outsider may give.

When you have someone who adds to this personal-history consciousness a literary bent of mind, your hope of getting a true picture of the subject becomes vastly more complicated. Now you have someone who not only is careful about what he puts down but is careful about how he phrases it.

The James Gillis of college and preordination years is one of these compound problems. He wrote self-consciously—and, therefore, cautiously. He wrote out of a writer's urge and, therefore, literarily. Fortunately there are friends still alive who were college and seminary associates of Father Gillis. They balance the diaries, corroborating many entries, correcting others, explaining a few that seem contradictory.

The eighteen-year-old boy out of Boston Latin School reveals from his first diary entry that he is a deeply serious person. The youngsters whom he met on his first trip to St. Charles might well have considered him stuffy and stiff, if we can judge from his recapitulation of the boat ride from Fall River, Massachusetts, to Baltimore.

James Gillis writes: "Met 3 or 4 other fellows who were bound for the college. . . . This was my first experience on board a steamer. . . . And it was an experience that I shall never forget, not because of anything connected with the sail primarily, but because of an acquaintance we made before we were aboard 15 minutes.

"We were sitting in the grand salon, when Grant noticed a priest, to whom he doffed his hat. The priest arose and came toward us and, after a few minutes talk, invited us to his state-room 'to have a talk.' . . . Immediately on entering the room, he threw off his coat, told us to do likewise and then to our astonishment asked us 'what would we have.' Suffice it to say that I took lemonade.

"After that this 'priest,' who said he had been having a vacation for a year . . . spent the night in singing and drinking. . . . I have come to the conclusion that he is a silenced priest. . . ."

This episode made the profoundest impression on young Gillis. It fixed him more firmly in his attitude on alcoholic drink. Jim had determined to follow his father's example of total abstinence. Even apart from that lead, he had been keenly disturbed by the many sights of drunkenness, its abuses and degradations, that occurred among the Irish neighborhoods of Boston. The wreck of good men and fine homes had made him bitter and firm in his opposition to liquor. There is some evidence to suppose that he had made some kind of abstinence pledge while only seventeen and still in Boston Latin.

Imagine the impact of this occasion! Any boy disturbed and unsettled on the matter of his priestly vocation would be shaken by being forced to spend time with a priest probably suspended because of alcoholism. Transfer James Gillis into the scene and you have increased the tension doubly. No wonder he wrote of his irritation over the incident, and no wonder the years ahead would bring a focus on him as an ardent temperance lecturer. An estimate of the shock the incident gave Jim Gillis was the fact that fifty years later he repeated this diary entry in his talks to students and retreatants. The same bitternesss that stung in his youthful lines colored the tone of the old voice as he retold the tale.

The spontaneous reaction to reading or hearing about his boat-trip affair is to label the young James Gillis a prig. There may be some justification for the reaction, but the appellation is not one that can simply be tagged on Jim Gillis and left at that.

James junior had been trained in an atmosphere that was the confluence of so many forces of restriction and restraint that it is a minor miracle he ever softened at all. Recall that his father, who was the boy's ideal, had been reared in Montreal under a spirituality leavened by a certain French rigorism and narrowness. The same boy grew up through the eighteen-eighties and nineties in New England, where even today Irish Jansenism and die-hard Puritanism continue to make some areas the height of insularity and constraint. Allow also for the boy's own callow perfectionist philosophy, which afflicts so many idealists in their teens. When scanned under some of these lenses, the tight-laced freshman headed for St. Charles deserves a better hearing than the summary tag "prig" would allow.

Monsignor Gibbons, who was a second-year man at the college when the young students arrived, says that the most noticeable trait about Jim Gillis was his standoffishness. "You could not call him a snob—no, he was not that. The word I always told Jim that struck me when we were introduced was 'Bostonese'—he was 'Bostonese' from crown to heel.

"I paid little attention to the new boy once the whole gang

was settled and never bothered much with him through the first weeks. I had my own chums—the Big Four, they called us, though we were all little fellows. . . . I had no need or time to be bothering with Gillis or any of the new gang. I just recall that he seemed to stand out or, maybe, stand apart from the rest of the students. I considered this as more of the 'Bostonese.' We were a rough bunch, pushing and shoving and scrambling all the time, and he seemed to hold off from any of this.

"Jim was a serious type, I thought, and he was deeply serious. Yet when I got to know him I saw that he was not heavy or boringly serious. He seemed older—older than the rest in ideas, attitudes, manners and purpose."

The St. Charles diary bears all this out. Young Gillis was writing ideas at eighteen that many men never come to at eighty-one. He has page after page of commentary on his reading; he analyzes at full length the sermons, conferences, chapel chats that sprinkled the St. Charles curriculum. There are extended notes on his reaction to the personalities of his teachers and friends; there are criticism and judgments on the benefits of the training the college provided. Pages are devoted to opinions on the political activities of the country at the time; more pages discuss the new trend in popularity of college football and the overimportance being accorded the college athlete. This is a midget index of the seven diaries—a more encyclopedic list would be the result if one tried to cover all the subjects on which Jim Gillis was thinking and making notes as a collegian.

Does one change much growing from boy to man? There is doubt that one does—the boy is the man, the student is the teacher, the seminarian becomes the priest. The littleness or greatness of our reach as a boy is the extent of our reach as a man. Usually, as men, we *reach* no farther—we just hold the original things more tightly or firmly.

James Gillis reveals a pattern of living and thinking at St. Charles that can be traced all the way through his life. The indignations, the ideals, the self-criticism, the political interest, the disgust with mediocrity, the zeal for temperance, the wish to be outstanding—these and more personal aspects fill his young writings. The same aspects can be found in his mission talks, his radio addresses, his editorials, his man-to-man contacts in his life as a Paulist. There might be many disagreements with James Gillis, the boy or the man, but give him credit for always having a very big reach.

Obviously, as the records unroll, young Jim Gillis had the potential for becoming a snobbish, tiresome, irritating know-it-all. Two great balance wheels, however, were turning and meshing with the other gears in the boy's make-up.

The first of these, humility, was to be developed more assiduously in the later priestly years of his life. As a boy he had the one touch necessary to keep himself from becoming a disgruntled, superiority-complex type of adult. His young writing is filled with references to his shortcomings in studies, deportment, industriousness, and even sports. Granted, some of the records are juvenile moments of wounded vanity and dissatisfaction with self—these are hardly humility—but the seedling of the virtue is still there in the effort shown to be fair and honest about his personal responsibility for all his failures.

The second saving grace of young Jim's make-up was his abundant gift of a sense of humor, the joke frequently being at his expense. He liked jokes and wit and humor all his life, and the record of its place in his temperament is established in his diaries. The entries of all seven books are liberally sprinkled with remarks and incidents that substantiate the recollections that John Gillis had concerning his brother's love of fun.

Consider this entry: "May 26 . . . Had a perfectly ludicrous mathematics class today. It seems that some mistake was made the other day when we made the measurements of the baseball field. Father C. tried to have the problem worked out on the board today. The snarl developed the further he went and the scene of confusion was exciting to say the least. At one time about 6 fellows were at the board trying to fix the figures and letters to suit themselves, Father C. playing a rather secondary part.

"The class in the seats meanwhile shouts and calls at the fellows, the din is terrible. Father C. smiles gently. Suddenly someone shouts, 'Let's go down again.' Immediately Mulcahy . . . grabs the surveying instrument box, slings it on his shoulder and starts for the field. Two fellows follow at hot speed, the rest restrained by Father C. During the absence of the 3 volunteers a variety of subjects is discussed, holidays, lectures, superiors general, etc. Finally a heavy tramp is heard in the corridor. 'Mul' comes rushing in with the box on his back, shouts out some unintelligible cry, and full of excitement hurries to the board, draws a figure shouting himself and accompanied by a din of voices from the class.

"After some minutes of this excitement, the data are found still insufficient and again volunteers arise on all sides. But it is too late, the hour is almost up. So ended Mathematics I for the day."

This is more than good writing by a freshman. It is good reporting by a person with an eye and ear for excitement and humor. The diaries sparkle with such moments, and the lines that describe them flow along, bubbling in the high spirit of the occasion retold.

James Gillis was appreciative of good humor all his life. His funny bone was a most sensitive thing, though there were some who thought his humor a little more apt for toga and forum than for the twentieth-century market place. He was not a comedian of the Jimmy Durante school by any means—gags and gagbusters he could take or leave and usually left them. The baggy-pants and toothless-grin comic could stir his laughter, but he had a too highly developed sense of dignity to assay the checkered-vest and snappy-patter manner when being humorous himself.

James Gillis liked a story, a light tale lightly told; even— may he be forgiven—a pun. He loved satire—dry, mordant wit that tested a man's power with words and ideas. He saw the laughable side of things in his own life, and how fortunate for James Gillis that he did. He learned not to take too grimly the sharp criticism and blunt broadsides that flew his way when he became a controversial public figure.

DAMASCUS ROAD, NEW ENGLAND STYLE

When the year at St. Charles came to an end Jim Gillis got a *summa* for his freshman efforts. He led his class in the over-all average for all subjects. More importantly, he had made up his mind to enter the seminary in Boston and study for the diocesan priesthood.

He entered St. John's at Brighton in September of 1896, and the first note in the new diary of that time states: "As to my general impressions of the place, they are most favorable. The seminary is a great improvement on St. Charles in every line except facilities for games, which here are rather poor."

The young aspirant notes how everything at the seminary induces application to study and a deep spiritual life. He resolves to be conscientious to all his obligations, but particularly he is concerned about his spiritual growth. His first step toward fostering his progress in priestly virtues is to select Father Gigot, the renowned Sulpician scripture scholar, as his director.

The year at Brighton skims along. Jim Gillis writes early in the term: "The days begin to go rapidly, contrasting strongly with the first 8 or 10 days which merely crept." Again he jots down the fact that "day follows day with a rapidity that seems greatly enhanced by regular life."

Such remarks as these are sometimes all that is written under a date line. Apparently, having found his vocation, he was more relaxed in his approach toward circumstances that formerly had irritated him and provoked comments. Again, he was more used to being away from home and thus less introspective and aloof; the inward-type world that formerly held his attention and got written down in diaries was now being shattered by a host of outside distractions.

Young Gillis is not entirely satisfied with this state. He says on one day: "Nothing of note. This might truly be said of almost any of the days now passing. I am afraid my diary is becoming very commonplace. . . . I have to make an entry by saying there are no entries to be made." His dissatisfaction was due in great part to the fact that he intended the diaries as practice in composition. He repined at the loss of literary exercise as much as against the loss of interesting things to write.

In this great calm that settled on Jim Gillis he faithfully continues to jot down something each day, even if it be but a line. Some of the single-statement entries are revealing, but most are routine.

A few of the notes are humorous, whether he intended them to be so or not. For example, here's one that briefly says: "Nothing of note today, except that I saw Uncle John, who is working a steam-roller on the boulevard close to the seminary." Or this one: "Went to the city . . . to have a tooth repaired. . . . Was agreeably surprised to find the tooth was all right. . . . This would seem a suspicious case, but I was entirely honest in my excuse to visit the city."

Not so humorous for James Gillis was this entry, which might bring a wry and sympathetic grin to others who have endured this same shock: "My thoughts led me to an attack of the blues. Another thing contributed—my hair, which has always heretofore been extraordinarily thick, is now falling out rapidly and I am getting to fear becoming prematurely bald."

The young man had years to go before baldness really retired his comb and brush. The little vanity Jim manifests is interesting, however, because it indicates a preoccupation with his looks that remained all his days. Even to the last sermon and the last lecture given, Father Gillis was careful about his appearance. He never faced an audience in slovenly or incorrect attire. The luxuriant hair left him, but his sense of being faultlessly groomed never did.

The days and months leaped to mid-term exams, turned 1896, to '97, covered spring and brought the final weeks of Jim's first year at Brighton. The diary shows no great moments, most of the entries falling in a pattern of minor interests and routine happenings. Examination marks, visits from his family, a letter from an old companion at St. Charles, catching cold, playing baseball—these in one form or another are repeated.

Suddenly and without warning a veritable human electric shock jolts Jim from the neat and quiet rut he and his diary are grooving at Brighton. The day is May 24, and under that date Jim Gillis writes his perfervid reaction to a lecture given that day to the students at the seminary.

"We had a talk today by Father Elliott, the celebrated Paulist. It was fine! He spoke for about an hour on the general topic of the Paulist work. . . . He explained how this immense country, most bountifully blessed in many ways by God, is peopled with millions who actually long for the truth and will listen to it . . .

"It seems to him, then, that all these favorable circumstances have been so placed by God, and for a purpose, the great purpose of the conversion of a mighty nation. In such a case our duty, he says, is obvious. Priests must be thorough apostles, they must be deeply penetrated with the conviction that the work is laid out for them and they must pursue that work with energy and devoted zeal."

Notice how closely this lecture was followed. Jim Gillis was taking notes as all the students were trained to do, but he is writing the spirit of the talk as well as the words. There is no further proof needed that the boy has been enflamed than the commentary that he makes on Father Elliott's description of a true priest.

"It is to be feared that there are far too few priests such as he describes. Would to God they all, and we preparing to take their places, were fired with the inextinguishable enthusiasm of Father Elliott and his Community.

"The impression left on me by his address was wonderful—for some time after I could hardly speak, being filled with admiration for the man and for his work. . . . Oh! how I should like to be such a priest! . . .

"Yet it is hard, extremely hard to rise out of routine such as leads through the seminary. There is too little opportunity to advance, too much waste of time and energy and (though I may be rash, and perhaps should not say so after only one year's experience) too much misguided effort. . . . Not that I am dissatisfied with seminary life, only I wish it were nearer perfection."

James Gillis admits in this entry that he is not blameless in much of the waste of time and energy he laments. He sees his own lack of firm resolution to pursue his course to the utmost of his ability.

His conclusion to this extraordinarily long record swings back to the speaker of the day. "What one must most admire in Father Elliott and the Paulists is their 'splendid optimism.' Never a hopeless word escapes them. They seem to be carried along on a blast of enthusiasm that permits them no time for pessimism and discouragement. It is like enjoying a refreshing breeze to listen to them, and the results are far more beneficial from one such talk than from a thousand 'spiritual readings.' "

The number of times that Father Gillis recounted this incident to lay people and religious, to seminarians and priests, in public and in private talks, is incalculable.

He would explain how he walked that morning to the auditorium, not knowing and not being vitally concerned about this speaker. He knew the priest had a fair reputation as a missionary and lecturer, but the man's present interest for Jim Gillis and the other students was that he provided a break from the routine of class. It did not matter whether Father Elliott was good, bad, or indifferent; he was the pause that refreshed, the time away from teacher that has been the hallmark of students from the days of Socrates.

"The seminarians, especially Jim Gillis," Father Gillis would say wryly, "had not reckoned correctly." Father Elliott was not the pause that refreshed, but rather a pause that shook and startled and compelled. There was absolute silence in the auditorium from the moment the tall, erect, bearded missionary stepped forward, stared penetratingly around, and said in a loud, clear voice, "My dear fellow missionaries." He spoke for an hour, and in that hour the figure never relaxed its look of urgency, the fierce eyes never wandered as they demanded attention, the voice never weakened in its driving message—America must be made Catholic.

Father Gillis, telling this story at eighty, would still indicate how the vividness of that morning's impression had remained with him. His own sonorous voice would take on some of the remembered tone of Father Elliott's, his eyes would become fixed in imitation of the missionary's, and he would quote passages of the lecture he had heard long years ago.

"My! How I can remember that morning as I walked from the auditorium," Father Gillis would conclude. "I think I knew I had to be a Paulist and I prayed I could be a missionary with half the zeal of Walter Elliott." He would shake his head, as if blaming himself for not achieving even that half portion of zeal. "That man became my beau ideal of the priesthood—I've wondered often how I've matched him."

The impact that Walter Elliott had on James Gillis was not unusual, because this young missionary was at that time in the prime of his mission career. The bishops, priests, and people who had heard him speak judged him an outstanding member of the Paulist Mission Band and one of the foremost speakers of his day. Descriptions of Father Elliott indicate that he had the great voice and manner of a prophet—and commanded his audiences with something of a prophet's authority.

In his personal life Father Elliott was a rigorist, criticized by some as being too much the martinet about his own spirituality and that of his fellow priests. As one Paulist of his day has said, "He practiced poverty to the point of pauperism, was chaste to the degree that women could call him unfriendly, and lived obedience (as he had learned it in the army during the Civil War) with the strictest adherence to the regulations of the Church and the Paulist Society."

If some of this sounds unflattering to Father Elliott, let us balance it with the fact that Father Gillis saw the man as a great priest—and Father Elliott was all that. The commentary above, which makes the missionary sound grim and baleful, does show him withal to be a man of great demands on himself, with a high sense of duty to his pledged vocation and a deep sense of responsibility to God.

The apostolic zeal of Father Elliott became the great magnet for James Gillis. The lecture was over, but the dynamism of the lecturer, the pull of the Paulist spirit—these tempted the mind and disturbed the soul of the young student.

The student diaries of the period do not cue us in to the deep thought James Gillis was giving the matter of changing to the Paulists. All we read is that he closed the first year at Brighton with one of the highest averages in his class. He starts his first vacation as a seminarian and the diary is left untouched for the months he is free. When the Brighton term opens in September of 1897, Jim is at St. John's gate—the Paulist attraction seems to have died, as if it had been a youthful enthusiasm that vacation had snuffed out.

The only clue that Father Elliott's impression has not faded entirely is in the early pages of the 1897 record. Young Gillis recapitulates the summer days and examines his conduct as a vacationing seminarian. He lists some of his activities on his extended holidays and describes a trip to Niagara Falls. En route, Jim had a day in New York City and he writes: "I took a room at the Grand Union and spent the day . . . seeing all that I possibly could . . . St. Patrick's Cathedral, the Paulist Church, 5th Avenue, Broadway, Central Park and many other things."

The single mention of the Paulist church is all the attention the Community received in his summer thinking. As Jim takes up the burden of his second year at Brighton his diary notes contain nothing further on the men he admired so much. The thread holding him to the Paulists seems to draw to a finer and finer strand as the days rush by. No word is entered about the Paulists. The conclusion one draws is that Jim Gillis had settled on the diocesan priesthood as his life.

Mid-term passes, and interest in the diary itself has languished. Not even the arrival of the new year of 1898 is noted, the last entry of '97 being at Thanksgiving Day.

Suddenly the pages come again to life. February 21 has a long statement about the sinking of the *U.S.S. Maine* in Havana Harbor. To those who know the Father Gillis of the nineteen-thirties—James Gillis, editor of *The Catholic World*—this entry on the Spanish-American contretemps would be most revealing. The seminarian of twenty-one years is foreshadowing the columnist of decades hence.

The quotation that follows and the analysis behind it are worthy of the frank, direct, argumentative editor who was to take on Hitler, Mussolini, Stalin, *et al.* "I think the protestations of friendship and sympathy which have proceeded from the Spanish newspapers are sincere. There are a group of warriors in the U.S. Senate who would delight in a safe encounter with unfortunate Spain. Perhaps they are trying to make things look suspicious for the Spaniards, but I imagine the sentiment is against war . . ."

The apprentice editorialist was very wrong in his estimate of the country's temper as it shouted, "Remember the *Maine!*" War came on April 25, 1898, and ended with almost breath-taking brevity in August as Spain surrendered after a disastrous sea battle.

Jim Gillis later notes his error in judgment regarding the war, but the entry is made as if in passing to more important matters. He is more concerned about the need to do a little surrendering of his own. In Lent, almost on top of his mention-ing the Spanish war possibility, he has an entry in his book which shows the Paulist Community had been with him more than he had allowed anyone to suspect.

"In my last letter to Sister M.," he writes, "I mentioned the matter which is nearest to my heart and which most occupies my mind at present, my possible call to the life of a missionary priest. This is a subject of which I have written nothing in these pages for several reasons."

Jim Gillis does not explain the reasons that determined him to exclude references to the conflict that went on in him con-cerning the Paulists. He concedes his uncertainty that Brighton is the correct choice for him and remarks: "I think that in what-ever sphere of priestly life I may eventually be placed, I cannot forget the enthusiasm I have felt for the Paulists."

One line of this record deserves to stand alone: "I have had a longing desire to discover in myself a calling to that Congregation."

This longing desire became Jim Gillis's first plea before the throne of God. "I shall make a lengthy novena which shall continue throughout the season of Lent, begging particularly of God to make known to me . . . just what is His will in the matter."

As so frequently happens with souls who press themselves upon God, God made no answer for the time being to the emergency plea. In the same mysterious way of Divinity, as matters became more complicated, the want of an answer became more urgent; the soul of young Gillis labored in deeper tangles of confusion and contradiction. Here in the moment of trying to see God's finger pointing him to the Paulists, Jim Gillis received the call from his own bishop to prepare himself for tonsure, the first step toward the priesthood.

His journal during the retreat for tonsure is filled with remarks about his certainty that he should be a priest—it is filled as well with misgivings on his being in the place God wants for him. Father Gigot, his spiritual director, advises him to proceed to the reception of tonsure. The priest assures Jim that nothing can be lost by moving forward to the altar. If a change is to come and God means him for the Paulists, the step will be well taken. "Paulists receive tonsure too," remarks the man humorously, hoping probably to break young Gillis out of the sober mood that held him.

The joke worked, Jim Gillis reveals. He was able to kneel before the bishop, submit his locks for the cruciform clipping, and savor the moment in reverence, rather than in the turmoil that had marked his retreat. Paulist or no, he was supremely joyed to know he had made his public declaration to serve God as His priest.

No clearing comes to split the haze, no light breaks the

gloom, and the days drag on for the young man begging God
for knowledge of His way. Again, God tests him in this ex-
tremity. Under the date of June 19, as the second year at
Brighton comes to the final exams, James Gillis writes of a new
problem: "Dr. Garrigan . . . speaks of me and my possibility
of going abroad to study theology. . . . [He] expresses the
wish that I might go to Germany . . . If I am offered the opportunity of a foreign education . . . I think France would be
my preference among places."

Jim Gillis was truly dazzled by the information that he was
being strongly talked of as a student deserving of a European
training. This would mean more than mere learning. It would
mean the chance to see and absorb the flavor and air of the
finest cultures available. In the future it could mean preferment
in the diocese, could lead far beyond the point of being a
teacher or rector of a seminary—it could lead to the very throne
of the diocese itself.

He might have dreamed a little about being a Doctor of
Theology or of Canon Law or of Sacred Scriptures. He could
see those letters, *S.T.D.* or *J.C.D.* or *S.S.D.*, set handsomely
behind the name James Gillis, and he knew they'd raise an
eyebrow or two as he scribbled them. But Jim wasn't sure these
were the letters he wanted behind his name. He had learned
to practice three different ones, as he shows in his entry that
laments: "The whole matter is the merest possibility. I have
still to decide my great question, 'Am I called to the missionary
religious life in the C.S.P.?' "

Suddenly the diary leaps, almost bounds forward as you
turn the page that holds these lines above, written on June 19.
The large scrawls seem to shout at the reader: "August 14—This
is written in New York, in the house of the Paulist Fathers. I
am not yet a Paulist, perhaps I am as far away from being one as
I ever was. Still, I am making a sort of retreat . . . My particular host and director is Father O'Callaghan . . . He treats

me with every possible kindness, yet in such a way as not to make me feel that he is trying to influence me to become a Paulist."

This was true—up to a point. Father O'Callaghan was patient and earnest with a troubled young man. The priest was also forthright and firm and not inclined to waste his or the young man's time by prolonging this special retreat. Jim Gillis records the one-two-three solution that came for his troubled soul after a few days of special conferences.

"Father O'Callaghan came in and interrupted me as I was writing . . . a different phase has been put on things. Immediately he began to treat my case summarily and I saw that something was coming."

The retreat master told Jim to state quickly and frankly all the objections to becoming a Paulist that came immediately to his mind.

"I did so," continues the young diarist, "he counted them up, considered them all as unimportant, and then said flatly that he believes I am called to be a Paulist!"

Jim Gillis's reaction to the uncompromising declaration was one of admiration for the priest. "I thank him . . . for treating me so fairly and squarely. I feel that he has dealt with my case in a kindly, indulgent, yet fearless, masterly way."

The most surprising thing in all this period of soul searching that Jim Gillis was undergoing is the obvious and tortuous uncertainty of his mind. This is an almost unconceivable condition to posit about the Paulist of future years. Anyone meeting, reading, or hearing the Reverend James Gillis in his prime would never accept the story of irresolution these diary pages tell. Some renowned religious, political, and social figures would shake their heads and swear that this confused seminarian is some other person. As they tenderly finger the lumps so positively and resoundingly raised on them by Father Gillis, they would deny he has any connection with this vacillating boy haunting the Paulist rectory in 1898.

But the young changeling and the old unflinchable are the same despite the inability of the former to be sure of his vocation to the Paulists. The surprise at his interior wrangling is something to be remarked on—yet, in fairness, many vocations reveal the same disturbed, unsettled course.

Deciding to serve God totally is no small resolve. The glorious leap to heaven that is made in religious profession or in receiving Holy Orders is not a blind jump into the darkness. Candidates are *schooled* to all that the vocation involves. Emotionalism or "feelings" are ruthlessly cautioned against. Nothing is to be allowed to color or diminish the sense of grave responsibility that must be developed if the candidate is to succeed. Young men or young women wishing to embrace such a dedicated life are never fooled about that life. They are permitted even to make a trial of the life in a novitiate or seminary. In that trial period they live as fully as possible all the severe obligations of the vows they'll be expected to pledge. If the preliminary does not suit them—or they are found unsuitable—they quit the trial. Under no circumstances do they move forward in ignorance or confusion or doubt about the high estate they are attempting.

What soul doesn't pause warily when considering the possibility of committing its whole life to one purpose? The lover, the poet, the medical zealot, the legal apostle—anyone eying the prospect of the total sum of his days dedicated to one person or one enthusiasm trembles under the realization that right here—at the moment of declaration—is the end of the road. His greatness is in the moment of his vow; all the rest of his life must be given over to the grim business of living up to the height he held for the briefest instant—that short moment of the vow made.

Add to this in James Gillis's case, as in so many others, the possibility that God was trying him at this time of consideration upon his vocation. Is it entirely unthinkable that James Gillis was not being permitted this confusion for many reasons that God alone could reveal? If the boy pressed forward in the face of such discouraging uncertainty, if he fought to find his answer despite the pain, the embarrassment of being thought unstable, wouldn't he be the better soul and priest for it? And later, when he reflected on these days, wouldn't he have reason to be patient and humble and sympathetic toward others who asked his help as they fought similar difficulties?

God had His purpose in the travail that Jim Gillis endured and He had His purpose in extending it. Young Gillis did not settle down even after Father O'Callaghan told him to become a Paulist.

Here is the young seminarian writing of his uncertainty even after the strong directive of the priest to whom he'd come. "Confronted with the statement that . . . I ought to be a Paulist, what am I to say? What am I to think? As near as one might judge, this appears to be the expression of the will of God. . . . I have tried to place myself in the attitude of entire submission to the will of God. . . . I intend to give my final decision Thursday evening, unless something really a hindrance comes up before that. May God help me!"

There is no climax to the story as Jim Gillis records it. Almost like an anticlimax as the August entry ends, there is no new date of comment until Friday, October 7, 1898. Two months have sped by without a word having been written. Then it becomes apparent why the extended omission—James Gillis has been too busy as a Paulist student to write in his diary! He is at Washington and is happily occupied in studies and serenely confident that he is "at home at last."

The young Paulist reviews the rushed days that had prevented him from keeping his daily record. He had accepted Father O'Callaghan's advice in August. Immediately he was swept up in filling out entrance papers, making the Paulist student retreat at Lake George, hurrying back to Boston to pack his books and personal effects, and saying his farewells to home. Once all these things were accomplished, he entrained for Washington and began his Paulist student life on September 11, 1898.

The adjustment to the new surroundings was the usual trial that it is for all. In the depth of his spirit Jim Gillis was at peace, but superficially, emotionally, matters were different. "I have not spoken of my impressions of my new home," he writes. "They are good, in the main. All is not perfection of course, not all is intended to be perfect. I have had some little 'blue' streaks, in fact not a few. Coming away from home has affected me now as never before. . . . I have felt and feel the separation most keenly . . . but I reason myself out of all gloominess and regret, for have I not foreseen that my joining the Paulists would necessarily lessen my chances for natural happiness . . ."

With this rhetorical question and on this externally unpropitious note Jim Gillis ceases to be a faithful diarist. There are no more daily insertions of the trifling events (or the important ones, for that matter) that happened in his new home.

Analyzing the reasons behind the surrender of this daily routine which he had built up in the years covering 1895 to 1898 is folly when sixty years have gone by since then. Jim Gillis terminated keeping this kind of diary, and that was the end of it. Fortunately, although this "Dear Diary" mood passed into the limbo of forgotten activites, he did not stop writing occasional records of events in his life. The notes written hereafter are more indicative of the maturing man than are any of the wordy, schoolboy diaries James Gillis kept.

The paper-covered notebooks that treat of St. Charles and Brighton are filled with accounts of games and sports and holidays. They labor the 90 and 95 averages Jim Gillis got when he topped his class in competitions. They lament the rain, the snow, the sleet, the ice—all the inclemencies of the weather that young, short-focused, narrowly bounded seminarians are so concerned over. They tell of coughs and colds, wheezes and sneezes, and pains of teeth and pains of toes. They sing gaily over a well-stocked box from home, carp about a heavy class assignment, exult about a great gathering of friends and family on visitors' day, moan over the poor meals provided by the institution's culinary experts.

The early books do have their reflections of more weighty moments than these, yet they are more truly mere gropings and stirrings toward maturity. The grave entries of the pre-Paulist days seem not to have true spontaneity and naturalness. They appear rather the writings of a boy who wanted to be serious—felt he should be—and self-consciously wrote gravity into his records, naïvely thinking this made important things more important. The failing, possible in any young man of deep spirit, tends to make unimportant things sound ponderous rather than significant.

The few notes made by the neophyte Paulist are more genuinely enthusiastic, more honestly serious than all the copious scribblings of former days. The fact that he was a little more advanced in age does not account entirely for the difference. Added years are no gilt-edged guarantee of a person's growing maturity.

James Gillis seems to have formed some resolve to live out and away from the daily trivia that bogs down many seminarians. He writes now infrequently, but on these few occasions he appears determined to snap out of youthfulness (even his gravely inclined type of youthfulness) and determined to snap himself into manhood.

In the main, retreat times become the only periods which

James Gillis records. The priesthood, Paulist mission life ahead, the conversion of America—these are his prayerful concern on retreat and he details these meditations fully.

Page after page of the retreat notebook of 1899 are devoted to these subjects. Father Walter Elliott conducted this retreat and he had the same effect on Jim Gillis in that August of '99 as he had the day he'd unhorsed the boy at Brighton. This time, though, the impact of Father Elliott was no one-shot matter. Day after day for seven days and in four long talks each day, Jim Gillis sat alternately mesmerized by admiration for the retreat master or stirred to excitement by the prospect of being a partaker of this mission vocation Father Elliott described.

His pen flies to note down the words, stories, exhortations, counsels, ominous warnings, and *obiter dicta* of the great preacher. The writing is woeful, sloppy, seems splashed on the pages as Jim Gillis forgets his precise penmanship in this eagerness not to miss a syllable.

When it is over, there is this summing up of all the weeks of talks: "Thank God for this retreat. I think I shall never forget it. I hope I may look back to it as the beginning of a new epoch wherein I shall have devoted myself to pursue faithfully my ideal of the priestly, religious, missionary life."

This quiet close to the feverishly scribbled, enthusiastically filled notebook tells us that the retreat was a success. The contented grasp of ideal and the fixed and single-eyed view of the future are implicit in such a minor-key paragraph as Jim Gillis wrote. The proof that he had come to true complacence in God's will and to a deep comprehension of his vocation is the life he lived afterward—he never let slip the standard raised at this student retreat. James Gillis was ever a devoted man in the priesthood, the Paulist religious life, and the Church's missionary activity.

Jim Gillis was not "living" in the chapel at St. Thomas's in these late years of the eighteen-hundreds. Paulist student life is not one long, spiritual tube through which the aspirant is processed and out of which he is duly squeezed on the world like tooth paste on a brush—a neat, bland-looking, minty-flavored kind of priest who brightens up his corner of life.

Paulist student life is fully explained in the last word of the phrase—"life." As with any religious institute, the basic ingredient of the course at St. Thomas's (now St. Paul's) Seminary is deep spiritual direction. Isaac Thomas Hecker, founder of the Paulists, in 1858 had set personal sanctity as one of the two great enthusiasms around which the Paulist life turned—the other was zeal for apostolic works. With these objectives before him, the young Paulist was then and is today trained and developed. Filled with the love of God through his own spiritual development, the Paulist overflows into apostolic activity for the conversion of souls to God. The particular direction of this convert activity in the ideal of Father Hecker was to be toward non-Catholic America. Being American in foundation and development, the early Paulists naturally saw in America the fulfillment of their missionary goal.

No seminary life, however, would sanctify its members or prepare them for effective work with souls if the intellectual, social, and recreational factors were eliminated from the course. The eminent good sense of the early Paulists led them to emphasize this complete regimen for their students. They wanted good priests, but not at the expense of turning out enfeebled ignoramuses with the manners of roustabouts.

"Play ball" was meant to be as relatively important a cry as "Keep the Rule"; and "Get your studies" was meant to be as relatively crisp a dictum as "Have zeal for souls." Proportion was the secret of each factor working most efficiently to make a very special priest—the Paulist.

James Gillis neglected none of these, not only because of his own good sense about being the balanced, well-rounded priest, but also because his Superiors would see to it that he neglected no part of his training.

He was sent to class in these student years at Catholic University. The university at Brookland in the District of Columbia was not always the hub around which all the religious communities revolved. In 1898, when Jim Gillis enrolled for courses, it was about eleven years old and struggling mightily to maintain the spark of life breathed into it by the bishops of America at its foundation.

The Paulist Fathers, themselves only twenty-nine years old when the university began, were the first religious community to settle at Brookland and the first to support the university venture by enrolling their young students in the classes. The practice continued until 1914, when the university was well on its way to success. By that time the Community had expanded to a point where a new seminary housing its own faculty and affiliated with the university became a reality for the Paulists.

James Gillis studied under the pioneer spirits of Dr. Thomas Shahan, Dr. Charles Grannan, and Dr. William Kerby in these years and could not help imbibing some of the rugged good sense and courage these men demonstrated in their venture of making Catholic University succeed.

One important note that was recommended for the young Paulist in his training was social graciousness and good manners. This fitted well the ideal Jim Gillis had for himself. Early in his youth, in the time at Brighton, he had written about the need of being a gentleman. The practice of this quality became a resolve of his and he strove to achieve it.

He could not have selected a more apt Community than the Paulists in which to pursue this want. They had long been called "the gentlemen priests" by their clerical and lay friends alike, and the ideal was stressed with each aspirant. The older men to whom the original compliment was paid were careful to distinguish for their students the severe difference between being a worldling and a gentleman. They cracked down hard on any student who mistook the idea of being a gentleman priest as an excuse for foppery.

The Paulists desired products from their seminary who were gentlemen in the Newmanesque ideal of one who never gives offense. They wanted priests who were articulate and cultured, men of many interests and developed talents. The ideal was a priest of God who could move like Christ into the market place and the hall of the king—never patronizing the poor or the little people nor being patronized by the famous or well-to-do—all the while commanding attention by manner, presence, and ability for the message he bore.

Jim Gillis was the very best material for what the Paulists had in mind when they developed this training program. He brought to the student life an eager soul, a quick mind, a supple body, and a gracious manner. One by one these basic qualities were enhanced by the Paulist training program to produce the outstanding priest of the future.

Would Jim Gillis have been all he was without the Paulist background? The point has been debated hotly, but the answer and the debate seem unimportant. The fact is, he did become outstanding and it was as a Paulist—the credit is his and the Community's: his in that he used the opportunities provided, the Paulists' in that they have a system of life that can develop such men.

Student days were tapering down for Jim Gillis. He was moving nearer and nearer the three final steps that would bring him to the face of Christ in the priesthood. It had been four years since the boy from Boston Latin had pushed open the sanctuary gate and had begun the long ascent to the top step of the altar.

The clock of the world clicked at midnight, December 31,

1899, and the twentieth century slipped into place. Jim Gillis might have been awake when the world moved across a century marker, but it is more possible he was sound asleep.

There is a real scarcity of horn blowing and cowbell ringing in seminaries on New Year's Eve. The rule of silence and the 5 A.M. rising make revelry a handicap to anyone so inclined. Jim had been asleep since about 9 P.M. on the moment the century turned, but that was to be one of the few times he'd ever be caught napping in the twentieth century. The next fifty years were to be golden ones for him, and he would stride across the decades with a tempo that increased as the numbers of the century moved higher and higher.

In 1900 Jim was called to the first of the major orders. He received subdeaconship and was admitted officially into the Paulist Community. In those days the aspirant was considered a novice from the time of entrance until the eve of subdeaconship. The night prior to the reception of the first major order, those candidates who had survived the student training period were vested with the Paulist habit after making their promise of fidelity to the Community Rule and Constitution. Pledging themselves to the practice of the virtues of poverty, chastity, and obedience, they were invoked by the Superior to don the habit and take their place among the other members of the Community. *

The new Paulist had resumed his diary keeping for the retreat preceding his vestiture and subdeaconship. His sentiments on both occasions are witness to the stirringly earnest moments he experienced.

The entry on the evening of his acceptance into the Paulists reads: "Thursday night. Dec. 20, 1900. James M. Gillis, C.S.P.! Received into the Community tonight after a day of unspeaka-

---

* Today acceptance into the Paulist life follows the making of a one-year novitiate. The candidates take a temporary promise, renewable for three years, and at the end of that period they make their final and perpetual promise. The system that saw Jim Gillis admitted was modified in 1923.

ble blessings from God." Much as a young girl before marriage practices writing the name she will assume soon, Jim Gillis has written this opening signature and, after it, dashed in flourishes the initials *C.S.P.!* It's a small sign—but an important one—of the pride and elation that filled him on having achieved the goal of becoming a Paulist.

He was not giddy or childish about the significance of attaching the great history of the Community as well as its initials to his name. He writes on that evening: "O my God, keep me secure for the future. Let me never stray from thee, for I have thrown myself, heart and soul, into thy hands and I wish never to be released. . . . O my Good Shepherd, go thou with me and teach me how to act and where to go and how to call thy straying ones. . . . Give me a . . . courageous soul and a heart overflowing with the love that thirsts for sacrifice. Make me and keep me . . . a good priest, a devoted missionary—a worthy Paulist."

The following day, December 21, James Gillis was ordained subdeacon. His heart is filled with such joy at this climax coming on top of the one of the previous evening that he finds difficulty in expressing his feelings. He writes hurriedly: "All my best expectations of the fervor of soul . . . and of love for God flowing warm from my heart have been realized. I feel, actually feel, the presence and the blessings flow so strongly that I could not have imagined it possible. . . . Make me understand, my good Master, make me understand more and more . . ."

One year to the day, the young Paulist was ordained a priest at St. Paul's Church in New York City.

The touching story that attends the moment of Jim Gillis's becoming a priest is the one concerning his mother and his fears that she would not see him ordained. While he was a student at Brighton his mother suffered a slight stroke that he felt was the harbinger of more serious ones to come.

Catherine Gillis seemed to recover from this initial shock. She went about her duties as previously, but it was obvious that she tired more easily now and lacked the drive that had been her trade-mark in the earlier days. Except for these signs, Mrs. Gillis was a well woman when Jim left Brighton and entered the Paulists.

Not until the last months of his student life was Jim made aware that his mother was weakening badly. The family told him that she might not be able to go to New York for the ordination. They begged Jim not to worry and assured him that they had no doubt his mother would be strong enough to be at the First Mass.

Young Gillis swallowed the bitter news but did not like it. He had dreamed too much of the glory of being made a priest with his mother and father watching and sharing the joy. Jim's notebooks are replete with references to the goodness, the lovableness, generosity, and self-sacrifice of these two people who had made so much of his priesthood possible. He wanted them to have this moment and he had begged God to make the wish come true. Now the word had come that God seemed to be denying the wish.

Despite the keen disappointment, he pushed on in his course. Often James Gillis must have turned to God and asked that if there was any chance—any chance—please let his mother come to New York and share with him the most glorious day any mother and son can have, the day her boy becomes a priest.

The chance appeared. Mr. Gillis wrote and said Jim's mother was picking up and feeling fine. At the rate she was improving, she would be able to make the great morning.

The children at home protested the danger for the mother when the father announced finally that Mrs. Gillis would accompany him. The protests were useless. The valiant couple were determined to travel to New York for Jim's ordination.

Young Gillis marched through the ceremony elated at the tremendous graces being conveyed on him. His mind was resolutely fixed on God and the splendid gift of the priesthood being placed in his hands. However, there was also the warm, tender glow that crept into his heart as he thought of the favor granted—his mother and father present at his elevation to the sacrament of Holy Orders.

When the ceremony was completed the men ordained turned to bless the throng in the church; then, as is customary, each new priest walked to the altar rail to the section assigned to family and friends. Father James Gillis hurried forward and started down the sanctuary steps. He went to his section of the rail and probably fought to restrain his steps that wanted to rush toward his mother and father.

Suddenly he paled as he searched the faces, the reverent, eager, smiling faces. Neither his mother nor his father knelt at the rail waiting his first blessing. The horrible thought came that neither had made the ceremony. Where were they? What had happened? Did he go now and bless some casual friend or distant relative with the blessing so often daydreamed of as especially for his mother?

As the new priest paused, a little stir occurred in the crowd at his section of railing. James Gillis's heart leaped as he looked through the shifting people. There was his father, firmly but gently bringing his mother through to the rail. Father James didn't hear all the explanation about his mother's feeling faint and having to step outside for a while—he didn't want any explanations as he gazed on his mother's face, where brightness and pride shone as she stared at her priest-son. She knelt humbly and dropped her head to hide the tears that filled her eyes.

Father James Gillis didn't bother to hide his own as he lifted his hand in a first priestly blessing over the bowed head of his mother.

One of the oddities of this whole last year that led to ordination is the fact that there is no journal of any sort for any part of the year. There is not even a retreat diary by Father Gillis for the days prior to his reception of the priesthood. The strangeness of this omission is noted as an oddity because there are thirty-two notebooks extant in Father Gillis's hand and they cover the years from 1902 to 1925. These writings comprise daily meditations and retreat diaries. Of all the years recorded from the day the boy, Jim Gillis, began searching for the priesthood until his silver jubilee as a Paulist, the one year missing is 1901—the year he was ordained a priest.

A lead on the mystery of this missing journal might be a tiny scrawl that is easily overlooked in the extensive set of notes Jim Gillis took during his combined Paulist reception and subdeacon retreat. Buried at the end of his resolutions are these three words: *"Dixi: nunc coepi."* ("I have pledged: now I begin.")

Reading his resolves, you grasp the meaning of those words and their import. You sense that he intended there was to be no need for more resolutions within a year when he became a priest. These determinations of 1900 covered the rest of his life, and already his purposes for the priesthood ahead were set.

When he stepped out of the student world and assumed the full responsibility of priestliness, Jim Gillis meant to be fixed in this stated program:

I resolve, God aiding me—
1st. To pray with constancy and fidelity.
    To give myself to the best kind of
    prayer that God shall make possible
    for me. Hence, in particular
    (a) To avoid sluggishness whenever
        I pray . . .
    (b) To prepare for meditation
        always conscientiously.

2nd. As an assistance to prayer, two things,
  (a) Mortification. Patient endurance
      of all little trials arising from
      Community life. Some voluntary
      bodily mortification. To begin
      with a controlling of my appetite
      at meals, and prompt rising from
      sleep.
  (b) Recollection. Solitude, making a
      retreat of my cell. The door of
      my room to be a barrier against
      distraction.
3rd. Work. Patient, painstaking, conscientious
     study.
Beyond these some minor matters. Principally:
  1. I will *never* speak of the faults of others
     unless called upon by duty to do so.
  2. I will be a gentleman in my conduct to all
     . . . putting some affection and reverence
     into my heart and manifesting it in my
     deportment.
  3. I will try to be perfectly unselfish in the
     ordinary meaning of the word. Always
     treat others and every other better than
     myself. May it please Almighty God to
     enable me to keep these resolutions.
     May Jesus Christ my Saviour who has
     deigned to make me His friend and His
     companion, always guide me and
     prompt me, and may His Blessed
     Virgin Mother, Mary, my mother, pray
     constantly for me and consider me as
     her child most especially.
God bless my resolutions.
     Dixi: nunc coepi.

One point should be made clear as we read these resolutions
and the fervent pleas that beg help in keeping them. James

Gillis is not listing his virtues. He is listing his problems in virtue.

Too often when reading about those who aspire to perfect goodness, people accept the person's mere desire for holiness as holiness itself. They do not realize that the subject's long self-exhortatory passage on charity or some other virtue is not always a sign of the subject's possession of the virtue—it can as well represent a consciousness of a glaring lack of the virtue. Much as a Romeo might apostrophize his Juliet, many an earnest, intelligent, godly person can laud faith, perseverance, zeal, or a hundred other spiritual talents. Romeo did not possess Juliet, and neither do these souls have the talent praised.

Resolutions are like this. They indicate our admiration for some important gift of soul, for some virtue that we either fail in regularly or do not practice at all. If the resolutions are not made in the field where we have problems, they are useless determinations. To fix our will on achieving conquest over something that presents no difficulty would be as salutary as an alcoholic's swearing off popcorn as a step toward sobriety.

Read this list of resolutions as if they were refusals being made to God and you have the picture of James Gillis's future struggles in the priesthood. Allowing, of course, for the neophyte fervor that led him to exaggerate the faults against which he purposes to work, you have a long list of interior difficulties.

Young Gillis saw his need of prayer, and he knew that his tendency to sloth in preparation and pursuance of prayer could be a serious handicap to priestliness. He had concern for his lack of self-discipline both in the rub of Community give-and-take and in the matter of denying his appetite its gratifications. The last of his major problems was his need to live more in solitude, breaking himself of the desire to be with people and thereby losing valuable time for reading and studying.

The minor resolutions were also his problems or problem,

since the three statements boil down to one great difficulty—uncharitableness. Each of these minor determinations is some phase of Community life against which he erred, and they all express the one lament: I've failed badly in living the Common Life.

Father James Gillis would agree with such an analysis as can be seen by those last three words, "*Dixi: nunc coepi.*" To make a beginning, as this motto avers, means logically to be at the beginning. The young man was ready to start being the Paulist priest he knew God wanted him to be.

MATCHING THE FOOTSTEPS OF PAUL

chapter IV

Christmas of 1901 was the merriest that the Gillis family had had in many years. Father James returned with his parents to the old Back Bay home and offered his First Mass at St. Cecilia's, their parish church. The usually busy holidays were made doubly hectic for the new priest by the round of activities that pressed into every hour of his brief vacation.

Vacation over, it was time for good-by—another good-by in that seemingly endless series that families of priests and religious must suffer. The son or daughter comes back, but never comes home. There is always an end to the visit and the sharp reminder to the family that a visit is all it has been—and all it can ever be.

Father Gillis returned to Washington and awaited the orders of his Superiors. He speculated on the rumors that he had heard concerning his future. Every newly ordained has lived through the rumor stage—dreading, enjoying, fearing, hoping—his reaction changing according to the latest gossip that flies his way.

"Gillis is going on the missions." "Gillis is going to Europe." "Gillis is going to teach." "Gillis is going to be stationed in parish work." "Gillis is going to study for a degree at the university." The name was always the same, but the rumor of the assignment was always different. Young Gillis held on, counting the rumors, wondering how wild they'd get and praying he'd do a good job of whatever task finally was set for him.

There was little sense getting involved in the gossip, because that could mean letting yourself want one thing more eagerly than the rest, and if it did not materialize you began the job you did receive in keen disappointment.

As one priest cautioned the students on the eve of their priesthood: "Forget the rumors about your future assignments. Do not become enmeshed in this chatter about you're going here, you're going there, you're going to do this, you're going to do that—you're going, going, going. Men, forget it, or you'll be just plain gone!"

Father Gillis was striving to follow this counsel when his appointment came. He gave no sign of great elation or dejection, and no one knew whether or not the Superior's letter pleased or disappointed him. The Paulist General, Very Reverend George Deshon, wrote to inform the new priest that he was to continue his studies for a degree in theology and also to teach a Church history course to the students at the Paulist college.

Teaching and studying *may* have been James Gillis's great interests, but there is room for grave doubt on the matter. He was born to preach, if we can judge from the recollections of friends who remember this early period. Father Gillis's own record of his preaching engagements—a date book that carries entries from 1901 to 1956—bears out the friendly recollections.

His student-teacher career is covered in a single sentence on the first page of this book; thereafter follows line after line of the places where Father Gillis was preaching through 1902 and 1903.

If this sermon and lecture record proves little concerning the real interest of James Gillis at this time, Monsignor Gibbons' memory can certainly establish the fact that Father Gillis had equipped himself as a preacher.

Joseph Gibbons had left St. Charles a year after James Gillis entered Brighton. He was sent by his bishop to study at San Sulpice in France and was ordained in 1902. During the years of separation the two men had continued their friendship by a lively correspondence. When Joe Gibbons returned to America as Father Gibbons in July of 1902, he headed straight for the old Paulist rectory on Fifty-ninth Street in New York. James Gillis had come to the Motherhouse to rest after an attack of typhoid.

"I landed in the city and went on up to see Jim," relates Monsignor Gibbons. "He was recovering from typhoid, as I recall. Well, I spent the day with him and told him I'd decided that I wanted him to preach at my First Mass in New Bedford.

"He laughed at the idea . . . disbelieving me . . . but I insisted. So he came on and was superb. There had never been a First Mass before at St. Lawrence's in New Bedford, and the church was packed. It seats about twelve hundred people . . . it's the main church in town and every seat was taken.

"Jim came out for the sermon and I sat amazed to watch him—erect, self-possessed, completely in control as he walked to the pulpit. He told me in later years how hard it had been not to burst out laughing at the thought of his welcoming me into the ranks of the priesthood and he being a priest only six months himself.

"Maybe Jim felt it funny, but he never cracked a smile. I think everyone thought he was ordained for years the way he stood in the pulpit and surveyed the crowd. My! The aplomb of a seasoned veteran was his at that time. He'd swing to me sitting on the bench and address me—then he'd go back to the people. Never a word, never a gesture out of place. He was all preacher, even then in 1902, only seven months out of the seminary . . . almost perfect, I'd say."

James Gillis returned to Washington in the fall of that year of 1902 and continued his courses at the university. If he was "all preacher" he gave no indication that he thought his present work was not to his liking. He did not show by word or mood that he must be allowed to capitalize on his abilities as a speaker.

That he liked to preach and wanted to preach, however, is fairly obvious. What better signs can one give of such attitudes than having great talent, polished, poised, ready to be employed?

The Paulist Superiors were not unaware of the young orator who was knocking down all the pins every time he took his turn in the alley. They could well use him, but first, they reasoned, let him finish the degree work at Washington.

In 1904, a year after receiving a Licentiate in Sacred Theology at Catholic University, James Gillis received orders to transfer to Chicago. He was to assist in the parish of Old St. Mary's, the Paulist church in that city, and be trained gradually in the mission work of the Community.

James Gillis felt he was now on the real task of the Paulists. His reaction is understandable, but not very accurate, and he could admit the error later in life. Training the students, teaching the future priests, is the great work of any Community's members. Pope Pius XI brought this out clearly in his encyclical on the priesthood when he advised Superiors and bishops to send the ablest men to their seminaries.

That the young priest did not fully grasp this is forgivable in the realization of the zeal and zest that impelled him to join the Paulists. When he had settled a little into the mellower moods of the last twenty years, James Gillis was not so sure that his hastening to Chicago had given him any deeper participation in the Paulist vocation than his days at Washington.

But parish work and the mission tryouts are the life of activity around which any enthusiastic seminarist builds his dreams. There's more the feel of doing things when you are in a parish, more the sense of achievement if you are preaching a mission. James Gillis had had the dream and felt the lure of the active life. He was on his way to Chicago, and from what he'd heard, Old St. Mary's at 911 South Wabash in Chicago was the active-active life.

Among the retreat diaries and meditation notebooks that James Gillis kept in the first twenty-five years of his priesthood, there is one sheaf of unbound pages that is a collection of anecdotes, stories, and reactions that cover the years from 1904 to 1907.

His entrance to Chicago is described with no pretense at hiding his expectation or of his response to the sprawling mid-western city: "Sept. 1, 1904. Arrived in Chicago, prepared for the worst— Didn't find it. But many bad prophecies came true. Dirt, physical and moral, predominates. Parish takes in all of what was—and perhaps is—the most notorious vice and crime center in the country. The 'demi-monde' and the 'submerged tenth' in force all around us—squatty, ramshackle houses: poverty, misery, dirt, smoke—an ugly locality—yet including also, in the business section, the finest hotels and the greatest shops in the world perhaps. . . .

"Prospect for work—vast, endless— Central location good for our business—convert-making and the rest."

This was on a Thursday. The following Sunday the young priest wrote: "Kept Sunday school—God save the mark—22 un-disciplined youngsters. Preached at Vespers, a thoroughly lugubrious service. No organ. One man sang 4 psalms— Gillis did the rest— Melancholy! Disastrous condition if not mended."

The note on melancholy refers to his own feelings. James Gillis was an easy prey for the blues because he was a deeply affectionate man and needed people.

That last fact should be more definitely marked to heighten

its importance. The idea it expresses is a contradiction to almost every concept of Father Gillis that is held by his associates, acquaintances, and enemies. Only his dearest friends know the truth of the statement—he was a deeply affectionate man and needed people. They would be the first ones to bring the fact to light as they talk of their days spent with Father Gillis.

James Gillis was no aloof iceberg. Leaving home to enter the seminary is reported in his youthful journals as a wrenching of his emotions. He notes how the sight of tears in his mother's eyes brought tears to his own. The early days at Brighton show that he was longing for the companions of St. Charles; the early days at the Paulist studentate show him longing for the friends of Brighton. James Gillis could become easily attached to a place and its people, even if he did not make close friends of many. Following this pattern, we find him feeling the loss of the men with whom he'd been at Washington since ordination. His first Chicago days hold expressions of melancholy over the new and strange surroundings.

The fact that James Gillis had very few close friends is no strong argument against this proposition that he needed people. His own statements on why he made few friends explain his position. As early as his first year in college he lamented the hurt that some false friend had caused him. Almost like a jilted lover, he tells himself that he shall proceed slowly in life hereafter and test people until he can be sure of their friendship.

The expression "defense mechanism" is so chewed over and used up today that it seems as flavorless and dull as yesterday's gum, but that expression fits Father Gillis's demeanor with people most of his life. His seeming aloofness and his controlled, almost withdrawn aspect were born of fear that he'd be hurt should he express his true feelings toward someone.

His future active days will bear this out and his old age will strip the last shred of this pretense aside, showing a man deeply cherishing true friendship. The Chicago chapter is the little sign, the tip on what the young man grows toward in the years to come.

One other characteristic of James Gillis can be detected in these first jottings on his assignment. He uses the words, "Arrived in Chicago, prepared for the worst." And he says about the Vespers, "Disastrous condition if not mended."

Father Gillis suffered the constant ravage of a tendency toward pessimism. This is the most basic word to use in describing his temperament and disposition. His drift in life—not his usual or final resolution of life—was pessimistic. The distinction is made because some critics of his preaching and writing have labeled him a Jeremiah and felt that the word *pessimistic* summed up Father Gillis. That careless judgment does more disservice to the critics than to the man.

They refuse to analyze and discover that the marvel of James Gillis's life is the struggle he put up to overcome his proneness to look on the worst side of things. Just as the wonder of the Tower of Pisa has been its leaning without falling, so the heroism of James Gillis was his constant struggle never to permit his melancholic leaning to be his undoing.

Time here, too, tells us a different story. The disposition toward pessimism that afflicted James Gillis was to prove for him a great safeguard when he became a national figure. Properly balanced, this apprehensiveness was to help him judge some modern fanaticisms with a realistic and single-purposed eye. Adequately focused by the aid of Christian principles, his jaundiced responses to world affairs would raise an alarm that woke many a sleeping patriot.

The blues and the touch of dejection that soured the first week of the recent addition to Old St. Mary's staff were blown away in the next couple of days. There wasn't time for blues and there was too much excitement for feeling dejected.

The young Bostonian, Puritan-touched and seminary-trained, was heaved—not merely tossed—into the seamy tide that broke against Old St. Mary's parish door. On September 16, James Gillis writes: "First sick call in Chicago—man in 'red light district'—rotten hole—gave him last rites—God have mercy on him."

Two days later he was again on duty and notes: "Sick call in a genuine 'sporting-house.' Girl dying in consumption—poorly instructed, but seemed in such bad shape, I gave her all the sacraments—— House full of women—God have mercy on them."

One day later he heralds the year ahead: "Work coming faster . . . House crowded every evening—instructions increasing!" He had guessed correctly in that first look at the parish that the work would be vast and endless. He was excited at the prospect that the convert apostolate would be a major part of that vast and endless work.

This apostolic spirit is a theme that holds constant in all the varieties of Father Gillis's future experience. Though it was a long and troubled decision that brought James Gillis to study and train under the ideal of St. Paul, it was not from haphazard choice that he was led to preach and write under a rule dedicated to the great Apostle to the Gentiles. He pledged the Paulist life because, as he once said, he felt he had to be a Paulist or nothing. It was his opinion that only in the new and different Community of Father Hecker could he expend the zeal he felt for converting America.

This enthusiasm for the broad mission field that stretches between the Atlantic and the Pacific oceans was not an inborn thing. Father Gillis did not dream of the great white harvest from his earliest years. It might be stirring and piously thrilling to tell how as a boy he would stand on the Boston docks, face *away* from the ocean, and look toward California, all the while telling his childhood companions that his mission work lay not across the sea at his back but across all the land that lay to the west.

The fact of his life, as we have seen, is that James Gillis entered the diocesan seminary setting no more scope for himself than the lives that would bound the parish where the bishop might station him. He wanted the priesthood, but that ministry was envisioned as at home, near family and friends and among Catholics.

Then came Father Walter Elliott, and from the moment that first fire had been kindled in him as a seminarian James Gillis burned with the desire to bring Catholicism to America.

Chicago was the first chance he'd been given, and James Gillis set to work immediately to convert America—at least the tiny portion allotted him then. He knew there was no profit in delaying his apostolic work until he should be appointed to the mission band. He grasped the opportunities at hand, knowing that one parish in any city can be a world of souls if a priest is interested.

His first zeal went to the individual inquirers who dropped in at the Paulist rectory on South Wabash Street in Chicago. Father Gillis spent hour upon hour in these early days of his priesthood instructing prospective converts or debating the objections of those who came looking not for light but for argument.

Few people know how taxing these hours of convert instruction can be, especially when they follow each other through a full morning or evening. Physical labor can never drain a man as exhaustively as facing three, four, or five successive inquirers, each one taking a different lesson.

This work, which today is carried on principally in the large Paulist Information Centers in major cities, is not glamorous, heralded, or humanly exciting. It is one of many simple, unadulterated tests of zealousness that Paulists are put to before their Superiors assign them to the varied specialist activities for which the newly ordained might have talent.

Father James Gillis had been marked for the mission band, but he could not achieve it unless he proved himself in his first parish assignment given him by his Community. His subsequent appointment to part-time missionary work within a year after his Chicago arrival was the seal upon his having passed the test. The hours given over to the patient teaching of simple catechism, the interest shown in the searchers who came begging truth, the zeal manifested in combating even one parlor debater proved to the Paulist Superiors that Father Gillis was ready for a broader convert field.

The Chicago mission work was not a full-time assignment for young Father Gillis. The schedule worked out for him was more in the nature of a training period or mission apprenticeship. He was gaining a small reputation at Old St. Mary's as an excellent speaker—that was no proof he would make an excellent missionary. There must be a trial of his talents in the work itself before any decision could be made that young Father Gillis deserved missionary status.

No contradiction exists in this policy of the Paulist training plan. That a man can hold a crowd's attention with a sparkling talk at a High Mass or on a great occasion means little in the light of what determines an effective missionary. A dazzling orator may please a congregation, delight its aesthetic sense with his performance, but not move anyone to go to confession. Even on this occasion, should he get them to the sacrament, he may not have the patience and sympathy to hear out the thousands of penitents that besiege a missionary in an average preaching year.

The prospective Paul may lack the simplicity of style needed to give a short, telling instruction—he may lack the temperament to adjust to the inconveniences of mission life—he may lack the disposition to be friendly and comradely with the

priests of the parish where he is preaching—he may lack pru-
dence and discretion in working with the problems that may
confront him on a mission. The list of possible points on which
a good speaker is not necessarily a good missionary is endless.

The shortcomings considered are not always under the control of each missionary hopeful. A boy may yearn with all his
heart to preach missions and not have the health to withstand
the ravages of the constant shifts called for by the missions. A
prospect may not have the voice, the drive, the particular x
quality that shows a mission spirit.

James Gillis had to be put to the trial and he was sent out on
his first mission. The initial test was in the fall of 1904 at Holy
Cross Church in Chicago. His older companion was Father
Elias Younan.

The young-old combination was (and is yet) a routine
practice of mission bands of all Communities. The young, untrained preacher is sent along with the master to learn the ropes.
The apprentice is schooled by first giving an instruction on the
Commandments or on the making of a good confession. He is
taught how to handle the announcements and to answer questions from a Question Box feature, which is a special part of a
Paulist mission. After a few months of this he may be permitted
to tackle one of the main subjects of the mission sermon schedule. With one sermon prepared and delivered, he moves on in
time to a second major subject. Finally he has a full course of
mission sermons and is ready to take his regular turn on a
mission, alternating the main sermon from evening to evening
with his partner.

An interesting side light on this coupling of James Gillis and
Elias Younan is the fact that Father Younan is the first Paulist
young Gillis had met. Long before the impact of Father Walter
Elliott's talk, Elias Younan had lectured at St. Charles when
James Gillis was a student there. The priest was certainly the

key in the lock, if not the actual door through which James Gillis came to the Paulist Community.

Father Gillis never said this, but in the psychology of how his vocation grew, it is difficult to see how Elias Younan can be omitted. The boy at St. Charles who kept the steady record of events wrote in enthusiastic terms about Father Younan's visit and lecture.

Under May 14 of the St. Charles year he says: "In the evening we were treated to a most excellent lecture . . . The lecture was on India by Father Younan, a Paulist." There follows a blow-by-blow description of the fascinating talk that must have left the young students on a high key of excitement as they retired for the night.

Young Gillis sums up the evening by writing: "The lecture was simply marvelous. I cannot attempt to describe it. It created a profound impression on me. Even making allowances for youthful inexperience and the power of an eloquent speaker on my mind . . . it was the most interesting lecture of the kind that I ever attended."

The lecturer of 1896 was now the mentor of the boy who had written those paragraphs. James Gillis was fortunate to begin his training under the vivid preacher on India. Father Younan was as colorful as the talk he had given the students. Syrian by nationality, he had been born in India and lived there for forty years. He had been a Jesuit but left the Society to join the new Community founded by Isaac Hecker.

Younan's presence was compelling—so much so that his fellow missionaries used to accuse him of hypnotizing the people. Piercing eyes gazed steadily from a handsome, swarthy countenance that was topped by a great bush of jet-black hair. He is described as one of the great missionaries of the era by today's old Paulists who were students in those days of Father Younan's glory.

Whatever natural gifts James Gillis had were going to be

tested well and improved under this master. Father Gillis
learned, as any wise young man learns, by watching and listening and asking questions. He grasped after and assimilated the
little knacks a finished speaker can teach an "almost perfect"
one, as Monsignor Gibbons called his First Mass preacher.

The test pleased Father Younan and he reported that James
Gillis should be kept on the missions. That was no problem for
the Paulist Superiors. They had more calls for missions than
they could fill and they were most willing to follow Father
Younan's recommendation.

The new life was not any easier in its peculiar burdens than
had been the static career of the parish convert-maker. Mission
work brought a whole new set of demands to the young priest.
Parish life at Old St. Mary's had meant being settled, being
known, making friends, having a life with the Community. The
new life afforded none of these opportunities to James Gillis as
he made his first trial with the mission band.

Missionaries are never settled, because two or three weeks are
their longest tenure in any parish. They are God's gypsies or
traveling salesmen, living out of a suitcase, always temporary
guests, ever geared to pack and move on when one parish mission ends and the next one on their schedule falls due. Father
Gillis learned in short order that there would be no great
friends or solid contacts made in this new life. He saw that the
matter of knowing people and being known by them was a
thing of the past.

He once described how shocked he was to have this lesson
of the missionary's anonymity brought home. "I had preached
what I thought was a bang-up sermon and left the pulpit with
no little sense of elation at the attention the huge throng had
given me. Imagine my devastation when two people among
my first dozen penitents that evening confided to me that they
were coming to confession because of what *I'd* said *in the in-*

struction. I was flattened properly that they didn't even know *I* hadn't given the instruction.

"My companion had given the instruction. He was a foot taller than I, so you can imagine how closely the people must have been following who was who and which was which!"

Father Gillis's experience was a baptism which all aspiring preachers must suffer. As any missionary can relate, there are hundreds of times in a mission career when a man receives comments akin to the one Father Gillis describes. They are the little stumblers along the way that hurt the vain but amuse the truly humble and help keep them humble.

That James Gillis was chuckling as he recounted the incident is obvious. His ability to tell it on himself is a good warrant of the humor he found in the experience. A vain man would never have spoken of his unknownness. He would have buried the slight and recounted something more glowingly descriptive of his excellence as a preacher.

Actually the people were more discerning than Father Gillis knew. Father Albert Murray, editor of the Paulist magazine, *Information*, tells of a mission in those early years when Father Gillis was assigned to preach with Father Thomas Burke, the acknowledged pulpit orator of the country.

Father Burke was doing the burden of the preaching, assigning his young companion two main sermons for the week. The two appearances were convincing enough for many of the parishioners, and they said so to the pastor. They told him that they wanted to hear the young preacher as well as the old one. The second week found Father Burke being requested by the pastor to alternate evenings with the junior missionary. Father Burke agreed readily to the suggestion, and James Gillis was a regular on that mission duo from that time on.

In his first round of mission duty James Gillis conducted a mission on the outskirts of Chicago, then one in St. Louis, another in Chicago, one at Logansport, Indiana, and a final one at

La Grange, Illinois. This tour completed the first part of the
Chicago Mission Band's schedule for the season.

There came a respite for the Christmas period, but in January
1905 James Gillis was drafted again to help fill the rush of
calls the Paulists had received for parish missions.

The end of that year was the end of James Gillis's test. No
questions remained in the mind of the Superiors as to whether
or not the new man had a missionary's qualities. He was given a
full schedule in 1906, and that was the official recognition that
he was a regular member of the Paulist Mission Band.

Talent will out, it is true, but in Father Gillis's case we can
trace his quick ascendancy to the regulars' ranks as due to more
than talent. He loved the missions and put his heart and soul
into the work. Zeal was merely finding its way and breaking
to the surface of this life. The glow and spark of the young
man's sermon delivery were coming from that fire that had
been lighted years before when he'd sat before Walter Elliott
and had risen from that encounter converted to the mission
apostolate.

In his personal and Community life during these years Father
Gillis was not having the same glorious success that he had in
achieving full-time missionary stature. Two matters caused him
heartache and discouragement. The first of these revolved
around his Community life. By that odd crisscrossing of circumstances that frequently puzzles all of us in life, Father
O'Callaghan, the man responsible for James Gillis's decision to
be a Paulist, was his Superior in Chicago. His reaction now was
to look with disfavor on his protégé!

Within four months of arrival in 1904, James Gillis, new,
untrained, looking for and needing approval, straining to
develop confidence, wrote: "Preached in evening . . . on some
prominent intellectual aberrations of the day—à propos of a
good many things appearing in the newspapers . . . Do not

know with what success . . . Father O'Callaghan says nothing at all. Apparently disapproves of my sermons. . . . Acts and looks unsympathetic—I must struggle along alone—making or marring myself for lack of good criticism."

The estrangement that widened was not recorded by James Gillis until the affair broke on him like a hurricane on a helpless ship. An important mission had been scheduled in Chicago and James Gillis wanted a good partner for the work. He begged John Harney, a young Paulist contemporary, to come to the city and work with him. Father Harney agreed but asked that the mission be postponed a week to allow him to finish the job he was on. The pastor of the Chicago church was agreeable and the mission was shifted to a week later, a change to which James Gillis assented before he broke the news to his Superior.

"I was not prepared," he states, "for the outburst that came. Father upbraided me most severely, and took the occasion to make a summary of my disobediences of the year—a kind of blanket indictment of all the evidences of my lawlessness. The attack was almost entirely unjust. He raked up cases in which I had acted from absolutely conscientious motives, and without the slightest notion of disobedience.

"In fact he charged me with that sin in cases where I honestly was working tooth and nail and under great disabilities for the good of the missions and of the people, and without anything that a reasonable man could consider disobedience.

"However, I got the dose, and it was a bitter one. . . . And this after my having . . . worked as never before in my life, have been again and again on the verge of exhaustion—and have had no thanks for it—rather blame—my motives have been vilified and my spirit of obedience questioned. It is a pretty how-de-do. . . .

"Perhaps this is unfair and even sinful, so I had better write no more. . . . The whole year has been clouded with these misunderstandings . . . All these things are compelling me to reconstruct my views of men and of life, especially life in a religious community."

The long entry covers three more pages, and it is evident that James Gillis is getting up a good head of steam. The pen races wildly along the lines, and the writing, which long ago had lost its fine and precise stroke, is worse than ever.

The conclusion of the bitter penman is the saving kind that James Gillis managed in all his dark moments. It is one of those paragraphs that demonstrates clearly the urgent struggle and the frequent success that attended his bouts of dejection.

"I am weary . . . chagrined, disappointed—and pained beyond expression . . . I must pound away tho'. . . . And may God give me some spiritual courage and patience and tolerance—in all of which I have been woefully lacking, as the very existence of these notes must give evidence—and God help our Community, send us men with zeal and detachment, and give us wise, efficient, and reasonable Superiors."

The wound had been made in a very sensitive spirit. Youth, with that fairly miraculous recuperative power, healed the lesion quickly, but the white scar tissue remained to show the place of the hurt. The danger ahead was in the question: How well or how often would the spirit show this resiliency if the years to come brought more and more severe wounds?

The misunderstanding with Father O'Callaghan seemed not to affect the mission work. What lists and records there are show the same drive and will that characterized the work of the beginner.

There was a little change, however, noticed by the young Paulist himself. His preaching at times became sessions of impatient and intolerant scolding, and this worried him fearfully. The dread he faced was that the bullyragging was an indulgence of his personal pique at the unfairness of the position in which he'd been represented by Father O'Callaghan.

James Gillis was honest, bitingly honest, in his knowledge

and admission of his weakness at this time to "leave everyone for dead." He knew he expected a great deal of people, knew a flick of disappointment over an issue could send him into a scorching sermon against those responsible, and he prayed that he could overcome this dubious talent for "really giving it to them hard."

His first weeks at Chicago had proved how disastrous this talent could be. James Gillis tells how "my sermon Sunday . . . incidentally arraigning theatres, has aroused much comment. Many actors and actresses in the congregation. One of them, Chauncey Olcott, left his card. Much offended. Sexton says a hundred people took exception to my remarks."

The early incident did not please the priest any more than the new outcropping of testiness that he was showing. James Gillis comments, "My belief is that I shall mellow down—not because the conditions that disclose themselves on the missions do not call for vigorous and even vehement treatment, but because I am beginning to question the usefulness of such means."

The "means" he describes in another entry as "my blunderbuss methods." The opinion about whether he ever controlled them, even to the end of his life, is greatly divided. In later years more artistry and finesse attended his preaching—the style of gun he used was no longer the blunderbuss. Most people, especially those on the target range, felt he still packed the new arsenal with the same old heavy charge of dynamite.

A second circumstance, of a very personal nature, was another contributing factor to this scolding style that had overtaken James Gillis's preaching. An August 1905 visit to his home had disturbed him thoroughly—left its tremors in his soul even to the last year of his life.

"My visit to Boston is marred seriously by the growing infirmity of my mother. She is fading considerably. Naturally, she feels that the end must come—and her mind, which used to be so sprightly, seems to incline to melancholy, though not quite to gloominess. She is turned old with these several years of virtual invalidism—her spirit is gone—her brain does not work always accurately, and there can be no doubt that she is not very far removed from her end."

James Gillis faced this future trial as inevitable. In some small way he was able to accept the future and thus steel himself when it came. There would be sorrow and dismay when his mother died, but her passing would not be the shock and surprise that accompany the earthly separation of some parents and children. This future moment was certain to occur even if the date was not established.

The greater and more prolonged trial that he fought over was his family's future and his own inability to be of any financial assistance.

"Besides Mother's condition," he continues in this entry, "my visit to Boston unearths some very disconcerting facts. My father works too hard—he is not as strong as he was before his serious illness of last year. Katie, doing the housework, is overexerting herself . . . Mary is plodding along with her work in the photograph studio—John is not yet settled . . .

"It makes my heart ache to see the girls both slaving and my father working along against a heavy debt on the house, while I have placed myself in a position where I can be of no financial help to them. I suppose I ought to have more faith in Divine Providence but I cannot help feeling that it is cruel in me to make them bear the burden.

"I feel now very keenly what I have felt formerly less sharply—that when a man goes for the priesthood in a religious community, it is not he himself that bears the cross, but very frequently, the folks at home.

"I need guidance as to what to do in this matter."

If he sought and received counsel there is no sign that it

proved effective. The problem grew beyond reasonable proportions and must have devastated him for the next year. It almost took him from the Paulists, but as the year sped by absorption in work seemed to overpower his concern for the family.

The journal is sprightly at times, beams with pleasure at a mission or retreat successfully completed. There are notes and descriptions of interesting places and people as he swings through his tour of duty.

An example of the mood that appears to show his improved spirits is this story that indicates his fascination and delight with a youngster who played at being a priest.

"Met . . . a remarkable little boy . . . who lives in the convent. The Sisters, visiting in Lowell, Mass., in search of vocations, noticed this boy who can say Mass like a priest, knowing Latin, ceremonies etc. He is clever, sharp but modest, unassuming and childlike. The people in Lowell used to go and hear him say 'Mass' in his own home after the real Mass in the church which he served.

"He immediately fell in love with the Sisters, and when they were gone wept, would not be consoled, wrote and begged to be allowed to go and live with them. He was so persistent that they answered—and the boy's father agreed. Sent him to Chicago—and now he would not leave on any account.

"Strange fascination for the Religious Life. Plays with nothing but holy things, indulges in no sports and repels the little girls who try to flirt with him. But lives, the only boy in this house full of girls.

"Served my Mass, delightfully well. Dignified as a little pope. The bishop rather balked at allowing him to continue 'saying Mass' but the Sisters had him do it in my room. He has all the paraphernalia—rather startling thing . . . brought him to Chicago . . . to give him a chance to be among the boys at the altar for one day at least.

"Now of course he wants to be a Paulist and nothing else. Maybe some day—But, at all events, a remarkable boy."

The good humor of this occasion is repeated, rather increased, with the recounting of the retreat he conducted at Loretto Academy near Niagara Falls. "This is the time of my life," he exults, "like a foretaste of heaven . . . This is joy— and I am revelling in it."

He should have collected and boxed the joy rather than be so profligate with the retreat days. The family problem swarmed him in a month and, like a man breaking a hive of bees, James Gillis was stung brutally and savagely.

The critical issue which he seemed to have lost or sublimated since his last visit was rife with thorny angles when he arrived in Boston. His own pages are the narrative of a heart in turmoil. James Gillis came to the edge of his Paulist life and wondered about leaving the Community.

"A grievous trial and difficulty—— My father has had a falling out with the priests of the parish . . . I called on the pastor and got a 'freeze'. . . The only solution of the difficulty is that my folks must move away. . . .

"But this is a drop in the bucket of my disappointments that are just now brimming over.

"My mother's condition is a trial— She has grown very weak since I saw her last—failed dreadfully. It is a pain every time I cast my eyes upon her.

"Katie, caring for the house and nursing Ma, has had a breakdown . . . Mary plodding away . . . without any prospect of release from the daily grind under a tyrant of a boss. . . .

"A big debt, far bigger than I imagined—$4500—on the house . . . and consequently my own mind dubious as to whether I am doing my natural duty—and add then my own tussles with my Superior in Chicago . . .

"Out of the cloud of difficulties and uncertainties one thing becomes evident. I must investigate into the financial condition of the family and determine once and for all whether I can in conscience remain in a position where I can be of no assistance to them.

"It is hurting me—in spite of my difficulties on the inside it would upset me dreadfully to leave the Community. Yet the problem must be faced and the question demands an honest answer."

The honest answer did not come quickly at all—it took one year to arrive. When it landed on James Gillis's desk he was not sure he wanted the answer this way—his Superiors appointed him the master of students at Washington, the job to become effective in September 1907.

The critical problem of wondering whether or not he should remain in the Community was never to arise again. Yet this family matter and his fears about their being supported persisted until he died.

How extended was this irritation and how intensely it must have pressed on James Gillis through the years can be guessed at from a letter found at the time of his death. The letter begs the Superior General of the Paulists to keep a kind and solicitous eye on the members of the Gillis family who survive Father Gillis. Father James feared that if extreme illness attacked any of them their small savings would be exhausted and they would have no means of subsistence.

Mary Gillis confirmed this brooding concern over the family that depressed Father James in his late years. "Every visit he made found us getting on the same subject, how would we manage in the future should serious hospital expense hit us? I told him to stop worrying, we were all right, and God would provide as he had for eighty years."

The strange aspect of this problem was the height and depth of the strain and fretting it caused James Gillis all his life. The mood was incompatible with the life of faith and trust that he preached. When he would confront his conscience with this inconsistency, he would upbraid himself for a woeful lack of confidence in God.

How poorly even the most intelligent souls understand themselves! Father Gillis's real problem was not doubt of Divine Providence and not entirely worry over the family's future. His trouble, more accurately seen, was his own frequent shortsightedness at the contribution he had made to his home. A spiritual giant in many phases of his development, he seems at times not to have grown up at all in this one.

On how many occasions must he have advised other souls who worried over the question of their vocation versus family support that silver and gold were like straws in the building of a home when compared to the divine riches a vocation would bring to a family. James Gillis knew this as well as he knew his name, but his written accounts of the problem never include this kind of reasoning on his own case. The matter presents no great chink in the armor of a formidable soldier of Christ; rather, it shows that emotions can outdebate on occasion even the most consistently logical of minds.

VARIETY IS THE SPICE
OF EXPERIENCE

chapter v

Father James Gillis received the Superior General's assignment to the position of student master with the words, "God have mercy on me!"

The words sum up fairly well the actual despondency that flooded his being as he realized the magnitude of the new job. He was almost overpowered by a strong temptation not to accept the work. He did not want to head the scholasticate at Washington for many reasons, the main ones being: first, his sense of inadequacy at guiding and forming future Paulists; and second, his pleasure, satisfaction, and joy with the active life of the missions.

The fear that charged his soul as he contemplated himself teaching students the basic elements of the spiritual life and being forced to decide their acceptability for the Community was understandable and valid. He reasoned that a saint would tremble at being made responsible for one soul; what then should he feel being asked to take the burden of thirty aspirants to the Paulist priesthood?

Here he was receiving this appointment within a few months of having questioned his own intention of remaining in the Paulists—and that difficulty still persisted! Suppose he found finally that he must leave because his family needed him. How

would that affect the youngsters he was training? You couldn't
spend a lifetime explaining to each student that your problem
had nothing to do with your love of the Community. Students
preferred rumor and speculation, something exciting about
your departure. The impression they'd derive would be the
worst and, therefore, in some cases the most harmful—if he himself eventually had to leave and aid his family.

Again, if his own soul was this unsettled, if out of his own
prayer-life was coming no great trust or faith in God, how did
he form priestly souls to strong, fervent prayer and saintliness?

These perplexities were in the world of his spirit. But equally
as bothersome were the temptations against taking the position
that rose from his love of the missions.

Going back to Washington meant forsaking a wonderfully
satisfying work, the preaching of missions and retreats as well
as the busy, exciting activity of the parish. The studentate
meant just that—becoming one with the students again. You
followed their narrow boundaries, lived their close, bell-ridden
days. You waked, walked, prayed, ate, studied with the seminarians. Not much time on the missions was needed to knock
you out of condition for such a tight regimen.

James Gillis felt this phase of the problem more acutely
than the spiritual side of it. The mission life was a tangible, real
grip on the apostolic work to which the Paulists were dedicated.
The missionary is no doctrinaire about souls and conversions.
He doesn't theorize about the evil of sin or the presence of the
devil in the world; he wrestles with these matters in his
apostolate.

The missionary knows, sees, counts the gains for the kingdom of heaven as much as is given anyone in this world to
know, see, count. James Gillis was in the middle of the battle,
and his spiritually martial sense reveled in the struggle. He
groaned to see himself returning behind the lines to stand and
urge others to go out and fight.

That summer of 1907 was a miserable one for James Gillis. He had become increasingly concerned over his family's need for support, and in the Community he was faced with the need to give word on the decision of his new appointment.

James Gillis made his own yearly retreat at Lake George that summer. He pressed for a solution to his dilemma, making each hour of his seven days of recollection count. His prayers and Masses were earnest pleas that the Holy Spirit, who had directed him thus far, would lead him again to the right choice.

Once again he sought counsel of a trusted friend among the Paulists, and the advice received was simple but telling. James Gillis was informed that the Community had special need of him. It was implicit in the fact that his family had not requested or even indicated that their condition required his help. The Community had indicated it required assistance at Washington; in fact, the Paulists had made their demand explicit—he had a letter from the Superior General appointing him to the student house. The will of God was being manifested in the word of his Superior.

Father Gillis took the counsel readily and humbly. The latter virtue should be stressed to offset the question as to why he couldn't have figured this out for himself. The issue seems so uninvolved, why any great interior hassling over it?

To such a question one can only answer: Why any disturbed hours or moments for anyone in the world? The person comes up so close and enters so emotionally into his crisis that judgment is destroyed. The perspective of the coolest and most balanced soul can be misted when emotions rise and fog the values that have hitherto seemed clear.

All personally involving issues ensnare each of us, and thus James Gillis was prey to this trap in the matter of deciding his new assignment. Widely recognizing the soul blindness that had ensued because of his nearness to the whole business, he sought advice—humbly, he accepted it; earnestly, he pledged to God that he would try to fulfill his call.

In the main, Father Gillis kept that pledge. Priests still active, who were students under the young master of novices, state with deep sincerity that James Gillis did an excellent work.

Father John Carter Smyth, who was later to be ordained and to join James Gillis on the missions, says without reservation, "He was one of the finest teachers we had in my time at the scholasticate. I thought in after years Father Gillis had taken over a pretty desperate situation and pulled it together manfully. He handled our theology with the surety and confidence that were needed at that period."

The problem of the Church—flagrant and dangerous enough to cause concern—was the affliction of Modernism. Called by Pius X the "synthesis of all heresies," it had infected some European and American churchmen. In this July of 1907 while James Gillis puzzled out his true place in God's scheme, the Holy Office condemned in the decree *Lamentabili* some sixty-five propositions of the Modernists. Pius X followed his condemnation by an encyclical in September of the same year. The Pontiff's letter stripped the heresy of its pretensions and exhorted all to the vigorous use of the remedies he prescribed to combat the evil.

The Church realized wisely that seminarians, and especially men advancing to receive major orders, could have been susceptible to the influences of Modernist writings and periodicals. She stressed the need of watchfulness in scholasticates and subsequently requested that an oath against Modernism be taken by all men advancing to the priesthood. The past half century had showed the Church that the taint could creep into a student if a firm, well-grounded course in theology was not pursued. All seminaries were instructed to be sedulous in their care of the future priests of the Church.

The Paulists had made an ideal choice when they selected

James Gillis. He brought strength and certainty to his spiritual counsels and his classroom work with the Paulist seminarians. He was all champion on the side of the Church and demonstrated forcefully the integrity of his Faith. The young minds and hearts under him rallied to this quality of leadership and responded to it willingly. Modernism got not even a toe hold on the students in the care of Father Gillis.

As could be suspected, the mission activities played a siren song to the young master of students. He read, he talked, he reminisced about the mission life. It was not going to be too hard to tempt James Gillis back to the pulpit and the traveling, the new places and exciting activities of the missions.

Temptation is not even a good concept of James Gillis's desire to return to the missions. He was *looking for* a chance to conduct some parish revivals around the Washington-Baltimore area.

Within the first two weeks of the September opening of the term he was eagerly accepting an invitation to assist Father Peter Moran of the Paulists on a small, one-week mission at Barnesville, Maryland. In October, Father Gillis took on a retreat at St. Paul's parish in Washington and preached again for October devotions at Holy Comforter Church in the same city.

Another request for mission assistance came in, and Father Gillis wrote to assure the priest that it could be arranged. Suddenly he realized that taking the job would mean shifting some classes and begging someone else to assume his burden. The knowledge of the inconvenience this would mean alerted his conscience to the responsibility he had assumed. It *was* his duty after all—not anyone else's. The missions were not his charge or worry. When he faced God he would answer not for them but for his failures as student master. James Gillis tore up the letter of acceptance and wrote his refusal.

He buckled down to the teaching of dogmatic theology and Church history. Each week he gave a conference to the seminarians or varied the diet for the young men by bringing in one of the other Fathers of the house. Especially did he lean on Father Walter Elliott, now aging and virtually retired from any active work, who was in residence at the studentate. The older man gladly took his turn at giving conferences and spiritual direction to the seminarians.

The year slipped along, each day belying a remark that Father Gillis had made at Lake George: "My success at Washington would be a miracle, considering my youth, inexperience, and lack of special aptitude."

None of these faults he listed was affecting his management of the scholasticate. If there was any difficulty outside of the attraction James Gillis had for the missions, it was his demandingness and hyper-expectation where the students were concerned.

A retreat note Father Gillis made just prior to the end of his term of office as master reads: "I have had my eyes opened in this retreat especially in regard to the necessity of gentleness, meekness, sweetness of spirit in my dealing with the students and with myself.

"I am inclined to be raspy, harsh, caustic, easily disgruntled, pessimistic (in spite of the fact that I always disclaim pessimism) . . .

"But the severity and asperity and discouragement if men did not meet my exacting demands, my conclusion that demoralization was at hand if some little accidental fault took place—these things were only too evident. They must be—will be—changed."

James Gillis tried to change. He did succeed in tempering that tendency to hold a sharp critical attitude on the students. The men who grew to the priesthood under his guidance do not recognize this self-complaint he makes. They admit no feeling existed in their student days that their master was a Simon Legree.

Interestingly enough, the criticism that James Gillis makes of himself proves more to his credit than his condemnation. He must have worked wonders in his nature (which he knew so well) to achieve gentleness and understanding.

Later years show the deep-grained streaks of all this critique he made in 1908. The raspy, harsh, caustic, easily disgruntled, pessimistic moods dogged his life, filled his soul, influenced his writing and speaking. The unremitting struggle to overcome himself could well be the great lesson of his life—it certainly was among the major conflicts in his striving to develop maturity.

The sorrow James Gillis had been expecting but dreading for years struck him in the summer of 1909. He was at Rehoboth, Delaware, with the students. It was the first vacation at a new property which Father Gillis had begged the Community to purchase.

In the midst of becoming acclimatized to the new surroundings, settling the boys, and taking charge of St. Agnes Church in the vicinity, James Gillis received word that his mother was dying. Quickly he arranged for one of the Fathers to take charge and he hastened home.

Catherine Gillis lingered on gravely ill for four days after James's arrival. He fretted about the students and their settlement at Rehoboth but feared leaving Boston with his mother so critical. Yet no change occurred in her condition to show her worsening. After consulting with the doctor Father James was dismayed to learn his mother could last weeks or could last minutes.

The priest-son decided that he must take the chance of returning to the students. He prepared to leave, telling the family he would check with them as he traveled to Delaware.

Mary Gillis describes the remarkable incident that happened as her brother was about to take his farewell of them. "Pa went in to see if Mother was alert enough to say good-by, and when he came back to us he said to Jim, 'You'd better wait just a little while before going.' Jim agreed and we sat around talking while Pa returned to the sickroom.

"Not long after, Pa hurried out and called us. 'Be quick,' he said, 'and start your prayers for the dying. Your mother's going.'

"We ran to the room and all of us fell on our knees. Jim went over and took Ma's hand and we didn't know if she recognized him, but at that moment she died. We were as shocked by Pa's sixth sense on that afternoon as we were by Ma's death."

James Gillis was overwhelmed, as could be expected of anyone so bound to his mother and father and family. His sorrow was deep inside, buried in one of those recesses of his heart which he never brought to light.

One single entry records the separation. "Mother died. The passing of the dearest and the saintliest. God grant her immediate rest. Mother, pray for me!"

As quickly as he could Father got back to Rehoboth. The leaving of his father and sisters and brother was heartbreaking, but the student master knew a sterner duty. He had decided once and for all that his Paulist call was the important one. He wanted to be with his family in its worst hour, but God's indicated responsibility was that he be with his seminarians.

Father Gillis wondered if he was being tested too severely as he arrived at Rehoboth. A scarlet fever epidemic had broken out. The town was feeling the scare as quarantine closed home after home. Visitors stopped coming to the resort for their vacations; the streets were deserted as residents stayed indoors to avoid contagion. Rehoboth was like a ghost spot.

The fear that the students might contract the fever worried James Gillis. He checked with New York, and it was decided to send the boys back to the college. Father Gillis had to remain at Rehoboth to assist at the local church where he had promised help. He must have smiled grimly as he sat out the final days at the empty student camp. He had hurried back to Rehoboth— to be alone.

The old lure of the mission life crept back to woo Father Gillis as he entered his third year in Washington. His preaching journal shows a rapid succession of entries for individual talks, retreats, and missions.

As the pages carry the story of work and increased work outside the studentate, the question arises: What caused the change? The man of two years back had decided resolutely to fulfill his commitments to his job at Washington. The journal now shows that he could not be doing justice to this decision.

One extenuating circumstance for the renewed mission work was the fact that the Paulist missionaries were receiving more jobs than they could fulfill. The small group working out of Fifty-ninth Street in New York was overscheduled. They were being promised in more places than they could handle. Work was taken always in the hope that somehow the schedule would be met.

That "somehow" usually meant filling in the job by asking an experienced man involved in his own work to take a week here or there. James Gillis was an example of this. His ability and proved performance were known. The mission would not suffer if he conducted it. Thus the extra jobs were placed before him for his consideration and he took them.

This problem was not peculiar to the Paulists. All missionary Communities faced the issue of more calls than men. Refusal was not easy when pastors relied on you or begged immediate emergency aid. Again, within a Community, sickness or death depletes a mission band and substitution becomes necessary.

No Community wants to overschedule itself. Certainly the Paulists of 1910 didn't want it. They totaled only sixty priests at that time, and these sixty were spread thinly as it was. Yet the calls came in, owing in great measure to the vigorous, popular missions for which the Paulists were becoming famous throughout the country.

The Paulists had tried valiantly to eliminate the problem of overscheduling. In 1902 they had founded the Apostolic Mission House in Washington under the direction of one of their men, Alexander Doyle. Father Doyle, who would be aptly dubbed on Madison Avenue today as an "idea man," had conceived the plan of training diocesan priests in the technique of conducting missions. If each diocese sent a band to the Apostolic Mission House, that group could be schooled in mission-giving and return to its central location ready to supplement the few religious missioners in the area.

The present Apostolic Mission Band of the New York Archdiocese stems from one of these original groups that began under Father Doyle in Washington. Its success and perpetuation in parish missions are proof of the workability of the Paulist idea. Sadly, other dioceses were not able or did not care to offer men for the training. The idea foundered and died, not so much impractical as untried.

James Gillis did not have to take the extra work that fell to him. The conditions under which it was brought to him were if it were feasible or if it did not interfere with his classes or counseling. He did not think it interfered. His conscience must have justified the acceptance, because he was inclined to be scrupulous where the studentate duties were involved.

There was no doubt some rationalization on his part when doubt flagged down his mission zeal and directed him to look inward. Perhaps he told himself that he needed to distract his mind from troubled thoughts over his mother's death. A mission or two couldn't harm anyone and would help him. Perhaps he argued necessity for gaining income for the Washington house. After all, the student house could use extra money, and missions kept him from having to drain New York for necessary funds.

There are a carload of "perhapses" and it does us no good today to speculate on them. All of them did James Gillis little good either; he broke down under the strain of these two absorbing, draining interests. Split between the missions and the student house, he collapsed in December 1909.

His journal notes: "Health broke badly . . . Speaking in whisper for 6 weeks—— Many preaching engagements for Lent, including 3 series, all given up."

James Gillis recovered his strength sufficiently to resume classwork at the studentate. His voice resisted treatment and continued to be too weak to permit more than the intimate lecturing in the classroom. Toward spring his throat eased a little and, thankfully, he was able to sense the vigor coming back to his tone.

The decision was made that he should go to Lake Placid for the summer and rest. There, while reading and resting, pondering his condition and reviewing his years at Washington, James Gillis took a big step. He sent in his resignation as student master.

The action seems sudden, precipitous. No hint of it is given in the spiritual notes James Gillis left on his retreat of 1909. Out of all he wrote, only one line covers the momentous determination: "Summer 1910— Adirondacks . . . Voice recovered. . . . Resignation accepted."

James Gillis had fully argued himself into the rightness of this step. He has left extensive considerations on the virtue of obedience, about which he wrote in his retreats of 1907 and

1908. In these paragraphs can be read his definite opinion that he had full justification in making known to his Superiors his incapacity for the Washington work.

"I have maintained for some years past," he wrote in 1907, "that teaching is not adapted to my nature . . . If I cannot rid my mind of this judgment, why should I not—acting in all honesty for the good of the Community, for the good of souls— in conscience speak my doubt on my condition to my Superior that he may be better informed?

"I think Father Hecker allows this—I think Father Baker allows it—Father Lallemant and all that school . . ."

James Gillis's conviction was acceptable to the Superior General. The now ex-student master was appointed to the New York Mission Band.

In 1910 Father Gillis was told to report to the Paulist Motherhouse at West Fifty-ninth Street in New York and take up his new work with the missionaries. He packed and left Washington, feeling, as all religious do, that this would be one of many moves he'd make in a lifetime.

He recalled how he had been saddened to leave the many converts and friends he had come to know in the few years at Old St. Mary's in Chicago. Each time he raised the chalice they had presented to him on his departure, he remembered them but he realized the pain of remembering was not as keen as it had been.

Now he was saddened to be leaving the students and faculty at Washington. Eager as he had been to be relieved of the responsibility, he was not overjoyed to make another separation.

He philosophized at that time about "the turning wheel of religious life." He remarked, "I cannot say that I am happy to be leaving all that has been so precious in these years. Yet, I think of other men who have come and gone and returned to this spot as they move on this turning wheel of religious life. Perhaps, I too shall return to a place here in the years ahead."

James Gillis was many-talented, but, at that writing, prophecy was not one of those talents. The transfer to New York in 1910 was to be the last until death sent along the next change of venue. West Fifty-ninth Street, fifth floor, Room 31, was to be home, confessional, court, den, study—all the possible places one room can become for a priest who lived the diversified existence of Father Gillis. In this room he prayed, wrote, gave counsel, confessed priests, debated Community policy, fought his stormy life's crises, entertained his friends, suffered his last illness.

A reading of the list of activities that took place in Room 31 could give an erroneous impression. The list means no more than that James Gillis was stationed at the Motherhouse; he did not spend all his days there.

The records show that his room was used for the activities mentioned—when he was home—which in the next forty-seven years was seldom. He crossed the United States on dozens of occasions, the Atlantic Ocean and Europe about five times, the Pacific Ocean and the Orient at least once. Add to these world-wide east-west, west-east journeyings the trips north and south and the lecture treks to hundreds of cities fanning in any direction, and you have a good estimate of the mileage on the travel meter.

James Gillis's preaching journal embraces fifty-seven years. The book has about five hundred pages. Only thirty-seven pages are used to cover the first nine years—a little more than four pages per year. This means roughly that, once assigned to New York, Father Gillis moved at more than twice the rate he traveled in his early years. Little wonder that there could be a false impression given if his room at Fifty-ninth Street were considered the dwelling of a sedentary person.

The places visited, the talks and number of talks given are
dry statistics. There is little sense in listing or counting them.
Mission year succeeds mission year, parish follows parish, as
the schedule is completed.

Out of the journal, however, come stories—gems in themselves—that divert the routine of mission-giving. These are the
different, the odd, the fascinating experiences that from time
to time lift the book of solid entries into the field of classic
mission annals.

There is his tale of being the Arkansas Traveler for a brief
period. The time is spring 1914, and he writes that he began
that year with a trip to Arkansas. It was deliberately chosen as
perhaps the most unpromising field in the United States and the
most benighted and bigoted. Father Gillis was advised not to
send word ahead or to advertise the coming missions for fear
that he might not so much as get into some of the towns. He
agreed it was very sound advice but dreaded the embarrassment of stepping off a train in Arkansas and announcing a mission!

The young missionary decided to start at Fayetteville, the
largest and best town in this section of the state. Upon arrival
he stepped off the train and went to a wretched hotel for breakfast. Afterward he checked with the clerk about Catholics in
the town. The man was noncommittal and told him to see a
Mr. Ucker. The clerk finished the brief interview by directing
Father Gillis to a store on the next street.

He found Ucker, or the Brothers Ucker, and explained his
presence. At first they were suspicious, and with reason—
Fayetteville, with the rest of Arkansas, had been the stamping
ground of every bogus priest in the United States.

The Uckers were not the final judges on whether or not
James Gillis was to be accepted as genuine. They turned to a
Mr. Healy who was sitting by a big red stove in the middle

of the store. "Father Gillis, Mr. Healy. He *says* he's from New York."

Mr. Healy did not look as though he believed it, but after a little chatting he seemed convinced. At any rate, he agreed to assist in the work of getting the mission started. Tom Healy and the Ucker brothers eventually became three of the best friends the priest had in Fayetteville.

The little church of the town seated about one hundred and fifty. Father Gillis lived in a dreary room in the house next to the church. He described his situation tersely: "Wood fire—damp—cold bedroom—rats under the floor all night—roosters in the yard very early in the morning. I stuck to the room and read until late in the night after mission services."

The mission was well attended, and the missionary was elated at the interest shown by the non-Catholics who came. He remained a week at Fayetteville, which seemed to him an oasis in a desert of bigotry and inhospitality.

Then came the real penance when he moved on to Bentonville. In a town with a population of about twenty-five hundred there was one active Catholic woman, a Mrs. Foster.

The plan was that he should lecture in a store. But the place proved too dreary and the mission site was changed to the courtroom—if the judge agreed. Father Gillis chased about looking for the judge. He finally discovered him by waiting in the lobby of a cheap hotel until the judge was finished with his supper.

From the dining room came a cripple, no higher than the priest's waist, walking on his knees, his legs or their relics tucked under him, arms and hands shriveled. It was the judge, "Bud" Smith, who turned out to be, as James Gillis said, "a bigger man than many a giant."

Judge Smith asserted he had no objections if the priest could persuade the other judge to go along with the idea. "We did persuade the other judge," writes Father Gillis, "though he had been holding night court."

This did not solve all the problems, because there were difficulties and obstacles owing to the opposition of bigots and the absence of any alert Catholics except Mrs. Foster. Some unknown turned people away, saying that the lecture had been called off. Another man, a lawyer, told many that there would be no lecture that opening night because he himself was to argue a case before Judge Humphrey.

Father Gillis spoke between two fierce red-hot stoves while immediately in front of him a group of men sat, "chawed" tobacco, and spat at the stoves. Commenting on this scene, James Gillis said: "The sizzling of tobacco juice was perhaps the best imitation of the hissing they may have wanted to give me."

He made no converts and, disheartened, went to Rogers, which proved worse than Bentonville. He had bargained for the "opry" house for half a week and the school for the other half. After getting started in the school he was told by the superintendent that he could not use the building. This proved more than Father Gillis could accept and he writes: "I simply gave him a good scolding—a few hot shots very politely—and told him that we had decided not to move."

The man retaliated and blurted out that he knew the town better than Father Gillis did and he was sure that 85 per cent of the people did not want the priest in the town anyway.

To cap this rejection, the editor of the local paper refused to accept ads for the mission. James Gillis was discouraged but not whipped. With the aid of sympathizers who knew his predicament, he got the story of these prejudiced actions circulated around Rogers. The people rallied to the underdog. James Gillis sensed the swing in sentiment and rehired the opera house. He had the satisfaction of knowing he had beaten the bigotry of the two men who had opposed him—the opera house was jammed as he came on stage to begin his mission service.

When the round of these missions was completed, James Gillis returned to his home base for a rest. The weeks had not been good for him in many ways, the worst of these being in his spirit. He was depressed by the lickings he had taken in no-priest land and he spared no one's feelings in his commentary on his adventures among the people of Arkansas.

Fortunately the depression was a mood, not a way of life. James Gillis rose from it and was ready again to go out and carry on his Paulist vocation. He reasoned that some other approach must be used in the fields that he had left, but while working to find that approach, conversion could be made in the places at hand.

In the months following the Arkansas debacle James Gillis was teamed on missions with Father Bertrand Conway, a young contemporary. It was an unusual arrangement that two young priests would be sent out together, but unusualness always has a great place in the plan of God for the souls He would use.

Father Conway was an almost direct opposite of Father Gillis, except in one thing: he too wanted non-Catholic mission work and was impatient to be doing it. He had preceded James Gillis to the Paulist priesthood by five years and had been preaching missions from his first years in the priesthood. The non-Catholic apostolate was his special dream and he prayed for the day when he could conduct that work exclusively.

Bertrand Conway is a book in himself. Born of a Jewish mother and an Irish father, he combined the gifts and aptitudes of those two strains to a remarkable extent. Volatile and clever, a Gatling-gun conversationalist, he mixed in everywhere, made friends swiftly, and found it a challenge always to go where he was least welcome and to do what he was told was most impossible.

Father Conway could be audacious in his proposals and equally audacious in making good his boasts. Once, long after these ventures with Father Gillis, the Superior General cautioned Father Conway about the need to balance the numbers of his Catholic and non-Catholic missions. Bertrand Conway's answer was that if he had his way he would do nothing but non-Catholic work.

"But you couldn't support yourself," was the protest.

"I'll bet I can," asserted Father Conway. "You let me sign up a complete non-Catholic mission schedule and I'll do more than support the work!"

He argued his point, and finally the Conway persistence and enthusiasm won out. Permission was granted.

At the end of the mission schedule Bertrand Conway came to the Superior. He held out a sheaf of statements on the previous year's work. Every mission had been financed handsomely and he had money left over, ready to be used on undertaking another year's work of the same nature!

Obviously Bertrand Conway was not a conservative by temperament or intention. Stating that he was the direct opposite of Father Gillis would be considered a mild comparison by many Paulists. Father Conway was as lively and effervescent as James Gillis was measured and controlled. If James Gillis had fire in his preaching, Bertrand Conway had fireworks.

Both were attractive personalities to an audience, but for the antipodal effects produced. Father Gillis was admired for what he said and how well he said it; Father Conway was relished for what he got away with saying and how breezily he related it.

Father Conway was the dash of daring that was needed to propel the non-Catholic mission ventures. Father Gillis wanted to do the work; Father Conway decided they should take the chance. As they worked together they discussed plans for making a trial of an exclusive non-Catholic mission to be held in New York City.

They obtained permission to start in St. Paul's Church and opened their mission to a mixed audience that included from eight hundred to a thousand non-Catholics! This is January 31, 1915—the audience was gathered without benefit of radio or television plugs, billboard, magazine, or newspaper advertisements. Ninety converts came from the group, and that result left no doubt of the possibilities of such missions in the minds of Fathers Gillis and Conway.

James Gillis had a page in his preaching journal that describes the plan used at that time to reach the non-Catholic audience. "Credit due Knights of Columbus—42 councils voted $10 to $50—70 pastors contributed circulars—300,000 in all. 13,000 pamphlets given away—2500 books (Question Box and Plain Facts)—500 Catechisms—first big effort of the K of C in New York."

The success of the idea was underlined when John Cardinal Farley appeared in the sanctuary of the Paulist church on the last evening of the mission. Seemingly he had come to do more than lend approval. Subsequent developments saw the same kind of mission requested for St. Patrick's Cathedral and a date set for January 1917.

The bantam missionaries—so they were dubbed, since both were short, stocky men having a confident stride—were elated with the accolades their experiment brought. Joy was heightened when bids came from all over the country to conduct this series of spiritual exercises styled for non-Catholics.

A mission was scheduled in St. Louis, Missouri, one in Newark, New Jersey, and a third at Paterson in the same state. An engagement in Torrington, Connecticut, came next, followed by one in the Sioux City cathedral in Iowa and one in the Denver cathedral in Colorado.

In March of 1916 the men were back at St. Paul's in New York and repeated their original triumph of the previous January. A second year of the work ensued, and the two men were busy up to the end of 1916. They were due for the assignment they had accepted at St. Patrick's Cathedral for January 1917.

On this mission Fathers Conway and Gillis intensified their coverage of the city and its environs. Letters and leaflets were directed to a greater number of churches and church groups. More councils of the Knights joined in supporting the extensive effort. The step-up in the campaign made for a highly successful mission—and a greatly taxing one for James Gillis.

He was a badly fatigued preacher when the last evening of the cathedral's mission came to a close. Unhesitatingly the doctor advised rest. Father Gillis was told to go to California for an indefinite leave of absence.

Now check this schedule James Gillis followed. He left New York on February 25, 1917, for Old St. Mary's, the Paulist church in San Francisco. In March of that year he was lecturing at the Paulist Newman Club attached to the University of California at Berkeley. On April 6—the day America declared war on Germany—Father Gillis preached the *Tre Ore* for Good Friday at St. Mary's. April 22, he was on a three-week mission with Father Owen McGrath, one of the Paulist missionaries on the Pacific Coast.

He continued this work until the summer, and in September resumed preaching missions along the coast at parishes and in the soldier camps springing up in the Far West. The next twelve months show no abating of activity—if anything, the tempo is increased. In 1918 and 1919 the same high level of work and travel, preaching and lecturing continues as James Gillis covers the coast from Portland, Oregon, to San Diego, California. More completely stated, the whole United States seemed to be the priest's mission territory, because listings are made of missions given during this period in ten different states.

This was what the missionary on sick leave was doing from the time he left St. Patrick's Cathedral an ill man in 1917 and returned to New York in 1920! The leave of absence for a rest had itself been so hectic that James Gillis was forced now to quit all his preaching work. In the summer of 1920 he was sent on a voyage to South America. It was felt that he could not possibly work up a mission schedule on the high seas. He would be forced to relax.

The suspicion arises that James Gillis was either a hypochondriac or a man too frailly constituted to carry the burden of mission life. Three rest leaves in one decade incline one to think that the priest was thinking too much about his health or working too hard to be thinking about it at all.

Checking the broad spate of activities that followed immediately upon the trip to California for sick leave offers grave doubts that Father Gillis was a hypochondriac. No one who was morbidly anxious about his well-being would throw himself promptly into this mission maelstrom if all the while he was fretting that the missions were destroying his health.

Admittedly James Gillis had more than average—but not morbid—anxiety about his health. In the diaries of St. Charles and Brighton Seminary, there are concerned references to colds, laryngitis, twisted ankles, and the like—those run-of-the-mill boyhood afflictions and sprains that are so much a part of our growing up. Few people note these things in passing, let alone in youthful diaries.

An example of this boyish anxiousness would be an item such as the following written when James Gillis was nineteen and a freshman at St. Charles: "Last night I was very sick, for the first time since I came. . . . I find that I shall have to be more careful of my stomach now than I have heretofore. This morning . . . I went to the infirmary and remained there, taking a sleep and resting until bedtime. Then I went to bed in the regular dormitory, not caring to sleep in the infirmary for there are two or three fellows there who are tainted with consumption."

This was the entire entry of December 4. On December 5, the very next day, the boy wrote, "In my anxiety to take enough exercise out of doors, I overdid the thing today and this, together with my sickness yesterday, made me very weak. . . . Father Duffy asked me how I was feeling. I told him and suggested that it would be a good plan for me to go to bed. He agreed and I went and had a good, long, heavy sleep."

The early notebooks are replete with such references. The same items—less specific but as frequent—crop up in the jottings of the young priest. Tuberculosis seemed to have been the young Gillis's hobgoblin; sore throat, colds, loss of voice, the middle-yeared bugaboo; loss of mental alertness and faculties, the aging Paulist's nemesis. There appears always to have been something weakening or worrying Father Gillis all his life.

Yet had he been a softy and sobbed in self-pity about his lumps and bumps, Father Gillis could never have achieved the place he carved for himself in these past five decades. The awe-inspiring number of talks, sermons, and conferences he delivered, the unbelievable total of the reams of copy he composed—these declare that if this man had a drift toward being a medicine buyer and hospital hunter, he overcame that drift with vengeance. If James Gillis was a prescription collector, he certainly didn't allow himself much time to get them filled at the corner drugstore.

The second important consideration on the matter of Father Gillis's problems in health is that, hypochondria or no, he suffered embarrassing, prolonged, and serious illnesses all through his life. These were not imagined or induced disabilities but real and painful ones that were crosses he bore patiently and heroically.

The first of these struck him around 1917 and was probably

a contributing factor to his gaining the leave of absence previously mentioned. A good description of the affliction would be to use the expression one priest ventured when he termed it "Gillis's psoriatic passion." James Gillis suffered the red blotch and white scale of psoriasis for over thirty-five years.

Anyone meeting Father in the late years of his life would notice the small blush-colored patch over one ear at the edge of his tonsure-like hairline. This was the last, the end of the skin disease that had tormented and embarrassed him for the greater part of his life. From 1917 on, his body was spotted with the red blotches and at one time they covered him from head to toe. This was disturbing enough to what normal vanity was in Father Gillis, but the cross did not end in having to bear this scarlet-spotted visage and body. Psoriasis has a crueler twist than mere angry rashes on the skin; it develops scales—fine, white flakings that break from the sores.

If no other cross were asked of James Gillis, this one would have been heavy enough in itself to make a great burden. He was sensitive about himself, his appearance, careful in personal grooming and cleanliness. Imagine the agonized embarrassment of this temperament out on missions, tormented in the knowledge that his disease made a repugnant sight for those who tended and cared for a rectory.

Mary Gillis describes her own reaction on Father's first visit to Boston soon after the psoriasis had become acute. "I remember going into Jim's room to make the bed and straighten up. All around the bed in a great circle on the rug was this snowy-looking sift or powder. I wondered what happened and looked up at the ceiling, thinking perhaps the paint had chipped, fallen, and broken across the bed. The ceiling was perfect. Then I went to the bed and saw the sheet and pillowcase a mass of these little white flakes. I realized, remembering how Jim's face had been when he'd arrived, that his body must be like his face, and these flakes proved it."

This was the reaction at home—comparatively mild and simple to take. What when the housekeeper or cleaning girl in a strange rectory entered your room and was confronted by the same sight? James Gillis must have dreaded this situation day after day on the constant rounds of missions he fulfilled through the years. The clue to his feelings might be grasped in the revelation that he carried his own bed linen with him on missions rather than cause difficulty with the help in the rectories he visited.

Father Gillis lost precious time in his efforts to combat this condition. Heat lamps or the sun seemed to be the most beneficial remedies he had found through years of seeking medication. Hours would have to be spent under the lamps to obtain some little relief. The sun was the strongest assistant of all, but even here, after a summer of baking in the hot rays, the disease could return inflamed and ugly as ever. It resulted usually in having to suffer the thing, and James Gillis did that until the late years, when the disease finally disappeared.

Two other prolonged and irritating handicaps round out this picture of steady physical inconveniences that Father Gillis bore. These, it must be remembered, are apart from the emergency or critical infirmities that occurred as he became older. The first of these complaints was a misplaced vertebra on the upper portion of the spine, the second a weakness of the intestinal walls—both maladjustments requiring leather straps to afford strength and protection.

His heavy schedule of travel and preaching, lecturing and writing, in season and out, had to be done under this chafing set of harnesses. Add this to the years of psoriasis and you have a picture of James Gillis's high courage and patience as his monumental life was lived out—hypochondria or no.

The last in the variety of experiences that were pressed into these years was the voyage he took to South America in 1920.

The trip was much like anyone else's trip to the lower American continent, but time would prove it to be the turning point in James Gillis's life.

A respite had come to Father Gillis in the summer of 1920. He had an opportunity to make a voyage to and beyond the Caribbean. He sailed from Baltimore on June 23 on the Grace Line ship, the *S.S. Santa Rosa*.

Father Gillis wrote on the front page of his private log the names of the captain, officers, pursers, steward, engineer, and last the assistant freight clerk. Opposite the latter title is written: "Gillis!" Apparently he traveled at the courtesy of the line and had to be checked in as a member of the crew. He does not reveal whether he officiated at the post, but imagining him on the deck running the freight department on the S.S. *Santa Rosa* presents a delightful picture.

Apparently he was not too heavily involved in the baggage room, because he lists thirty-four books that he read on the trip. As someone said when hearing of this: "Gillis had every right to the title of assistant freight clerk if he carried that many volumes around with him."

Despite the facetiousness of the comment on their number, these thirty-four books became the pivot of James Gillis's life. As you run along the titles which are all dutifully listed in the log along with the number of pages in each volume, you spot the future taking shape.

A partial list shows:

> *Now It Can Be Told*
> *Inside History of the Peace Conference*
> *Biology of War*
> *Guesses at Truth*
> *Errors of Democracy*
> *Greed*

There are twenty-eight more—Shakespeare, Locke, Doyle, Eliot, Chekhov, Butler, and others. His thinking concerned the six books listed above. The long days at sea and the quiet nights were bringing forth comments like this in the log: "Reading Philip Gibbs all day long—*Now It Can Be Told* . . . one paragraph concerns me—'I, as an onlooker, hated the people who had not seen and were callous of this misery . . . the clergy who praised God as the Commander-in-Chief of the Allied armies and had never said a word before the war to make it less inevitable.' "

James Gillis makes no comment on this statement of Gibbs, but it had buried itself deeply in his heart. How deeply this and the entire book had touched him is read in the résumé of his feelings when he concluded it. "[Gibbs] is pacifistic as a result of great observation of the war—and seems to be almost Bolshevist in the good sense. Fierce against . . . all who profit by bloodshed, bitter at times and—I am inclined to think—justly so—— A powerful arraignment of war and of warmakers. I have read the book principally because I am concerned that I must henceforth preach against war as long as I live, or can speak, and I am ashamed of some things I said in public during the war . . . All who had voice or pen should at long advance argue against war."

On July 5 James Gillis is reading Macaulay's essay on Frederick the Great. He notes that the essay is an arsenal of weapons against war.

These are the only forthright remarks on the long list of books James Gillis read. He notes the day when he begins and ends the reading of others, such as Dillon's *Inside Story of the Peace Conference*, but there are no further considerations set down.

How arrive at the fact that these books became the point on which the future turned? James Gillis wrote two comments, and that hardly makes a future career.

Two comments do not make a career, but they can—and did—begin it for James Gillis. The time at sea was a time for deep meditation; he was isolated, marooned with his thoughts, the thinking bit deep, cut a pattern of resolve like acid on an etcher's plate.

The shipboard reading was the beginning of a way of thinking, a lead toward new subjects and convictions. Father Gillis didn't jump from the voyage and become a street-corner ranter, but he did disembark with a wider horizon for his speaking and writing. James Gillis did return to land wanting more facts and more information about topics he had known only cursorily before.

Anti-war idealism was not the entire future he would make. As he put the voyage behind him, the drive to preach against war may have been the main thought that now clouded the hitherto clear stream of Father Gillis's priestly ideal and purpose. But beneath the murky, troubled stream, justice, honesty, truth were the crystallizing ideals.

The hypocrisy, venality, dissembling, and pretense that attended the war and the peace had shocked James Gillis. He was spurred to a watchfulness against these sins in all of life. He took the hint, the clue, from the debacle of 1914–18. Looking around in the years ahead, he would see that these evils were as dangerous in our everyday existence as they were in the time of the first great world war.

He would develop along this tack and soon be searching out the bogus, the sham, the corrupt in politics, labor, religion, sport, theater, economics, science—every phase of our society.

Thus a career was taking shape under the impact of reading that was performed as a recreation on a Caribbean cruise.

Twin aids would give impetus or splendid occasion to the career. First, James Gillis himself was temperamentally most suited, dispositionally most apt to become a righteous crusader and moral champion of causes. With dynamic presence as a speaker and superior talent at dialectics, he had a rich vein of moral indignation just waiting to be mined. Add to these a trait

of perfectionism that demanded things always at their best—
and a bent toward pessimism that saw things always at their
worst—then give all this a platform, and the world is in for a
sound spanking.

The second aid to the future career was that the platform
was given to James Gillis. Within two years he was to be
appointed editor of *The Catholic World*, the Paulist Fathers'
and America's oldest Catholic magazine.

The world was to be spanked collectively—in some cases,
individually—for close to twenty-six years.

THE TEMPESTUOUS
TWENTY-SIX

chapter VI

James Gillis's head must have spun a little as he read the words of praise and reverence that filled the letters and notes piled on his desk. He had every right to savor them and, at the same time, cherish the tone of regret with which each correspondent ended his letter of praise. Father Gillis had announced his retirement from the editorship of the Paulist Fathers' *Catholic World* magazine. These complimentary lines and phrases were the response to that announcement and they were welcome reactions.

A hard, frequently bitter, and sometimes unhappy twenty-six years were being totaled up by this mail. There had been good times, pleasant days, glorious moments, but these he didn't wonder about. He had known, he'd felt how right he'd been then. The unpopular things he had written, the strong positions maintained, the abuse and vilification he suffered—those were the things that made him wonder about the kind of job he'd done. This mail was a warm, resounding "Well done!" for which anyone would be thankful and pleased.

The sad part of the announcement about retiring was putting it into effect. There was the work of moving out to be done. Twenty-six years of gathering papers and books and notes and correspondence had developed a formidable set of files.

An editor's career is contained in his files, and each man who faces the emptying of these cabinets must spend haunted hours. James Gillis was triply haunted then because in his years on *The Catholic World* he had lived three careers. They mingled, they crossed, at times they parted and ran like parallels, never meeting; but, interwoven or separate, he had kept three individual files.

He had been a leading radio preacher, he had been an editor-lecturer, he had been a weekly columnist syndicated in Catholic papers. Each of the careers faced him with its history as he tackled the job of moving out of his office.

No one can know what James Gillis experienced as he flipped folders and sorted papers on each of these activities. People speculate, offer ideas that one thing more than another evoked his memories and caused him to dream. Speculation is useless, because James Gillis took to his grave whatever moment in all the files he thought most memorable.

There is more than a good guess, however, that of all the folders he lifted and glanced at, one bulging folder opened the sorest wound. When his hand closed over the envelope marked the *Catholic Hour*, James Gillis must have bled just a little more from the cut that never really healed.

The mystery of his removal from the *Catholic Hour* schedule of speakers was never answered to his satisfaction. One priest humorously suggested that the problem was among the first questions James Gillis asked of God when he faced Him. Who—if anyone—had been responsible for unceremoniously dumping him from network broadcasting in 1942?

The travails of James Gillis and radio broadcasting are of a strange pattern when the over-all design of his life is studied. He had troubles and he made troubles for himself in many phases of his career, but the radio work seemed a special packaged brand of nettles for this Paulist.

When Station KDKA of Pittsburgh made its first radio broadcast in November 1920, the Paulist Fathers were more interested than the average group in radio's possibilities. From the time of Isaac Hecker's foundation of the Community, it had lived his ideals and exhortations on the practice of the Paulist vocation. Father Hecker had urged personal sanctification in his subjects and laid this down as their main work. His second request of the new institute was that it be characterized by zeal for apostolic work.

"Our vocation is apostolic," Isaac Hecker told his men, "conversion of souls to the Faith, of sinners to repentance, giving missions, defense of the Christian religion by conferences, lectures, sermons, the pen, the press, and the like . . ."

There was no mistaking the meaning of Father Hecker's expression "and the like." He intended that his men not only see but seek out every *new* technique and means possible for achieving their apostolic purpose. His own example was brilliantly before them in his founding of the Paulist Press, which was to become the leading Catholic printing firm in America. Even prior to this, Father Hecker had launched *The Catholic World*, followed this with a magazine called *The Young Catholic*, and never stopped dreaming of someday beginning a Catholic daily newspaper.

This was a man who blazed new trails and worked out new ways. The Paulists didn't need much convincing in 1925 that had their Holy Founder been around he would have beamed beatifically as the Community opened a switch and announced: "This is Station WLWL, owned and operated by the Paulist Fathers." That was the reason behind their more than average interest in radio broadcasting. They believed that they should be doing it. Five years after Westinghouse had announced its KDKA, the Paulists were in radio—the twelfth high-powered station filed in the United States.

The first broadcasting was performed in the main section of

the rectory. Equipment, studios, offices were squeezed in at a happy sacrifice by the men who manned the parish. You might fall over wires and bump into a microphone, but you were proud that you were in a wonderful growing world of opportunity for the Community and the Church. It was a thrill to be able to say: "WLWL is the largest Catholic station in the country."

Patrick Cardinal Hayes initiated Paulist broadcasting on September 24, 1925, and James Gillis followed him within a month. Soon the regular schedule swung into operation and programs were being carried on a day and night log.

The first year was hard work, but excitingly satisfying. Letters and cards poured in from all over the United States. Often enough the mail included letters that proved broadcasts had been heard as far away as England, Ireland, Germany, Alaska, many sections of Canada, Texas, Bermuda, and Greenland.

That was a wonderful year, and then came the radio war. It came to the Paulists in all the literal meanings short of bloodshed that the word can have. In October 1926 the Department of Commerce licensed another station for broadcasting on the same wave length as WLWL. The new station belonged to the Starlight Amusement Park of the Bronx. As Father Gillis expressed it, "Apparently the Department of Commerce considered Starlight Amusement of more consequence than religion!"

The Paulists were forced to surrender the wave length. They applied for a new spot on the dial and received it, renewing that license in 1927. In February of that year the Federal Radio Commission was created and placed in charge of broadcasting. The Commission revised the whole radio-station arrangement and WLWL was told it would have to share a channel with WMCA—WMCA being allowed to fix the hours to be used by WLWL. The blow was a hard one, since WMCA, a commercial station at five-hundred-watt power, could have the lion's share of the broadcasting day, while the Paulist station at five thousand watts was pared to fifteen and a half hours a week!

The Paulist Fathers fought valiantly to preserve even this small allotment of time. They could not understand the summary and discriminatory treatment that they were receiving from official sources. No doubt existed in their minds that the contribution they were making to radio history was as valuable as that being made by the growing commerical operators who seemed ravenously hungry for more air time.

If any fear existed among the Paulists that WLWL was not doing its job, that fear was buried by an avalanche of fan letters during this period of controversy. The bulging mailbags were a result of a happy misunderstanding on the part of the listeners who were tuned in one evening. The director of the station in signing off mentioned that WLWL was due to appear in Washington for a hearing before the Radio Commission. The hearing was to be in reference to the station's demand for more time on the air.

Many listeners mistook the meaning of the words and thought WLWL was being summoned to Washington to be read its discontinuance as a station. During the succeeding week, sacks of cards, letters, notes were bouncing on the Paulist doorstep and the station help stopped counting them when the tally reached sixty thousand! This was in 1931, before star-frenzy and fan-clubbing had become a professional occupation. The more than sixty thousand protests over the possible ceasing of WLWL was the spontaneous, unplanned, and very earnest response of people who desired to aid the station in its effort to remain on the air.

An old WLWL program booklet—far ahead of its time and imitated today by some cultural-educational stations—carries a page of these letters that came in answer to the misunderstood announcement. The five-thousand-watter of the Paulist Fathers had friends all over the continent—Ohio, Montana, Missouri,

North Carolina, Minnesota, Newfoundland, Prince Edward
Island, Quebec, Nova Scotia. WLWL had friends everywhere
but where it counted most.

This was proved time and again to the Paulists as they not
only saw their broadcasting hours dwindling but found themselves bouncing along the radio dial like popcorn in a vending
machine. A run-down of the broadcasting frequency assignments of WLWL reads like a Toonerville train schedule with
no one sure when and where to get on and off.

In 1925, the opening year, 1040 was the dial spot; in 1926,
780; 1020 and 810 were the frequencies assigned at different
times in 1927; finally in 1928 WLWL was placed at 1100 on
the dial. Every new shift was made stupidly or callously in favor
of some other station—each a commercial profit-making venture.

Some of the most indignant prose ever written by James
Gillis flowed under the nib of a very busy pen in those days of
discrimination to which the Paulists were subjected. One passage he delivered over WLWL at the height of the controversy
causes a gasp at the picture of righteous rage and stinging con-
tempt that it implies. This man was no man to have against you!

[The Paulists] have been fretted and harassed and tor-
tured with delays and reversals of judgment apparently
intended to wear down our patience until we should cry
"quits." But through it all we have labored at vast expense
and with considerable self-sacrifice to provide an educa-
tional and cultural program for persons of intelligence and
good taste, for those who recoil with disgust from the bun-
kum, the hokum, the vulgarity, the asininity, the crudity,
the imbecility of the usual commercial programs. . . .

It would seem that those whom the Roman poet called
the *vulgus humanum*, the vulgar horde, those who lack
good taste and intelligence and ambition for culture, the
moronic mob, the kind that patronize "Scandals" and "Fol-
lies" and other such indecent and shameless musical come-

dies . . . the kind that laughs loudest at smutty jokes in plays brazenly advertised as "bawdy"; the kind that prefers the more lascivious type of motion picture, seeking from the screen sexual titillation or a substitute for it; the kind that devours mountains of salacious fiction and buys the obscene periodicals exhibited brazenly at the corner newsstand; the kind that demands jazz and more jazz and nothing but jazz from the radio; this element of the population —the "hotcha" element—I say is articulate: it knows no modesty; it is a total stranger to reserve of manner; it knows what it wants and gets it . . .

Meanwhile, the quieter people, the unobtrusive who still cherish old-fashioned virtues of modesty and decency and retirement, are crowded out, ignored, laughed at. They too know what they want but the mob won't let them have it. It is held a fault in them that they don't push and pull and scramble, don't get into the common melee and fight for what they want. They get no sympathy from the *hoi polloi* who believe in wading in and getting theirs, like pigs in a trough of swill.

The work, the rage, the prayers—the singular effort of James Gillis or the total effort of the Paulists and their friends—were not going to save the station. Father John Harney, Superior General of the Paulists, waged as steady and articulate a battle as Father Gillis. He wrote, he talked, he appeared in Washington to seek redress for the Community, but with no success. The war went on with conditions worsening for the Paulists through the nineteen-thirties.

A small hope flickered when Station WOV made a verbal agreement in 1936 to sell its stock for $300,000 to the Paulist Fathers. WLWL would then be restored to full operation and WOV, owned by John Iraci, would realize a handsome profit. All that remained was the written contract and transfer of stock.

Two clippings in Father Gillis's radio file state—if they do not explain—the sudden and mysterious debacle that struck this

deal. *Broadcasting*, the broadcast advertising magazine, in its
September 1, 1936, issue reveals:

> More confusion than ever now seems to prevail over the
> series of moves and countermoves made by parties associ-
> ated with the transaction whereby WLWL, New York
> station, operated by the Paulist Fathers, would acquire full
> time on a clear channel . . .
> Arde Bulova, New York watch manufacturer and
> broadcast station backer, who disrupted original plans . . .
> by purchasing WOV, New York, found himself the sub-
> ject of a vigorous attack at the hands of the Paulists in a
> letter filed with the FCC by Father John B. Harney, Su-
> perior of the Paulists, who objected to his intrusion in the
> negotiations. . . .
> The Bulova group stepped in by purchasing WOV,
> part-time Italian language station, from John Iraci, for
> $300,000 . . .
> Mr. Iraci . . . would become 80% owner of WNEW,
> New York, in which Mr. Bulova is heavily interested . . .

The reasons behind the sudden grab of Mr. Bulova for WOV
stock, which collapsed the Paulist hope of remaining on the air,
were hinted at more explicitly in *Light* magazine of the same
September.

> Everything marches on except the solution of the radio
> difficulties of Station WLWL . . .
> A few weeks ago it seemed likely that through the sale
> of Station WOV to Station WLWL . . . full time justice
> would be secured. . . .
> Contrary to the known and direct expressions and
> wishes of Station WLWL, Mr. Arde Bulova, chief
> owner of the Bulova Watch Company, and according to
> *Variety*, a generous contributor to the Democratic Na-
> tional Campaign chest, suddenly stepped into the picture.
> Time started marching backwards. . . .
> As far as Station WLWL is concerned, Mr. Bulova, with
> the assistance and cooperation of Mr. John Iraci, president
> of Station WOV, has ruined the most recent and practical

way in which the radio problems of the largest and oldest Catholic radio station in America could have been solved. It also means a continued financial drain on the resources of the Paulist Fathers, which, if not remedied, must inevitably result in financial disaster, and the defeat and elimination of the only exclusive means left for free and open public discussion of topics of vital interest to millions of Catholics and non-Catholics.

Light was so right. The inevitable result predicted took place —the defeat of WLWL was finally accomplished and the Paulist station was eliminated from broadcasting life on the night of June 16, 1937, between 7:45 and 8 P.M.

James Gillis delivered the final talk. His voice, usually charged and vibrant, was somber, close to mournful, as he expressed the sad farewell the occasion warranted. "I am a New Englander," stated the editor of *The Catholic World*, "and although I am not of Puritan stock some of my friends tell me that I am overreserved and even lacking in proper human sympathy. [Yet] when Father Malloy asked me to speak two or three minutes on this final and sorrowful program of WLWL, I hesitated . . . because I felt the effort to express myself under the circumstances might cause anguish in my heart, if not bring tears to my eyes . . . to me, it is a matter of pain—to you, I believe, it is at least a matter of regret."

The Paulist rectory was like a mortuary chapel as the broadcast closed. The silence pressed all around—and most heavily on those nearest the corpse of WLWL. No one wanted to flick the switch that would cut the transmitting power, each realizing the meaning of the action. Not only would a radio station die, but a channel of Catholic information, delivered in truth and with integrity, would be dammed up. The Paulists would lose a strong, far-reaching voice; another tool to effect their purpose of conversion would be blunted, broken, and cast aside.

Strangely enough, the files of James Gillis were to be piled into the old studio and control rooms that still remain in the Paulist rectory on West Fifty-ninth Street in New York. You can stand in the old control booth of WLWL and look down into the dead rooms that now hold the words and papers and books of James Gillis. It is fitting that one of the champions of the ill-fated venture remains with it yet. It's like having a silent challenge on the quiet, muffled scene. Perhaps the spirit of that courage waits only to be summoned in old studios for a new broadcast over WLWL.

The heartbreak attendant on the snuffing out of WLWL was felt deeply by all the Paulists. James Gillis experienced as keen a pain at the demise of the station as any Paulist. The pang at the loss of the Community's radio outlet was to be a mere pinprick when matched against that which he suffered in his controversy with the *Catholic Hour*. The latter issue was to be more like the sharp stab of a knife.

During the years of WLWL's harassment by the federal authorities over its dial status and time allotment, the *Catholic Hour* came into being. The National Council of Catholic Men, with headquarters at Washington, had conceived the idea of a regular weekly nationwide program. The National Broadcasting Company was receptive to the idea and offered time to the NCCM on Sunday evenings throughout the year. On March 2, 1930, Cardinal Hayes inaugurated the series that was to become one of the top-grade educational-religious features of the decades of radio programing.

James Gillis, established as an outstanding radio speaker through his work over WLWL, was invited by the NCCM to conduct the Advent series for the 1930 season. He was the twelfth speaker invited to appear on the *Catholic Hour* and he delivered a series of sermons on the moral law.

The reception to the talks was more than average. The NCCM foreword to the collected sermons of 1930 states that "the large number of requests for them is a compliment to the speaker."

A second invitation by the NCCM, requesting Father Gillis to take over the same spot on their schedule in 1931, was just as great a vote of confidence in the speaker. The solidity of such confidence was evidenced by the fact that this invitation was repeated for the next ten years. A letter among Father Gillis's NCCM files shows that one series no sooner ended than the following year's invitation was on hand. On December 19, 1939, Monsignor Michael J. Ready, later Bishop of Columbus, Ohio, who was then General Secretary of the National Catholic Welfare Conference, under which the NCCM operated, wrote:

> *Dear Father Gillis:*
> On behalf of the Executive Committee of the Catholic Hour I invite you to accept a series of addresses on the Catholic Hour. The period proposed is October 6 to December 8, 1940, inclusive. This period comprises ten broadcasts.
> May I express the gratitude of the Radio Committee for your present splendid course. Your influence on the Catholic Hour audience inspires the sincere hope that you will accept the period for 1940.
> With cordial good wishes for a blessed Christmas, I remain
>
> Very sincerely yours,
MICHAEL J. READY
General Secretary

This was giving the priest a year's notice! Within two years' time James Gillis would find there was no series being arranged for him on the *Catholic Hour* schedule. At the close of the 1941 set of talks no year-in-advance request would come for the Paulist to resume broadcasting in 1942.

In 1939, however, he was considered a *Catholic Hour* fixture, teaming with the increasingly popular Fulton J. Sheen to make up the one-two Sunday-evening punch of the nationwide broadcast. James Gillis had become an Advent fixture. "You could tell that the holidays were near," one Paulist remarked, "when Jim came on NBC. It was like seeing Santa Claus on the street corner, you began counting the shopping days until Christmas."

A hint of dark days to come was presaged in a run of letters that the NCCM forwarded to Father Gillis in 1940. The Paulist editor of *The Catholic World* had written an editorial in the November 1940 issue of the magazine. The piece was entitled: "The Third Term a Bugaboo?"

The paragraphs of the editorial were marshaled arguments against Franklin Delano Roosevelt and his bid to run for a third time. The article appeared in the heat of the campaign in which Wendell Willkie faced Mr. Roosevelt and made a desperate effort to become the White House tenant.

Father Gillis's editorial might have gone unnoticed or, at most, caused a minor stir that faded away except for one event. Someone reprinted the piece in its entirety and flooded the country with handbills. They were mailed to thousands and thousands of people; thousands more were distributed on street corners and in stores and shops; worst of all, the wily reprinters had them passed out at the doors of Catholic churches in as many principal urban centers as they could cover.

The *Catholic Hour* received many of these handbills with letters attached that excoriated them and their speaker, James Gillis. The NCCM replied to their critics in a form letter that explained:

> Your letter referring to the editorial written by our current Catholic Hour speaker in the November issue of *The Catholic World* has been received in this office. Since it is addressed to Father Gillis we are forwarding it direct to him. We should like to have it very clearly understood, however, that neither the Catholic Hour nor the National Council of Catholic Men is in any measure re-

sponsible for any of the views of Catholic Hour speakers, other than those expressed within the framework of the Catholic Hour proper. The Catholic Hour never has become involved in partisan politics, and never will.

The Catholic World office was dunned with the handbills—and more than a share of canceled subscriptions. Father Gillis was shredded by correspondent after correspondent—some of the letters were vile, some threatening, some bitter. The stacks of mail showed he had made thousands of enemies.

In the election that followed the celebrated or notorious (depending upon the political viewpoint) editorial, more than fifty-five per cent of a record fifty million voters disagreed with James Gillis. Mr. Roosevelt became the first President to enter on a third term.

Father Gillis continued his editorial opposition to the President. He lectured as frequently as he could to underline his attitude. He was a non-interventionist and constantly accused Mr. Roosevelt of leading us to war.

The 1941 invitation to speak on the *Catholic Hour* came like spring—a little late that year. Monsignor Ready wrote in May of 1941 and offered Father Gillis two series from which to choose. One was in early fall, the second was in Advent. Father Gillis expressed his preference for the pre-Christmas set of talks.

He began the *Catholic Hour* addresses on November 2, his writings still pounding savagely at Mr. Roosevelt. The title given to this Advent group of speeches was: "What Is Wrong and How to Set It Right."

A run-down on the dates and titles of this last group of sermons is interesting if we recall the American history that was written in the Pacific on Sunday afternoon, December 7, 1941:

Nov. 2 Cause and Cure: Deeper Down and Further Back

Nov. 9 Tell the Truth and Save the World
Nov. 16 The Fifth Freedom: From the Mass Mind
Nov. 23 Local or Universal: Patriotism or Internationalism?
Nov. 30 Total Reform or None: Economic, Political, Moral
Dec. 7 Politics in Religion? Religion in Politics?
Dec. 14 From Christ and to Christ

Father Gillis's preaching diary shows that he faced a little personal problem that could have been titled, as were his lectures: "What Is Wrong and How to Set It Right." There is a line scribbled in his book where he notes the date and delivering of his November 30 address. The scrawled comment reads thus: "First manuscript refused by NCCM and rewritten by Father Gillis." The NCCM thought a few things wrong in the November 30 talk and they told him how to set it right.

The Paulist was not resentful of this request—at least the correspondence during this 1941 Advent course does not indicate that James Gillis was acting like a rampaging dissenter. An exchange of letters written within two days of each other reveals rather that Father Gillis was fearful lest he fail the *Catholic Hour* in conforming to its program rules.

Monsignor Ready had sent a letter to all the NCCM speakers in October of 1941 in which he reminded them: "We are especially concerned that the definite religious character of the Catholic Hour be maintained during these fateful days. Accordingly, the Catholic Hour Executive Committee requests all speakers on the program to emphasize its religious purpose in the selection and development of Catholic Hour addresses. We believe that the presentation of definitely religious programs at this time is the best contribution we can make for the welfare of our country and the Church."

The date of Monsignor Ready's letter to Father Gillis is October 17. There was no hesitation on the part of *The Catho-*

lic World editor after he had read the letter. James Gillis reached for the telephone and called Washington. He wanted to pin down any fluttering suspicions about the meaning of this letter.

Two days later he wrote to the NCCM, and his correspondence tells what transpired on the telephone. His statements hold also his firm pledge of maintaining the policy of the *Catholic Hour:*

> *Dear Mr. Heffron:*
> Since sending you my first Catholic Hour talk of this series on October 13th, I have received a letter from Msgr. Ready explaining that all talks on the Catholic Hour should concern religion primarily and perhaps exclusively. Thinking that perhaps his letter had something to do with the program I had submitted and my first talk, I spoke to him on the telephone and discovered that his communication was a form letter sent to all speakers on the Catholic Hour.
> I took the occasion to explain hurriedly the method of treatment I proposed to follow. . . . The treatment will be philosophical and theological and therefore of universal application. . . .
> I say these things to reassure you if you have any fear that I would attempt to expose my own views of the Federal Administration in the present crisis.
> Yours very truly,
> JAMES M. GILLIS, C.S.P.

Whatever conflict developed over Father Gillis in this series of talks that was to be his last for the *Catholic Hour* cannot be wholly discovered from any evidence extant among his papers. From all reports, he did not destroy any material that related to what his file lists as "Catholic Hour Controversy."

The one letter that states any NCCM disapproval of the Paulist's work is the letter of November 21, 1941, that requests him to rewrite the talk for November 30. The *Catholic Hour* chairman wrote:

Dear Father Gillis:

Your address for November 30, "Total Reform or None," has been read by the members of the Catholic Hour Executive Committee, and all are of the opinion that it is chiefly political, only remotely religious; and, further, that the political considerations which are mustered are, consciously or unconsciously, of the character of "America First" arguments.

It is respectfully requested, therefore, that the address be rewritten so as to conform to the letter sent to all Catholic Hour speakers, by the Director of Speakers, under date of October 17.

With every good wish, I remain

Sincerely yours,

EDWARD J. HEFFRON

James Gillis had indicated in his preaching diary the return and rewriting of the manuscript. That is the sole reference his papers have to the incident. The file on the 1941 *Catholic Hour* series holds no further remark or indication that Father Gillis would not be listed among their 1942 schedule of speakers.

His current series concluded, the editor of *The Catholic World* continued about his very busy business. He was writing a weekly column syndicated by the NCWC and titled "Sursum Corda"—this stint had been his since 1928. He continued his magazine work and he preached as frequently as opportunity and strength would permit.

Checking over a list of speaking engagements that followed the close of the 1941 *Catholic Hour* work makes one wonder how James Gillis kept up the pace. Talks are listed under dates of January 4, 7, 11, 13, 18, 25, 28 A.M., 28 P.M. February, March, April, May fly by with just as dizzying a succession of lecture or sermon obligations.

Summer vacation presented a chance for James Gillis to relax.

Vacation should have been a quiet, easing time, but it developed into a time of irritation. He was being plagued by rumors, surmises, opinions from all quarters that he would not be on the *Catholic Hour* for Advent of 1942.

Friends protested that they had seen or heard about the list of speakers for the fall and winter and his name was not among those announced. This was August. Father Gillis explained that he knew nothing about the radio schedule—as far as he knew he'd be back—he had no reason to surmise he wouldn't be invited to return to the program. By September he was tired of making excuses.

He wrote to Monsignor Ready on September 8 and received an answer in ten days. A week later Father Gillis answered the General Secretary of the NCWC. These three letters are the heart of the controversy that flared and flamed between Father Gillis and the *Catholic Hour*. These three letters are the contenders' own dialogue on the subject. There is much to be said on both sides, and the parties of the first part and the second part say it well.

September 8, 1942

Right Rev. Michael J. Ready
1312 Massachusetts Avenue, N.W.
Washington, D.C.

Right Reverend dear Monsignor:
About a month ago I heard, in a roundabout way, that my name was not on the list of those invited to speak on the Catholic Hour for the coming season. I confess to some disappointment, not only because of being dropped from the programs but because I had received no official information of that fact.

I understand, of course, that no one has a right or even a claim to be invited annually. But it did seem to me that after delivering thirteen series of talks in succession I might have enjoyed the courtesy of being told directly that my engagement had ceased.

However, my primary concern is not with that fact or

with the manner in which I came to hear it. What seems to me of vital importance is the reason behind the action of the N.C.C.M.

I cannot say that I had made no surmise, and in the last few days word has seeped through to me that my guess was correct—that I am *persona non grata* on the Catholic Hour because of what I have written in *The Catholic World* and spoken on public platforms (before Pearl Harbor) in regard to American participation in the war, and in criticism of some of the measures and methods of the Federal Administration in its conduct of the affairs of the nation.

Will you, therefore, kindly set my mind at rest by telling me authoritatively if my surmise is either substantially or entirely correct. You will understand, I am sure, that no information will help me unless it be given with complete candor. I should not care for a perfunctory or evasive reply to my question. I feel that I must have the actual reason for the cessation of a work to which I gave my best efforts, and a privilege that I highly valued.

Very truly yours,

JAMES M. GILLIS, C.S.P.

September 17, 1942

Dear Father Gillis:

I beg to reply to your letter of September 8th. The Catholic Hour has followed the policy of annually inviting speakers for designated periods. I regret that this policy has caused you disappointment insofar as no announcement went to you stating that you were getting an invitation for the present year. If we have failed in proper courtesy, I offer our apologies. It seemed to the Catholic Hour Committee that, since invitations were sent to speakers for each period assigned, there would be no reason to send notice that an invitation was not being offered.

The Catholic Hour did not extend an invitation to you this year because, during your past two engagements on the Catholic Hour, your editorial and lecture work in a special manner identified the Catholic Hour with your own personal political opinions. I refer to your active support of Mr. Willkie in 1940 and to your lecture tour for America First in 1941.

Regardless of your own or our efforts to keep your writing and lecturing free and separate from Catholic Hour responsibility, the radio audience failed to keep your other activities in their proper category. We have endeavored to keep the Catholic Hour a religious broadcast. It was highly embarrassing to have it accused of supporting a particular political aspirant against another and of promoting a particular political opinion. We had no right to limit your editorial or lecture activities during your broadcast period. But since those activities by many were identified with the Catholic Hour, we decided that it would be best to prevent similar situations.

Personally I regret the decision which it seemed best for the Catholic Hour to make. You have contributed many excellent series to the Catholic Hour. We are deeply grateful for that long and favorable service and we trust that in the future we again may have the favor of your consideration.

With sentiments of esteem, I remain

Very sincerely yours,

MICHAEL J. READY
General Secretary

September 25, 1942

Right Rev. Msgr. Michael J. Ready
1312 Massachusetts Avenue, N.W.
Washington, D.C.

Right Reverend dear Monsignor:

I appreciate highly your candid and courteous reply to my request for the reason of my being dropped from the Catholic Hour after a continuous service of twelve years.

I beg leave to ask now a personal favor. I would like to have the following statement inserted, if you please, in the files of the N.C.C.M. I think it may be useful or at least interesting after two or three years.

First: permit me to quote a couple of sentences from your letter of September 17th: "Your [i.e. my] editorial and lecture work in a special manner identified the Catholic Hour with your own personal political opinions. I refer to your active support of Mr. Willkie in 1940 and to your lecture tour for America First in 1941."

May I observe that the phrase "personal political opinions" might be misleading. It seems to suggest *partisan* politics. My interest is not in "politics" but in the political philosophy upon which I conceive the American Republic to have been built and upon which I think it should continue to operate. My opposition to the present administration was based upon a fear that it was abandoning fundamental principles consecrated by a century and a half of tradition. I opposed that change not as a partisan politician but as—I hope—a good American. If Mr. Roosevelt had been tenacious of the tradition, and Mr. Willkie had advocated changing it, I would have written and spoken for Mr. Roosevelt and against Mr. Willkie. Political tags mean nothing to me. I would regret therefore having the statement about my "politics" stand as final.

Secondly you say: "Regardless of your own or our efforts to keep your writing and lecturing free and separate from Catholic Hour responsibility, the radio audience failed to keep your other activities in their proper category. We have endeavored to keep the Catholic Hour a religious broadcast. It was highly embarrassing to have it accused of supporting a particular political aspirant against another and of promoting a particular political opinion."

I should imagine that intelligent listeners would have recognized that my Catholic Hour talks were strictly religious and that the N.C.C.M. had no further control or responsibility for my utterances.

Furthermore, I have reason to believe that most Americans and most Catholics favored the position I took in regard to our foreign policy. Take the question of non-intervention in foreign wars (one of the American traditions referred to). An Archbishop had written in a pastoral letter dated July 27, 1940: "There is no moral obligation for our becoming involved in the present world conflict. America's blessed mission is not to destroy but to reconstruct. This opportunity will come when peace dawns. America can lead the way in proving the stability of our democratic form of government resting on fixed moral principles."

Commenting on that statement (a splendid example by the way of what I mean by fundamental American political principle) and upon a later newspaper utterance by the same Archbishop, a particularly well-informed bishop said to me that between 90% and 95% of the hierarchy were non-interventionists. My own observation had led me to believe also that an equally large proportion of the clergy and laity were of the same mind. The fact that in the November elections 22 million votes were cast for the professedly non-intervention candidate, and 25 million more for the candidate who had assured the people that we should not fight on foreign shores, would seem to support my opinion. Since December 7, 1941 I have made no speeches on the matter.

I need scarcely add that I never attempted to use the Catholic Hour for a political purpose. I kept strictly to the rules governing its speakers. My script was invariably revised and read as approved. I do not see why it should have been "highly embarrassing" to have the Catholic Hour "accused" of promoting politics, when such an accusation evidently had no foundation.

Just one word in regard to "America First." There was no profession of political faith required of the members or speakers of that organization beyond a belief in traditional Americanism. There may have been a fringe of extremists in "America First" just as there is a fringe of extremists in the New Deal. But the program of "America First" was indicated in the title. That slogan I thought patriotic and honorable. I am inclined to believe that in years to come the principles advocated by "America First" will again be brought to the fore, and that the nation at large will come to realize that the movement was loyal not only to American Democracy but to the best interests of the world at large.

This letter has gone far beyond the bounds intended. But since I am asking only that it be kept in the files as my reluctant valedictory to the Catholic Hour, I ask to quote one final statement of what I mean by traditional American political principle.

In reply to a committee that waited upon Henry Clay, then Secretary of State, to ask intervention in Hungary in the days of Kossuth, Mr. Clay replied: "It is a grave and momentous question 'whether any one nation should assume the power of compelling other nations to observe international law.' (We could not give official aid to Hungary without abandoning 'our ancient policy of non-intervention.') If we interfere in Europe, Europe would have a right to interfere in America." And he declared, "By the policy to which we have adhered since the days of Washington, we have done more for the cause of liberty in the world than we could effect by resort to arms. We have shown to other nations the way to greatness and happiness. We should adhere to our system of peace and avoid the distant wars of Europe. We should keep our lamp burning brightly on this western shore as a light to all nations, rather than to hazard its utter extinction amid the ruins of fallen and falling republics in Europe."

I regret the loss of the opportunity to speak on the Catholic Hour. But I cannot regret having advocated what Henry Clay called "our ancient policy of non-intervention." I recognize that it would be now unpatriotic to continue to cry out against a policy that has been abandoned by the nation. But at the time I spoke it was still legitimate. It may once again become legitimate and patriotic to advocate the "ancient policy." In anticipation of the time when that may come to pass, I ask permission to go on record with the N.C.C.M. as I have elsewhere.

Very truly yours,
JAMES M. GILLIS, C.S.P.

P.S. Many former listeners to my addresses on the Catholic Hour have already asked for information about my "next" series, and I anticipate a great many more queries when the time usually allotted to me (Nov. and Dec.) arrives. I plan to present the substance if not the text of this letter and of yours in *The Catholic World* and on a printed slip in lieu of a great deal of letter writing. I shall however omit your name unless you grant permission for its use.

Father Gillis's postscript became an editorial in the November 1942 issue of *The Catholic World*. The editorial never saw print. The copy was killed before the magazine went to press. Father Gillis had entitled it, "Paying the Penalty," and in it he had repeated the substance of the three letters that had passed between Monsignor Ready and himself. The former *Catholic Hour* speaker was riled to a fighting pitch and wanted to go all the way in finishing the battle. He was not so imprudent, however, as to forget that a little advice now and then is needed by the best of men.

As in so many critical moments, he sought the counsel of his spiritual director, Father Joseph McSorley. The answer he received on the editorial was: "Don't print it."

That was the spiritual side voting—now for the human, the friendship side. Father Gillis consulted his alter ego, Monsignor Gibbons. The session the two friends had is vividly described by the Monsignor.

"Father Gillis came in to me in my room at the rectory. It was the time he was eased off the *Catholic Hour*. He had the ears of the country. He was champion of the anti-war cause. He came into my room with an editorial, all typed, all ready to be set up.

"He said, 'Read this,' and I read it. He asked me what I thought of it. I said, 'It's very good, a lot of punch; it's good in your usual style. It's very interesting,' I said to him. 'What do you want to do with it?'

" 'I'm going to publish it,' he answered. I told him I wouldn't do that. He asked me, 'Why?' He was dead serious. 'Why not publish it?' he asked.

" 'You're just stung,' I answered. 'You're stung and you're eating your heart out. You're letting your feelings run away. It's in perfect order,' I said. 'You're justified in every word you say, but you'd be a better man in every word you say if you didn't publish. Be a man, be the man you are,' I told him. 'If I were in your place I'd tear that up.' He stared at me very seriously and said, 'That's what my confessor said.'

" 'That's the thing to do then,' I remarked. Jim walked to the desk and tore the editorial in half and dropped it in the basket. To me that was a wonderful thing to do."

Father Gillis slowly and only by the greatest of effort brought under control the great roaring blaze of wrath this conflict had ignited in him. The flame of anger never totally died. Until the day of his death any small dry twig of interest in the controversy when tossed his way could start the fire crackling again.

There were later radio appearances around New York and throughout the country. There never was another *Catholic Hour* broadcast by Father Gillis during the rest of his life. There are no letters showing that he was ever invited back. He left no notes indicating he ever cared to return.

A DOOR MARKED "OUT"

chapter VII

The files had been sorted after a fashion in the days following Father Gillis's statement that he would retire. He himself had felt there was no great need to be too careful about going through his voluminous notes and letters. He could move his things over to the basement of the rectory and work on the files at leisure.

The one disadvantage to such expediency was that it brought around the last day of editorial activity that much more swiftly. The moment for taking that short walk over the threshold and into retirement was staring at the priest from the wall calendar.

The arthritic, stooped, and tired-looking old man walking around the editorial office of *The Catholic World* magazine was as mellow and soft as he'd permitted himself to be in two and a half decades. He'd read how people had left homes or business firms and wandered in and out of rooms, staring mistily at pictures or furniture, wanting to touch a desk or a chair. He'd heard how they prolonged the moments before they would step across a threshold and seal off a part of their life. He had never dreamed he'd be acting that way himself.

James Gillis had never been a rank sentimentalist by nature or profession. He had been born with a deep share of emotions, but he'd studied and learned control of them; as a religious, he had promised God he'd channel them faithfully to His service.

Now, however, the normal, deep affection that he had hidden so well and shared with so few wanted to flood out to the walls, the windows, the books, the trappings of this place. And toward the people of this place his feelings surged in gratitude and joy for the years of patience and the lives of devotion that had been placed at his beck.

Father Gillis pushed back his thin shoulders as if squaring to meet a challenge and cleared his throat loudly. Both actions had become second nature to him in these last years. They were an old person's habits—reflexes indulged in by a man who'd known for some time now that he was about finished on God's job. The squared shoulders were like a jog to the mind that it must live—sharp, alert, ready for the conflict. The cleared throat was the prompting of self to keep the once strong sonorous voice clear, ready for answering all challenges.

For now the nervous mannerisms covered up the retiring editor's entrance into the staff room. James Gillis was sorry that he was not gifted with flippancy at this moment. He knew from long experience that he would be a trifle formal at this occasion of good-by; to an outsider he'd look cold and withdrawn. He thanked God that these helpers were not outsiders. Katherine Crofton, Edith Donovan, Alice Walsh, and Augusta Adrian were like a quartette of right arms, and they knew without his gushing from desk to desk how deeply he felt as he stood silently before them.

"This is not really a farewell, you realize," he began, and stopped. He had to admit that the words seemed to him about as dull and unoriginal a farewell as he'd ever heard. Odd how all the experience of almost forty-six years on the public platform got him no better a finale than that limping au revoir. He had talked before apostolic delegates, cardinals, bishops, governors, mayors, and people by the millions, and never a loss for words.

Here he was taking leave of his office staff with a line and scene that belonged in a badly written soap opera.

James Gillis decided not to try any further. He realized that he could not say a good good-by because he couldn't say good-by at all to this staff.

He hurried to the door, murmuring, "I'll be in every day for a while until things are settled."

The old priest stepped into the corridor and started toward the exit. He paused at the wooden single-slot magazine rack that stood at the head of the stairway. A copy of the current issue of the magazine was on display. James Gillis lifted it and fingered the familiar cover. Idly he flipped the leaves and then came back to the first page. The sober black ink said in four proportioned headings: "*The Catholic World*, September 1948, Editorial Comment, Valedictory."

James Gillis counted the pages he had used for his last editorial—one, two, three, four, five. Twenty-six years condensed in ten sides. That didn't seem a proper ratio somehow, but there it was—five sheets, ten sides—perhaps the most exciting, turbulent, stimulating two and a half decades the world had seen. Certainly the most exciting, turbulent, and stimulating two and a half decades he had lived.

He smiled to recall the first hesitant, somewhat guarded, patently non-controversial editorials he had written. Fresh from the missions, unschooled in managing a magazine, he had imitated his predecessor. He had ventured only on rare occasions a tack or approach of his own.

James Gillis knew he had had ideas and convictions that he had put aside for a while. Then came a time when he had felt issues demanded some rough handling and he'd given it to them. More and more of this kind of editorial appeared under his name. Soon it was his accepted manner—his style of writing.

He knew the development had not been accidental. Neither

the letters of commendation nor the people who bespoke delight over his attacks had geared him to this style.

He had been preaching in somewhat the same manner for too many years not to know it was part of his nature. He nodded his head as if confirming this opinion. It's the way I'm made or the way I've made myself, he thought. Commendation or no commendation, I'd have an opinion or attitude on things— especially when they weren't just right or when they were absolutely wrong.

The ex-editor glanced quickly at the paragraphs that spelled out his retirement. Names leaped from the lines—F. D. Roosevelt and Eleanor, Churchill, Truman, Stalin, Yalta, Potsdam, Teheran—each name bringing a flood of memories, a swelling tide of associations along with it.

The thoughts were hurting now, not because they themselves caused pain, but because they reminded James Gillis that he was old and no longer able to carry on the battle. There was a new man, Father John Sheerin, to succeed him, and he had handed over the weapons, the army, the field to the younger commander. He would be the sage on the sidelines. He was to be a consultant editor.

James Gillis muttered a characteristic expression, "Ye gods— consultant editor." He knew he had no more patience to be a consultant editor than he had to be a temporizer over injustices. His kind was better described in that song he'd heard some crooner caterwauling recently, "All or Nothing at All."

That was his young way, his old way, his life's way. Monsignor Joseph Gibbons often reminded him of that streak that had showed in St. Charles College. The two of them would go out to the ball field and he'd want to practice one thing over and over again.

"There's a right way and a wrong way, Joe, to doing everything," he'd say, heading for the infield. "Now you bat that ball at me hard until I get the hang of picking it up just right." And a hundred times he'd run and scoop and throw the ball until he was satisfied.

Joe claimed he was that way about classes too. James Gillis tried to remember himself as he must have appeared to the others. Most probably Joe was correct, because no one else knew the real Gillis as Joe Gibbons did. As he recalled the college days, Father Gillis had to agree that his lifetime friend was right again. He had been intense, competitive, anxious to be the *summa* student, and he'd won the award.

"I've wanted life to be the *summa*," he said firmly, softly. "I wanted the best—the very best for my soul, my family, my Community, my country, my world. Was that so wrong?"

The old man knew he hadn't been wrong even as he asked himself the question. Maybe he'd been wrong in some instances as he'd gone about preaching, writing, seeking the best—but to want the best so badly and so fiercely could never be wrong.

James Gillis turned and faced the long stone-topped stairway leading down and out of *The Catholic World* building. He hesitated, fully aware of the meaning of taking that first step down. Quickly he turned to see if anyone was coming. He was embarrassed to think someone might pop out of the office and catch him poised like a girls' academy senior filled with dread and indecision at the moment of leaving the old school.

Better to be out of sight, he rationalized, if he wanted to give himself a good, long, nostalgic binge before tackling the exit march. James Gillis slipped back from the stairway and eased himself into the reference room.

Why do we delight in such torturing reminiscences, he wondered as he walked to the far windows and gazed on the busy, noisy street below. There were not two people in the world who would suspect that he was indulging himself in this most mawkish farewell. He had hoped to avoid it himself, but here he was swimming freely in what he would have described in anyone else as the icky-sticky goo of sentimentality.

Again, however, that was how he was made. Father Gillis had known James Gillis very well all his days, and that soft-as-soap heart had not been easy to hide. Sure, he had managed it, but more because the pain of being disappointed in people early in life had developed a scar tissue on his affections. It had become like an impervious crust on his heart.

One person knew this softness, but he would keep the secret well. Joe Gibbons knew the story of loneliness, the want of affection and acceptance that he had felt all his life.

Only once had he even hinted at such things, Father Gillis thought as he turned from the window and sat back against the sill. How many years ago was that? Let's see—it was 1942. The time of the *Catholic Hour* argument.

He had been with Joe Gibbons and had poured out his feelings about the business of not being invited back to take his accustomed series. Joe had recommended that he destroy the editorial he had written explaining fully the position of both sides in the argument. When he had destroyed it he'd looked at Joe and said: "I need you. Always remember that. You are like my own flesh and blood; I need you more than you realize."

James Gillis shuddered slightly as he recalled the incident. What he'd said had been true, but wasn't it a terrible confession of weakness? God certainly was with him all through the hard years. Had he forgotten that? Had his faith been so weak that human friendship become more important than Divine?

The old editor knew he'd never really lost perspective. He'd kept the true balance in his friendship. If anything, he'd been given that one true companion for some small relief while tracking that vast dry stretch of loneliness he'd had to walk these last twenty-six years.

Father Gillis strolled from the window and squared his thin back as he stood before a reference shelf. His rheumatically crooked finger touched the first book on the ledge before him.

He ran the finger along the row of books—the bound copies of his magazine—twenty-six years of *The Catholic World*.

He slid the first volume off the shelf and sat at the desk near the window. The sunlight streaming in warmed the coldness that never seemed to leave his bones lately.

James Gillis leafed the pages and pressed the book open to the first page. His opening editorial fell before his eyes. The priest smiled as he read his neophyte statement of policy:

> First, we are, or we shall try to be, modern in our spirit and in our method of expressing the truth. This may seem difficult to those who think of the Catholic Church as merely the "old" Church. But the miracle of the Church is that she is the oldest and the youngest. And Truth, like God, and like the Church, though ancient, is ever new. . . .
>
> To us the past means nothing without the present . . . A backward-looking church, or a backward-looking society or individual is, to all intents and purposes, dead and buried. . . .
>
> Secondly, we are—not merely by accident of birth, but by conviction—Americans. . . .
>
> To paraphrase a line from Boyle O'Reilly, we "would rather live in America than in any other land." That will sound decidedly "Main Street" to the sophisticated, who enjoy the anti-American tirades of H. L. Mencken and George Jean Nathan, and perhaps to many others who have recently learned to affect a contempt for all things American. Be it so; we repeat that a sincere love and admiration for America is one of the corner-stone principles upon which *The Catholic World* has built, and will continue to build.

Gnarled hands slammed the book shut with firmness and finality. James Gillis pushed away from the desk and replaced the volume in its series. He was not going to continue this mood any further. He'd lived all those editorials and they'd been painful enough the first time around. He was not going to start himself picking at the old scars and cause irritation again.

The tired shoulders snapped back as he came to the head of the stairs. Firmly and resolutely he touched each step on the way down. James Gillis came to the vestibule and glanced at the sign over the left door: "Out." He shoved the door open and stepped to the street. Head rigidly forward, he did not glance back.

James Gillis would have had a lot of reading to do had he dared continue from that first editorial on to the end. A fascinating possibility is what his reaction would have been had any challenged him in reviewing his magazine writing and asked: "Did you ever think you were wrong about some of the things you said?"

Monsignor Gibbons was of the opinion that Father Gillis never considered himself wrong about any of the highly controversial opinions and statements that he had made. Criticized severely, even, as in the *Catholic Hour* squabble, penalized because of editorial remarks, James Gillis undauntedly maintained his viewpoint.

This has been termed his strength and condemned as his weakness. The opposing attitudes are vouchsafed according to whether the speaker was an admirer or a critic of Father Gillis. The space in between these poles is fairly barren land. Few people were undecided about the editor of *The Catholic World*. He was so positive that readers leaped in attraction to his side—or rose in rebellion against his ideas.

Bear in mind that James Gillis didn't tackle subjects that permitted a kindly shrug of the shoulders and a smile as if to say: "Oh well, that's just how Father Jim feels about things." He had a knack for dealing with the most loaded items the news could offer.

If the subject was not patently explosive, James Gillis seemed to have a built-in fuse finder that got directly to the dynamite. One editorial on the topic, and its TNT potential was no longer a hidden thing.

This two-pronged ability was peculiar to the Paulist. Many people criticize or voice opinions about a variety of matters affecting the world and its people. They write well—some of them so ably that they are collected among the literary pieces of a generation. But what they write is not composed in such a way that it starts an argument.

Not so Father Gillis. His *treatment* of a subject was as much the reason behind the hassles in which he was involved as was the subject itself. A case in point is the famous November 1940 editorial directed against Franklin Roosevelt and the third term. When James Gillis put the last period to that piece, you had to come out of your corner swinging if you were a Rooseveltian admirer. If you were against him, you wanted everyone to know how *you* felt had *you* been able to put your feelings in words. You quoted this man's bitter, driving, punishing sentences.

The *Catholic Hour* controversy proved this fact. The ardent anti-Roosevelt people quoted the November editorial in its entirety, had it printed and distributed all over the country.

Partisanship aside for the moment, these lines reveal how the style of James Gillis was as much an incensing factor as was his criticism of the popular Democratic leader:

> If I must choose between two political evils, I would prefer the "smear," dirty as it is, to the violence done to logic, and good sense, and good taste, and elementary truth, by those who are determined to put the "audacious," "dangerous," "reckless" President in the position where he can do most harm. . . .
>
> He admits nothing; retracts nothing; explains nothing. He doesn't confess his broken promises. In one of his earliest "fireside chats" he said, "If I find that any course of action we attempt is a mistake, I shall be the first to re-

port the mistake to the people." He has never made any such report. Rather he seems to sing with the Sheriff in *Robin Hood*, "I've never yet made one mistake; I'd like to for variety's sake." The man who never makes a mistake is too good to be President. No one enjoys that prerogative but a *Duce* or a *Fuehrer*.

If the friends of Mr. Roosevelt did not rise from their chairs spoiling for battle as they noted the linking of their candidate with Hitler and Mussolini, this conclusion surely did bring them to their feet:

> What interests me and puzzles me is that the President should say and do a hundred things, which he is not called upon by his office to do, judging, condemning, challenging, threatening other nations, all but daring them to war, yet blandly declare before God and man "I work and pray for peace." It is a psychological riddle. I confess I don't understand the man. A "dangerous," "reckless," "audacious," inconsistent, unpredictable man is no man to be three times President of the United States.

Notice at the end of the editorial the repetition of the adjectives used earlier. The dunning home of his point is like a taunt and was certainly a challenge to anyone who chose to disagree.

He would accept the battle, particularly if it was on the issue of Franklin Roosevelt and family. James Gillis had been hammering the Hyde Park family for a long time previous to the "Third Term" editorial. Down to the end of his tenure as head of *The Catholic World* he was unflagging in his prodding of them.

The matter seems to have been developed into an *idée fixe* with Father Gillis, especially in the days that followed his failure to be renewed on the *Catholic Hour*. A suspicion haunted the priest that he had been "fingered" by Franklin Roosevelt because of his writings, which, as noted, were associated with the NBC radiocasts.

Rumors, notes, opinions—all whispered confidentially but

always whispered, never openly declared—built up a mountain of indications that some official in Washington (if not Mr. Roosevelt) had pulled the plug on the Gillis microphone. The mountain was made of that spun-sugar candy sold at fairs and carnivals—it melted at the touch. The part that didn't melt was at best a sticky residue that was more wisely tossed away.

The balanced picture, however, must hold the fact that Father Gillis was writing strongly about President Roosevelt years before the quiet, restrained, get-lost note came from the *Catholic Hour*.

In the early years of the New Deal, James Gillis was writing strongly *for* the then new President. The March 1934 editorial of *The Catholic World* states:

> To his great credit be it said that Mr. Roosevelt, though a determined and aggressive man (I thank God we have such a one in the White House), has *not* closed his mind. He has proved again and again that he doesn't seek to be surrounded with "yes-men."
>
> The President has never declared dogmatically that the plan he proposes is *the only one.* . . . He is not fanatically devoted to one idea . . . he is not a monomaniac. Again thank God! . . . It is divinely providential that we have . . . a man who while he knows how to maintain his balance is not content to stand still but goes ahead and does things. He most certainly *does things*. He does things not rashly, not recklessly, but after deliberation and consultation.

This quotation is a stunning reversal of the picture so many have that Father Gillis was ever an unyielding opponent of Franklin Delano Roosevelt. Even knowing James Gillis only by a reading of the "Third Term" editorial would lead one to do a double take on seeing the above extremely laudatory appraisal of Mr. Roosevelt.

There is one sentence that follows this passage quoted above which cues us to the firm and articulate antipathy that grew in James Gillis. The line is a complete explanation of the next quarter of a century in which he criticized the four-term President:

> As long as he welcomes deliberation and consultation, our chief citizens and all thoughtful students of the situation are entitled to speak out their mind for his benefit.

The first sign of real disaffection was more than a year off. Throughout 1934 all was on the plus side. The editorial tone was in defense of President Roosevelt and against the critics who feared America was drifting toward dictatorship under F.D.R.

Oddly enough, Europe and Asia became the occasions for unsettling Father Gillis's forthright confidence in the President. Long ago the Paulist missionary had fixed himself in the ranks of the anti-war camp. Trapped by oversimplification, he reasoned that foreign entanglement—superficial or otherwise—was the obstacle to America's effort to stay out of world conflict. For Father Gillis the formula read: To avoid war, avoid Europe and/or Asia. The practice of the formula was called isolationism.

Father Gillis didn't like the shouts and gestures he was seeing in the 1933–35 newsreels of Germany, Italy, and Japan. He figured all that marching had to have a place to go, and going places in uniforms and tanks wouldn't lead to a genteel lawn party.

America's foreign policy became his concern when Mussolini flexed his biceps and started looking for little fellows to pommel. Hitler aggravated the issue because he had muscles just as fearsome as Il Duce's, and he gave all the signs of looking not for little fellows but big ones—the bigger the better.

With a prescience throughout these years that even his severest critic cannot reject, James Gillis started in May 1935 telling our calamitous future:

> Russia, France and England are determined to drag us into the next war. They will lure us, cajole, bluff, trick, frighten, shame us into it if they can. The barrage is on. From Moscow, from London, from Berlin, from Paris, from Lyons, from Tokyo, from all points of the compass the fire is concentrated upon our poor defenseless head. . . .
>
> Meanwhile news dispatches from Washington indicate a tentative, timid, noncommittal attitude on the part of the Government. . . .
>
> Those of us who have desired for these many months a clear strong declaration of the foreign policy of the United States are wondering if the reason it is not forthcoming is because it is nonexistent. . . .
>
> One thing is certain. All this irresolute "viewing" and "pointing out" by anonymous and therefore irresponsible subalterns argues incompetence in the administration.

At the end of Mr. Roosevelt's first term Father Gillis was still with the New Dealer in everything but his lack of a foreign program. After listening to the President's State of the Union speech in early 1936, the editor remarked:

> My displeasure and disappointment in the address came principally from what the President did *not* say. What he left out was even more significant than what he put in. . . .
>
> For example, take the matter of foreign relations. . . . What really concerns the American citizen is the vital question, "What does Mr. Roosevelt plan to do . . . ?"

History records the answer to that question. James Gillis didn't like the answer and said so throughout the late thirties and into the forties.

A study of the Paulist's editorial years reveals a much more diversified selection of subject matter than one man or one issue. The World Court, companionate marriage, birth control, labor, strikes, baseball, prize fighting, drama, literature—these and more were given the special Gillisan treatment.

An index of all the editorial materials manifests a diversified subject matter; yet, withal, there was one kind of subject that attracted him as if a constant magnet bore down on his soul. James Gillis was possessed of an interest in personages—national and international names caught his eye, his mind, his heart.

The person in focus was seldom there because of Father Gillis's admiration. James Gillis was hardly the type who flung himself at the feet of the master and swooned away in delight at the pearls of wisdom being dropped on his prostrate form. His fascination with names—big names in the news, national figures, international politicians and patriots—was for the purpose of giving them the dourest scrutiny.

As a quick check of the ratio between persons and ideas, take James Gillis's manner of dealing with four nations—America, Germany, Italy, and Russia. There are seventy-three editorials covering the problems and policies of these countries in 1925–48. Russia—or communism—is the only nation written of in impersonal or ideological titles. Russia holds twenty-five titles on the list. The other three countries have forty-eight, all referring to individuals—Hitler, Mussolini, Roosevelt. A two-to-one proportion of criticism scores the faults of names as against nations.

Il Duce was the bull's-eye that James Gillis shot at again and again. The shooting was not at all akin to that of the archer who aimed his arrow into the air and knew not where the shaft landed. Father Gillis was taking dead-sure sight on the future years and splitting the target. "Mussolini is running amuck," *The Catholic World* writer said in a piece dated March 1926. Father Gillis added:

The dictator is acting like a madman . . . His bulldozing and fire-eating, his particularly ill-timed militarism, his foolish and frantic speeches . . . make Kaiser Wilhelm, even in his most *Gott-und-Ich* days, seem like a pacifist. . . .

If the bulldozing dictator is not quite crazy, he will come out of his frenzy. But if he continues to plunge along, like a mad buffalo, with wild mouthings and threats of violence, he will ruin Italy and perhaps bring on another horrible European war. . . .

I hesitate to assume the role of a prophet, and most of all, a prophet of woe. But, barring the entrance of some entirely unforeseen element into the Italian situation, Mussolini's regime will end in something akin to disaster.

In 1945 ill-fated Duce was hanging by the heels, a battered, shamed shell of the pompous dictator for which Father Gillis predicted tragedy.

Between the forewarning and the fact, Father Gillis accepted no illusions about Mussolini. He decried any belief in Benito's dissimulation concerning war and war-intent.

If Mussolini is a great statesman, will he whole-heartedly and sincerely join in a plan to do away . . . with warfare? . . . Will he go the whole way, and join the United States and the other powers, in disarmament and the outlawry of war? I fear not, for he is too fond of what he thinks to be the likeness between himself and Julius Caesar and Napoleon. When a man wants peace, he doesn't select either one of those bloody warriors to be his beau ideal and his patron saint.

This was printed in 1928. Five years later, in the Holy Year of 1933, Father Gillis traveled through Italy and was firmly convinced that Mussolini could mean nothing but war as his future course of action. He realized in a quick sampling of the popular feeling that Mussolini had no choice but battle—the people had been sold well and there was no backing down now as they cried to assert their supposed military destiny.

Before war came against Haile Selassie's kingdom, an editorial concerning Italy was on *The Catholic World* press. It had been written a month before the Italian declaration of hostilities, but it could have been penned the day the invasion occurred:

> But what of *Il Populo?* I wish I could say—since I still hold to the democratic principle of the ultimate wisdom of the mass of men—that Mussolini is running ahead of and quite away from the Italian people. But they are keeping pace with him. . . . The populace is quite as eager for war as the sword-rattler himself.

The portent of those words was vindicated within the life of that issue of the Paulist Fathers' magazine. On October 3, 1935, Mussolini entered Ethiopia and joy burst over Italy that at last they were to take their share of the world's spoils.

Intelligently enough, Father Gillis did not follow up the point of his prediction by a jeering "I told you so!" His writings left off in their express personal attacks on Mussolini and pleaded for compassion toward the helpless natives of Ethiopia. Father Gillis was appalled at the plight of the victims of Il Duce's attack:

> This hideous slaughter of a naked people "huddled despairingly" with no means of defense, not to say retaliation, is the most shameful episode . . . in the history of war, ancient, medieval or modern. And this cruel carnage, this cold-blooded butchery was done in the name of civilization; even in the name of religion. If I were an Italian I should blush for my country, my Duce and my army. As a white man, it shames me to think what members of my race have done to the blacks.

James Gillis was close to physical revulsion as he pored over the accounts of the struggle between the mismatched pair of contenders. His feelings of helplessness were increased when he watched the League of Nations sit by and talk out the short war's duration. His own reaction was to fix for himself more boldly than ever before a driving opposition to war. The anti-war editorials may not number as many as those dealing with other single subjects, but they match any of his writings in fierceness and intensity. They partake of the spirit of a crusade—a one-man war against war.

The first step was trying to make people face hard facts and unyielding reality. Once the Italo-Abyssinian conflict ceased, James Gillis plumped this initial hard fact before his readers. At the start of the summer of 1936 he wrote:

> Now that the bloody fiasco in Ethiopia has come to an end, let us see if we can get any satisfaction out of it. Yes, satisfaction—the jewel in the toad's head, comfort in adversity, satisfaction in tragedy.
>
> First, then, the League of Nations is exposed before the world for what it really is, false, pretentious, helpless, cowardly. Conceived in idealistic ignorance, begotten of insincerity, it lived on fraud and died. . . .
>
> No organization, no matter how nobly conceived and hopefully inaugurated, can survive if it will not face reality. The League took a "sock-in-the-jaw" from Japan and then a blow in the solar plexus from Italy. It is down and out. Its prostrate form should be removed from the ring.

A substitute was needed for the League if there was to be some common point of alliance that could arbitrate disputes and outlaw war. James Gillis realized this because he described the idea of a League as "a magnificent idea." He did not have the substitute, but he refused to let that deter him from preaching and writing against war—and offering suggestions for eliminating its possibility.

Enthusiastically he spends a whole editorial boosting Paul Hanly Furfey's *Fire on the Earth*. The carping, biting tone is dropped—Father Gillis becomes lyric and sweet and extended as he proposes the theory of an uncompromising Christianity:

> "Follow me," says Stalin. "Not him but me," says Mussolini. "Neither of them but me," says Hitler. Medicine men! All of them. Mountebanks! As a cure for the ills that afflict the world we might as well carry a horse-chestnut in the pocket, kiss a rabbit's foot or rub a hunchback's spine. What we really need is a John the Baptist to run up and down through the nations crying out "The ax is laid to the root of the tree. Repent or perish." . . .
>
> If a modern statesman ventured, no matter how apologetically, to recommend religion as a panacea, men would ask, "Have the troubles of the times touched him in the head? Has he become balmy? Is there a visionary in the counsels of the nation? A mystic? Let's get rid of him before he does harm." But if a statesman advocates pacts, treaties, concordats, alliances, leagues, in spite of the fact that all these obsolete devices have been demonstrated futile, men call him "savior."

Father Gillis must have realized the impracticality of expecting a book, no matter how highly praised, to effect much change in the world. He very practically took his case to the people. Any occasion that presented an opportunity for speaking was eagerly accepted and applied to the crusade against war.

All the talks were fundamentally based on the one theme, no matter how they were titled or in what phrases they were set. The substance of the crusade was stated in the February 1937 issue of *The Catholic World* under the title, "Who Wants War?"

> I say no one wants war. Buttonhole any man, any hundred men, any thousand men you happen to see on the

street. Ask them, "Buddy, do you crave a war?" You
wouldn't get to the thousandth man, or the hundredth. At
about the tenth the officers would grab you and send you
to the psychopathic ward for examination. "You fool, you
lunatic, don't you know that nobody wants war . . ."

The puzzle, the contradiction, the anomaly remains.
Since no one in the world wants war, why and how shall
war come? I don't know the answer. The world as the
world is irrational. If that is what men mean when they
say "It is a mad world," we can all agree. . . .

We must discover the cause before we can expect the
cure . . . of war which is a kind of dementia. Now the
cause of war is mental. It is an *idea*. . . .

What is the *idea* that causes the fact of war? Not one
idea but many. "What is your name?" said Christ to the
demon. "My name is Legion," was the answer. . . . So,
too, a legion of devils conspire to produce war.

First is the idea of the superiority of one race above
another. . . .

I would not wish to convey the impression that race
antagonism, race hatred, invidious comparison between
race and race is the *only* cause of war. . . . There is the
devil of commercial rivalry, the devil of international
finance . . . the devil of politics . . . the devil of imperial-
ism. Yes . . . devils and more than seven devils must be
cast out of our civilization if we are going to escape war.

The conclusion to all his arguments and reductions to
absurdity that sprinkle the lengthy piece is this simple idea:

I have appealed only to common sense, human decency
and ethnological truth. But persons who believe in the
Bible and who take Christ for their Master may throw all
my ideas and opinions and statements . . . out the window,
and take as ultimate and infallible the fact preached by
Jesus that all mankind is one; that He is the Vine and we
the branches; that He is the Head and we are the members.

James Gillis had yearned for a John the Baptist and was one himself in this composition. As one Paulist said, he was doing no more with all his refined rage and cutting logic than pointing out over the heads of the people and crying: "Behold the Lamb of God!" His dramatic description of John running up and down the nation had omitted the fact that John's thunderous utterances had not saved his head nor the Jewish nation. Yet John's job was well done. He was the precursor, the announcer—not the Messiah.

No one knows if Father Gillis saw this point of comparison. In the ten years that followed this editorial and up to the day of retirement, James Gillis exhausted himself by a continuous stream of speeches and articles in which he lamented, condemned, analyzed, and castigated war, war leaders, and warmongers. No estimates were given by Father Gillis on the effectiveness of his campaign. Whatever good he felt was being accomplished by the years of effort was obliterated in one day's stroke by Adolf Hitler. September 1, 1939, German troops and planes gave a word and a war to the world as blitzkrieg struck Poland.

James Gillis was crushed as devastatingly as the Polish Republic under Ignace Moscicki, its president. The sudden, lightning-like attack of the German planes and Panzers shredded the Paulist editor's hope that reason and truthtelling, direct discussion and open debate could forestall a great war. Two months after Germany's action, England, France, Russia, and Finland were added to the imbroglio.

With surprising resilience for one so easily disposed to a pessimistic outlook, Father Gillis sprang back to his cause. If the world wanted war, he meant to preserve some slim thread of hope that America could remain out of it.

Actually, the Hitlerian smashing of Poland was not too overwhelming a shock to Father Gillis. His snapback to vigilant editorializing was more to be expected than not. Long years before—almost on the heels of tabbing Mussolini's intentions—James Gillis had marked Adolf Hitler as capable of the weirdest possible activity. Two years prior to the blitzkrieg the priest wrote:

> Adolf Hitler is quite probably insane: not merely mad in the loose rhetorical sense of the apothegm "whom the gods would destroy they first make mad," but in the strict scientific sense, a paranoiac.

Three months before the Polish war James Gillis told what pattern the paranoia would follow:

> Hitler's course of action, after keeping the world in an almost intolerable condition of jitters for two or three years, must inevitably produce war.

At the outbreak of hostilities he analyzed the problem and purpose of Adolf Hitler, prophesying through the analysis that war would not end until Germany's problem was solved or her purpose achieved.

> Long ago . . . I recorded my own cool calm conviction that Adolf Hitler is a paranoiac and more specifically a megalomaniac. But even a madman may have a lucid moment; and an habitual liar may once in a while step out of character and tell the truth. . . .
>
> Hitler said . . . "Wars will continue as long as the world's goods are distributed inequitably."
>
> Absolutely and everlastingly true. . . .
>
> The English may not know exactly what they are fighting for. Or they may know but not say. Hitler knows and says. . . .
>
> The English are dealing with a maniac, but a maniac with an idea, a fixed idea, the idea that underlies all discontent, social unrest, political upheavals, riots, rebellions, revolutions, class wars, religious wars, international wars, the simple idea that some people have too much and other people have not enough.

The one-man crusade redirected its sights now that Europe had drawn its lines and marshaled its power and men. The lurking dread in the isolationist trait of James Gillis was that we could not remain neutral despite the preachments of Mr. Roosevelt which exhorted Americans to maintain no bias.

The Catholic World editor could thumb back to a page in his magazine of 1935 which he had sarcastically titled: "Come On In: The War Is Fine." That had been a prophecy—the kind of prophecy one makes and, while making, cannot help thinking with some smugness: Suppose I guess correctly. When the guess about tragedy begins to fashion into fact and breathe on your neck, you agonize to reshape it. You don't want to guess that accurately.

James Gillis got to work swiftly on forestalling any possibility that America would be tempted to heed the siren song of Europe's politicians. Mostly he bore down on the pen when writing of the words and actions of Franklin Roosevelt. He felt his fears about the change he had noticed in the President around 1936 were being horribly confirmed in 1939. James Gillis groaned at the error of judgment Mr. Roosevelt made in stepping up his belligerency all the while advocating neutrality.

Only in a democracy could an editor write what Father Gillis published in May 1939. Before Hitler began his march, Father Gillis ripped into President Roosevelt concerning his handling of foreign affairs:

> The President of the United States . . . should have known better. He was full grown at the time of the World War. He had an excellent chance to learn. He saw Mr. Wilson go overseas. He saw Mr. Wilson come back. . . . He saw the Senate break the back—and the heart—of Mr. Wilson. But did the tragic outcome of President Wilson's obstinacy teach President Roosevelt anything? Apparently not. Like Mr. Wilson, he disregards the Senate, ignores

the people, makes speeches, writes notes, takes sides, scolds one side in the European controversy, promises help to the other, and commits us willy-nilly, all the while reiterating the purely fanciful phrase "measures short of war." There are no "measures short of war." . . .

If the full truth must be spoken, we are already in the next war. Without consulting us, the President has committed us. . . .

That "next war" began, and James Gillis repeated the title and ideas of his May 1939 piece a year later. In July 1940 he stated under the heading, "The President Puts Us In":

On the same day that Mussolini declared war, President Roosevelt projected us into the war. In that crucial "dagger in the back" speech, he said, "Let us not hesitate to proclaim certain truths . . ." The trouble is that he did not . . . proclaim more truths. . . . To supply the deficiency, perhaps we had better enumerate at least a few "certain truths" not mentioned by the President.

1. We are now in the war . . . from the repeal of the embargo act in the autumn of 1939. . . . And let us not quibble as to whether we are officially or unofficially in. . . . We are in.

2. President Roosevelt said in his fateful speech, "We will extend to the opponents of force the material resources of this nation" . . .

3. There are more fighting words in the original text. . . . If the Allies are beaten we may be called upon to stand by these words.

4. We cannot without national humiliation retract what our President said. . . .

5. We are not only in this war. We are from now on in every European war. . . .

The President says isolation is no longer possible. It is not real. It is a nightmare. And what can that mean but that henceforth and forever, for good or for ill, for peace or for war, for life or death, we are no longer America but a part of Europe, Asia and Africa. Indeed we are in the war. In deep. Now and forever.

The satire, the sarcasm, the pleading for logic, the dire predictions, the appeal to common sense—the whole gamut of oratorical and literary skills at Father Gillis's command was thrown into the breach. He slammed the political dilettantes who surrounded the President, he banged the rash and lusty jingoists, he criticized Eleanor Roosevelt's comments, he parried and thrust and finally clubbed Franklin Delano himself at every twist and turn of direction and phrase.

In the midst of all this activity came the famous editorial that scored Roosevelt's ambition for the third term. This was the piece that was to identify James Gillis in the minds of millions as a political-minded cleric. The reprinting and distribution of the editorial without any permission and beyond the control of the Paulist priest did him untold damage. The bruise to his prestige can be measured by the fat files of angry, scathingly abusive letters that slashed across his desk.

James Gillis was hurt badly, deeply, but he tried not to show it. He felt he was all priest; he could not believe that anyone would make him out to be a politician. He defended the ethics of his position as editor; he argued his right, his duty to deal in truth in all quarters—even that of the political arena.

It is doubtful the defense was heard or, if heard, accepted. Undaunted but obviously bloodied by the unsympathetic beating from his lay and clerical critics, he moved more deeply into the field of political associations.

Firmly convinced that he was doing his duty, James Gillis joined the ranks of the isolationists who had banded together and formed the America First group. The basic tenet of the group was the demand that the United States follow its traditional policy of non-intervention in foreign affairs.

Charles Lindbergh, Senator Gerald Nye of North Dakota, Reverend John A. O'Brien, Representative Hamilton Fish, Jr., of New York, were some of the men who mounted the platform to plead the cause of non-intervention. In some instances recriminations, accusations of "smear," and charges of anti-Semitism marred the clear-eyed view that James Gillis wanted to maintain regarding the role of the America First movement.

He pushed aside the charges leveled against the members of the committee. Fervently and logically Father Gillis pleaded for their right to hold this cause and their right to fulfill the faith they shared in it. He joined Senator Nye in Brooklyn, Representative Fish in Baltimore and Rockville Centre, Long Island, Senator Burton Wheeler at Springfield, Massachusetts.

The rallies followed one upon the other in the months of September and October 1941. The meetings smacked of hostility and bitterness as charges and countercharges filled the atmosphere. The impressions given of the rallies seemed to indicate that they were loud, brassy, and contentious. About the Brooklyn gathering, for example, the New York *Herald Tribune* of September 23, 1941, reports:

> . . . the inside and outside of the Academy were guarded by one of the largest police details ever assigned to a Brooklyn gathering.

It was the last—the famous last—*Catholic Hour* series that interrupted the American First rallying by Father Gillis. Had he thought of continuing with the group after his talks on NBC finished, he was able to forget the idea. December 8, 1941, America declared war on the Japanese after their sneak attack on Pearl Harbor.

What was James Gillis's reaction to this obliterating of his eighteen concentrated years filled with effort to hush, to reason with, to debate with the figures of this period's history whom he had labeled as bellicose?

His editorial at the time of the declaration of war ends on the keynote of idealism that spurred so much of his reasonable, high-minded writing of these decades:

> We have tried hard to keep out. We have failed, not because of any lack of sincerity or of honest vigor of argument, but because of that wicked and stupid action of the Japs in the Pacific. Now that we are in we must fight with honor and chivalry. We dread indeed to think of what may happen to our American institutions of liberty and democracy while we are at war. But a far greater calamity will happen if we abandon our ethics and our religion in the attempt to reestablish civilization.

THIS FILE FOR MISCELLANY

chapter viii

When James Gillis faced the last of the three sets of records he had kept on his activities, he must have realized that this one was not as specific as the file on radio work or the file on editorials. The third collection of papers dealt generally with matters pertaining to his weekly columns; more truly it was a catchall, a miscellany of news items, magazine clippings, comments, articles, reviews, private correspondence, personal spiritual suggestions, travel folders, retreat diaries—just about anything and everything a busy writer-speaker saves and stores in the hope that someday he'll use.

Monsignor Gibbons brought out this point in discussing the intense mental appetite of his Paulist friend. "Everybody and everything contributed to feed ideas to Jim—at least he made them contribute. We'd be out somewhere at a dinner or some great affair and afterward I'd be amazed at the suggestions for articles and pieces that Jim had drawn from an evening's conversation. Everything was grist for his mill."

Some hint of the truth of this can be gathered from all the previous pages that cover years as a teacher, a missionary, a lecturer, and an editor. Father Gillis moved from work to work always retaining, yet always expanding, the knowledge gained at his previous assignment. To this he added the new

facts and ideas of the next assignment and built a storehouse
of information that made him unchallengeably erudite.

Checking the hundreds of topics listed in Father Gillis's
preaching diary would tend to make one smile that any man
dared treat all these subjects. The smile soon disappears when
you slide open a drawer in his file and see folder after folder
containing a typed or handwritten copy of the talks he listed.
The volume of work that this suggests is incalculable. Even
allowing for the repetition of a speech or editorial on a couple
of occasions, the number of single and different compositions
is hardly believable.

A quick opening glance at James Gillis's preaching diary
demonstrates this forcibly. Flip it open at random. Two pages
spread out before you. The margin date is 1941. The first
entry is May 11, the last June 11. Here is what you read:

May 11: N. Y. Univ. Newman Club
        Mothers' Day Communion Breakfast
        "Nisi Dominus"

May 16: Butler, N.J., St. Anthony's (O.F.M.)
        Duns Scotus Unit, C.S.M.C.
        Franciscan clerics. "Nisi Dominus"

May 18: White Plains
        Westchester Holy Name Rally
        "Panaceas and the One True Church"

May 20: Belle Harbor—St. Francis de Sales
        Holy Name Forum
        "Keeping One's Balance in a Reeling World"

May 23: St. Walburga's
        Day of Recollection
        "Faith"
        "The Mass"
        "Brotherhood"

May 26: Four columns—Sursum Corda
        May 5–26 incl.

June 3: Rock Castle, Va.
        "Advice to Nationalists—You

Can't Take It with You"
June 6: Hackensack, N.J.
First Friday Club
"Nisi Dominus"
June 8: Brooklyn—Don Bosco Free Public Library
Communion Breakfast talk
June 11: Boston College Commencement
Delivered address—Received Litt D. Degree

In the ten entries listed on the two pages covering a month's activity the repetitions of the talk "Nisi Dominus" are more than balanced by the four "Sursum Corda" columns turned in to the NCWC, which syndicated Father Gillis from coast to coast. The total of different subjects treated in ten dates runs to thirteen!

"Sursum Corda" alone gives us a picture of a man who handled a multitude of subjects. This column was always pressure on James Gillis, no matter what he was involved in or how far his travels might take him. He had accepted the offer to write the column early in 1928. On November 12 he turned in columns one, two, and three. The variety of matters treated can be estimated when we realize that the last "Sursum Corda" handed in for January 1955 was numbered 1,368. Close to twenty-seven years of writing and well over a thousand ideas or their aspects discussed!

The story is told that when James Gillis was requested to write this regular column he was advised to keep it bright and optimistic. The Paulist was surprised that such counsel should be given but he promised with good grace to follow the request.

A news clipping of October 27, 1928, which announced the start of Father Gillis's column, made this promise to its readers: "The articles will be inspirational and dwell on the happy or good side of life." When the first pieces appeared they were light, bright, and just right. That mood lasted for a month or so, and then gradually the old somber tone crept into the paragraphs. As the storyteller summed it up: "Lightness went out and darkness covered the world of Gillis again."

It is difficult to shake off this constant and widely accepted critique that the priest-columnist was a writer who dipped his pen in dejection and wrote with a broad nib about the worsening aspects of everything. Yet there above his column—1,368 times—was the heading: "Sursum Corda"—"Lift Up Your Hearts"! And when a secondary banner was used to emphasize the Latin words of the original, the new heading was: "What's Right with the World"! If any man intended to confound the critics and cross up the opposition, he could not have managed it more dexterously than James Gillis in this selection of titles.

There is every good reason to believe that he did not think he was overstressing the dark side of the day. His own feelings seem to have been that he was being serious but not morose about the world and world conditions.

Perhaps one of the factors that leads to the easy assumption of his pessimism is that so much of his writing is of a prophetic nature. Many of these prophecies came at a time when Western civilization suffered severely from its own corruption, greed, and mendacity. What he observed and read and meditated over indicated only one course for our future—war and chaos in ever-recurring cycles until our culture was destroyed.

People do not always want to be told these things. The optimists, or more accurately the unrealistic wishful thinkers, resent the fact of horrible, terror-filled reality being pushed roughly in their face. James Gillis never pushed easily. Maybe this was his error, not his column or editorial content.

One analyst, a Paulist confrere of Father Gillis, claimed that he was impatient with world leaders and the peoples of the world who would not heed the simple, honest, direct methods he advocated for peace. It did not occur to James Gillis in a practical way that world leaders and most of the world's peoples were not reading his columns.

The critic-companion offered the theory that this impatience crept into Father Gillis's work and was taken out on the subscribers, who in the main read and agreed with him. The damage, however, was being done to his reputation by his overstressing the direct phases of global evils as if he thought repetition and dramatic writing could waken the world to its danger. Some of his readers cringed at the bitter logic, the sharp stinging language, the ominous future depicted. James Gillis may not have realized that they yearned to do all they could to prevent the tragedy but were as helpless as he. What these readers needed was courage and comfort against their future, and instead he gave them warnings that were better suited to an entirely different stripe of people. It is soon easy to call this kind of writer pessimistic.

There are many good points in the argument that James Gillis's vigorous, intransigent, dominating spirit leaned far over to the desperate side of causes. The people who consider Father Gillis pessimistic feel that all detailed arguments might be forestalled by listing the one criticism of him they claim carries the greatest weight. Granting that James Gillis quickly and devastatingly got to the flaw in persons and philosophies— that he could demolish anyone and anything in a stroke— his critics pointed out that he ended article after article seemingly satisfied with the devastation and demolition. Out of the rubble arose no new plan or better idea or braver world.

With that sentence the critics have had their say. They can sit back and wait for rebuttal. But there is no rebuttal. The Gillis protagonists aren't interested in the proposition in the first place. They see no argument concerning James Gillis and whether he was or was not pessimistic. They do not agree that the criticism is a fair distinction or a real thesis for debate. James Gillis to them was right and true and courageous when it cost something to be so.

His role, his purpose, was accomplished in his putting the finger on hypocrisy and pretense. He refused to be bought or forced into compromise; he would not be stampeded or bamboozled—he stood firm, saying what had to be said when nobody had the heart and will to buck the world's swift slide downward.

The supporters of Father Gillis don't read pessimism in the realities the Paulist preached and penned. They disagree that his years were years that needed high-blown theorizing or rapturous arrangements of life to make new utopias. The age of James Gillis was dangerous and close to diabolical, calling for a man who could spot the devil and drive him out. The defenders of Father Gillis don't think the man who steps into that kind of arena is any more a pessimist than Michael the Archangel. If heaven needed a hero of that sort, earth did too in the decades of James Gillis.

There stand the positions on Father Gillis's basic disposition as reflected in his writings and talks. Someday a broader, deeper, and more definitive treatise on whether or not this man was a pessimist may be written. Not enough history has flowed by since his death to allow a gauge on all he foretold or all the forebodings he evidenced. Today we must be satisfied with the decision that decides nothing. Was Father Gillis pessimistic? Some say yes and some say no.

How ironic that the priest who was so staunchly direct and outspoken in life is the victim of a "no decision" contest in death.

"Sursum Corda," for all its years in print, did not have the impact of *The Catholic World* editorials. As Father Joseph Manton noted when he compared the two features, the real

Father Gillis was in the monthly magazine, not the weekly column.

A cursory survey of Gillis readers would prove this to be true. People commenting on something the priest had written spoke more often about the editorials than the columns. Yet some of the finest and most influential writings of James Gillis are in these columns. Folder after folder bulges with the correspondence that showed the tremendous response "Sursum Corda" received. Some of the columns caused controversy and prompted sharp critical letters. But many of the weekly pieces were well received and bore their effect long after their printing.

An instance of this latter type of reaction was the column in which Father Gillis spoke of Bishop Ottokar Prohaszka's *Meditations.* Writing easily, conversationally, not dunning or demanding anything of anyone, Father Gillis lauded the Bishop's three-volume work, expounding its virtues and benefits to all interested in a deeper prayer life.

The mail response was one of the largest to greet any of the articles Father Gillis had written. Outstandingly prominent was the number of requests for information on how and where the books could be purchased. The queries came from lay people and religious, subjects and Superiors. Beyond the fact that so many were interested in prayer, this particular column proved that not all the Gillis audience was constantly squaring for battle.

But James Gillis could not keep "Sursum Corda" wholly free from the pulsing problems that raised his editorial blood pressure. "What's Right with the World" was bound to be influenced by the joustings that went on over *The Catholic World* editorial desk. Especially was this so as the critical issues leading to war became more and more absorbing. The columns were beginning to be the overflows of the editorials and they took on more and more of the sting, the blast, the riposte, the slash, the slug—the whole battery of literary maneuvers found in James Gillis's *Catholic World* writings.

The major irritant to this free-swinging battler as a columnist was the fact that the weekly piece was not his to control. Father Gillis wrote "Sursum Corda," but the NCWC managed it. Some weeks they managed it right back into a big return envelope for corrections. Other weeks they couldn't manage it at all—it just wouldn't do. Back it would come to James Gillis with a great "no-go" sign splashed across it. He would have to sit down and write a complete new column no matter what pressure was on him from other quarters.

How impatient he became over this problem and how suppressed but smoldering was his temper may be gleaned from the following letter, written during what was to be the last season he would ever broadcast for the NCWC unit, the *Catholic Hour*. Harassment had come earlier from the NCWC's radio committee when they'd made him rewrite the November 30 network address. You can almost hear the Gillis blood bubbling to a boil as he contemplates another rejection and rewrite job and wonders how much of this he can take. His entire letter is worth printing here since it makes many solid points that Father Gillis thought needed answering on more occasions than this:

December 13, 1941

Mr. Frank A. Hall
N.C.W.C. News Service
1312 Massachusetts Avenue
Washington, D.C.

My dear Mr. Hall:
   I do confess that your opinion on Sursum Corda ✳ 687, "Rules of Warfare," puzzles me. I would have imagined that this was just the time to insist upon right fundamental moral principle with regard to war and the waging of war.

It strikes me as being very strange if one is not permitted to quote the great theologians upon that question. I had thought and I still do think that in war time the Church has a deep obligation of keeping the people's minds right. Furthermore, I see no contradiction between my statement that our war with Japan is a just one, since it is obviously a war of defense, and the parallel statement that we must wage that just war according to Christian ethics.

I cannot possibly understand your impression that the article is "an invitation for persons to become conscientious objectors." But supposing it were: is it not Catholic to be a conscientious objector? I repeat, however, that I do not admit for a moment that there is an argument for conscientious objectors in that article. How could there be conscientious objectors if this is a just war?

One thing more: I wonder if you have been following not only the weekly Catholic press in England but whether you have consistently read such pieces on the morality of war and the means of waging war as have appeared in the *Clergy Review*. I wonder why it is that our Catholic press in the United States cannot grapple with these moral questions, even now that we are at war, when the Catholic press of Great Britain deals with them so directly and frankly.

However, since you state categorically that you do not think that particular Sursum Corda should be published, I am sending you another one. But you would have done me a favor if you had let me know immediately. I am always hard pressed for time and the end of the week generally finds me especially crowded.

Very truly yours,
REV. JAMES M. GILLIS

The clash of editorial judgments on the material to be printed raises an interesting question. How much would James Gillis have been allowed to print had he not been editor-in-chief of *The Catholic World?* Judging from the disparate opinions on his columns and lectures during the war years, some feel that had he not been in charge of a magazine little of his work would have seen the print shop. James Gillis's legion of followers argue that such steel never goes unbladed—such richness never goes unmined.

The priest himself seems to indicate a great dependency upon his editorial position for giving his ideas life and breath. At least he implies that his assignment, which could have been recalled by his Superiors, was encouraged and given free rein.

The "Valedictory" editorial remarks:

> My confreres, the Paulist Fathers, could always say, "It's only Gillis who speaks." As a matter of fact the Paulist Fathers never did disown me or disclaim responsibility for what had appeared in these columns. They must have been tempted to do so when, for example, in the early days of Mussolini they were warned that if *The Catholic World* didn't cease its attack upon the Duce and his Fascist system "the Paulists would be thrown out of Rome." Even at that risk, my Community didn't suggest that I desist. After the invasion of Ethiopia and Albania my Superior told me to go the limit and not pull my punches. When I reminded him of the threat he simply answered, "Even so"! Because of that and many similar instances of courageous devotion to truth and justice, the religious society to which I am happy and proud to belong deserves, I think, singular credit.

James Gillis knew the Paulist Fathers had given him not only encouragement but the greatest opportunity any man could want. He had a pulpit, a rostrum, a ready-made, wide-open place on which to stand month after month and speak out his mind. *The Catholic World* editorial corner was no pigeon coop—it was a place whose walls extended out to the boundaries of the earth and the kingdom of heaven. All that territory was under Father Gillis's pen, and his Superiors never took away his editorial chance to superintend it.

The strange point about James Gillis's being in such complete charge of his magazine was that he operated least within the sphere most directly under his authority. He is not described with exactness when called the editor of *The Catholic World*. A better denoting of his place on the magazine is to say he wrote the editorials.

Early in his magazine career he stamped the mark of individuality on his editorial opinion by saying:

> "We" have decided to dwindle to "I." The editorial "we" is awkward, clumsy, stilted, pompous, frequently misleading, and altogether absurd. . . .
>
> *The Catholic World* is edited by one priest (with lay assistants). It is published by a group of priests—the Paulist Fathers. . . .
>
> To tell the truth, I cannot even be certain that the political or quasi-political views that may happen to appear in these pages meet the approval of the majority of the Paulist Fathers . . . We do not all agree. One of our friends said he liked us because we had no "family smile." Likewise we have no family politics. . . .
>
> Therefore, from this issue forth, while the present editor remains, "we" shall be "I" . . .

The early years at the managing desk were not lacking in interest in the magazine. James Gillis had a "feel" for poetry, stories, and good articles. He read and checked and selected material, but he began delegating more and more of this work to his assistants.

His outside commitments piled up, took him away from the office for days, often weeks. This necessitated editing the magazine by remote control. "Jim Gillis can't run *The Catholic World*," a contemporary of his said in 1942. "He's not around long enough to take a swing in his swivel chair. *The World* is run by his assistants."

Scale down the exaggeration that goes into the causerie on any outstanding person by his contemporaries, you still face

this objective fact—the bulk of *The Catholic World* subscription list was made up of Gillis editorial readers. That was
their magazine. Even today you'll meet men who tell you they
never went beyond those first few pages.

Father Manton, in his eulogistic remarks on James Gillis,
spoke briefly about *The Catholic World*. He made this very
telling observation:

> *The Catholic World . . .* was highbrow and there were
> many of us who felt that a good deal of it seemed to be
> written by and for school teachers. It was dignified, didac-
> tic, and dull. But the Editorials! Though often they
> seemed to stretch from his swivel chair (they were that
> long!)— we looked forward to them every month. In
> those days, they *were* the magazine . . .

Apparently no one resented or faulted this situation. James
Gillis was considered worth a subscription. You bought an
editorial that was all comet and shooting star—the pages that
followed Father Gillis's editorial were no more important
than the comet's tail. They were like little wispy white dust
trailing after the brightness.

The emphasis on political questions and in particular those
questions that revolved around the politics and practices of
Franklin Roosevelt had a more unfortunate effect on Father
Gillis than merely keeping him sometimes from supervising
the whole magazine. They left an impression of him that is
woefully incomplete when his talents as a writer are estimated.

Some react to the name of James Gillis by recalling him as
"always interfering in politics" or "the priest who blasted
Roosevelt" or "the America First priest who should have
stayed in his pulpit." If the reaction is not so jauntily or decorously phrased, it is nine out of ten times limited to thinking
that Father Gillis wrote of nothing but the second world war
President.

James Gillis wrote often, but not entirely about F.D.R. If those editorials on the Democratic leader could be excised from the Gillis collection it would be a very good thing. Not to spare Father Gillis, but rather to leave for all to see, conspicuously excellent and timely, those pieces he penned on social, literary, economic, and moral issues. Among these are columns, articles, and sermons just as pregnant in thought, just as prophetic in tone, just as forceful in logic as any of the political writings that gained him notoriety or fame. And throughout this variety of subjects, the same lucid, flashing style, the highly polished phrases, the masterfully wrought sentences and paragraphs flow abundantly, universally, matchlessly.

His great crusade for temperance in the use of alcohol is one of these editorial and preaching markers that is frequently overlooked in Father Gillis's life. A total abstainer himself, he advocated the practice for all. The origin of his strong feeling against alcohol is not easily discovered. Mary Gillis thinks that her brother's abstinence was at first in imitation of the elder Gillis. James Gillis's own home never saw drinking either as a habitual occurrence or even occasionally as a means of celebration or geniality.

Father Gillis's sister thinks that Jim's animadversion to drink was engendered more by observation of the havoc wrought by drunkenness than by any specific home training. Mary recalls how troubled and angered the young Jim became at the sight of the degradation that overindulgence caused in talented, promising neighbors. The tragedies of broken homes, neglected children, and moral dissolution that drink brought to the immigrant peoples of that period sickened the young Boston idealist.

James Gillis's reaction to the silenced priest he met on the boat to St. Charles is typical of his feeling about intoxication all his life. It is also typical of the weakness of his personal campaign against liquor. He was intolerant, sarcastic, severe to the point where a man's resentment obstructed the chance of reform.

This was not true in other sins or abuses that might afflict people. He could denounce these evils and rattle the devil's hold on the world, but in doing so he did not give the impression that he was revolted by the crime. Drunkenness—and even drinking—seemed to touch off a special nerve that gave Father Gillis the appearance of being absolutely unreasonable where liquor was concerned.

Once he was preaching a mission in a parish renowned for the number and variety of its taverns. James Gillis was intense when he tackled temperance during the mission week. He was so powerful that a committee of tavernkeepers came around to the rectory and spoke to the pastor. They were indignant and wanted redress for some of the things that had been said. "I wouldn't want to interfere with the missionary," explained the priest. "I think you'd better speak to Father Gillis himself. Wait here and I'll bring him down."

In a body the owners rose and pushed to the door. "Never mind, Your Reverence," said the spokesman, anxiously eying his friends already departing. "Better to let the whole thing drop. We'd better not get him going again on the subject."

Some of this extreme seriousness when liquor was mentioned lightly can be verified by a 1925 editorial that Father Gillis wrote on Robert Ingersoll's eulogy on whiskey. Ingersoll had sent a gift of whiskey to his future son-in-law and wrote a casual, if poetic, letter to explain the gift. One of his sentences was: "Drink it and you will hear the voices of men and maidens singing the Harvest Moon, mingled with the laughter of children."

Father Gillis says:

Being rather a realist than a rhapsodist, I cannot help wondering how "the laughter of children" comes to be associated with the drinking of whiskey. . . . I have consulted some hundreds of priests and social workers, who have had endless chances to see and to hear what goes on in the whiskey drinker's home. But none of them remembers much about the "laughter of children"—except that it ceased suddenly when whiskey came . . . Wives and children have heard growling and snarling and quarreling, and smashing of furniture and profanity and blasphemy.

A grave disservice is rendered, however, in not admitting that despite this unyielding, humorless approach Father Gillis did incalculable good in his fierce campaign against drink. The evils and abuses, the heartbreaking conditions caused by alcohol, particularly among the first- and second-generation Irish, had to be scored and flayed.

The time in which James Gillis grew up around Boston allowed for no funny stories and no gay way with John Barleycorn. Also, as a missionary he heard the intimate confessions of men and women whose lives had been blighted directly and indirectly by drink. The answer to it all for him was total war against liquor manufacturers and sellers.

His mission records hold the figures that tell his effectiveness. He would preach on temperance and ask the people to take a pledge against alcohol. Pledge cards were passed out and picked up at the end of the evening. The practice was not his alone but one that was common on missions at that time. James Gillis carried the idea with him when he was transferred from the missions to *The Catholic World*. If he could not pass out pledges, he was intensely convinced that he must continue preaching and advocating total abstinence.

Prohibition was not a joy to him when it came. The fact seems contradictory in the light of his *constant* mood and *re-*

sponse to liquor and drinking and trafficking. He explains his greater distaste for the Volstead Act:

> It is my own conviction . . . that the prohibition law was the greatest blow ever given to the temperance movement. Before prohibition, the people at large were becoming more and more sober. Total abstinence had become the practice, not of a few, but of millions. . . . Under the Volstead Law, drinking became a popular sport. The passage of the law was a psychological blunder, and a moral calamity.

His substitute plan for curbing intemperance—the only one he ever used—was voluntary conversion of the person.

> The only way to make the country sober is to persuade individual citizens, one by one, to be sober.

This remained James Gillis's "way" after the repeal of prohibition. The "way" was a losing battle in the years following repeal. But to the end, James Gillis didn't make it any easier for himself or others by his implacable attitude on alcoholic drink no matter how, where, why, when it was served.

Major as was the temperance campaign in the Paulist's life, it was not the end of his enthusiasms or causes. These we have gathered were manifold, rising and catching his attentions whenever he saw evil or injustice being done. More often he was ahead of the trend, spotting the issue or the danger in the issue far ahead of his contemporaries.

The Negro question was one of these topics that Father Gillis treated long before the Little Rocks or Ciceros exploded in our headlines. In 1924, one year after the famous "False Prophets" series, with a New York audience crowding St. Paul's to hear again the priest who had captivated them, he demanded equality for Negroes.

"Illiteracy is the obstacle to the progress and development of the Negro," preached Father Gillis. In his remarks he pleaded:

> Encourage him, open the way to opportunity, help him to develop, and the so-called inferiority of the Negro will disappear. I believe some of the prejudice against the Negro is that of white men who fear that his development may make him equal mentally with themselves, or even superior.

The speech did not go unnoticed by the newspapers and periodicals. The New York *Times* gave it half a column, quoting extensively from the sermon. *Commonweal* used it as an editorial tie-in. The NCWC news service flashed it to their papers. Whether the country at large was stirred is doubtful. Preaching such ideas in 1924 was years before groups and interests would be making capital of such kind of oratory. Besides, Americans in 1924 were knee-deep in the dictionary. Crosswords were on us and *social philosophy* were important words only if they fitted six spaces down and ten spaces across.

Despite the manifold interests that hindered Father Gillis's giving himself completely to any one issue, his championing of Negro rights never abated. Other matters overtook this one in importance because of one emergency or another, but each occasion that could be turned to the cause of justice for the Negro was seized on and highlighted.

A review might appear on a Negro entertainer, and Father Gillis would feature some aspect of the review to dramatize the race's condition. Roland Hayes in 1927 gave a concert, and the New York *World* critic said the singer had a tender and deeply sensitive soul. Father Gillis featured this criticism in the February *Catholic World* and blocked off in bold type as a heading for his comments the words, "A Negro with a Soul."

On another occasion he would fix on some political news item concerning the abuse of Negroes and reprint it with a caustic comment. Senator George of Georgia made the blunt statement in 1928 that "we [in the South] have been very careful to obey the letter of the Federal Constitution but we have been very diligent and astute in violating the spirit of such amendments and statutes as would lead the Negro to believe himself the equal of a white man. And we shall continue to conduct ourselves in that way."

Father Gillis quoted that remark and gave one short comment in an editorial of May 1928:

> The New York *World* calls this "plain speaking." But it could be plainer. Instead of the phrase, "such statutes as would lead the Negro to believe himself the equal of a white man," he should have said, more simply and more frankly, "such statutes as permit the Negro to vote."

The Paulist editor had an extreme consciousness of the plight of the Negro race and the dangers that could be added to it by any carelessness on his part. Writing about crime in America in the June 1929 issue of his magazine and discussing the rate of crimes in sections of the country, Father Gillis pointed out the high percentage of offenses in the South. He must have feared that unfair inferences would be drawn from his statistics. Quickly he makes an aside:

> For fear that some of our readers abroad may suspect that crime in the South is due to the presence of the Negro in great numbers . . . the unimaginative statistician . . . declares . . . "even when the rates are worked out separately for the two races (black and white) it is shown that both races have in the South a decidedly higher homicide death rate than in the North . . ."

The great chance to foster his position on the Negro question did not arrive until 1932. He was in his third series as a *Catholic Hour* speaker. A good portion of the American listening public was tuned in to him from coast to coast. James Gillis opened the throttle wide as he spoke on the subject "White Man and Black."

The paragraphs are breath-takingly frank and begging for trouble. James Gillis knew this as he began. He introduced his topic to the fifty-seven NBC affiliates by stating that he intended speaking on "a ticklish problem and one generally considered too hot to handle." From there on he threw away the caution. He said flatly:

> We robbed the red man and killed him. But we kidnapped the black man and enslaved him. The traders in human flesh and blood who . . . swooped down upon the blacks . . . and sold them into bondage were guilty of as great a sin as that of Oliver Cromwell, who slaughtered thousands of the Irish and sold the remainder into slavery in the Barbados. . . . The stain if not the guilt of that sin against the black man is still upon the soul of the white man. It is for us to wash it away with the baptism of humiliation and with works of penance.

He spoke the hard words, the correctly righteous words, of the man who so often burned against injustice:

> On the whole the Negro is considered an alien, an outcast, and, as it were, a leper in our midst. He is ostracized if not exiled. He is the victim of such discrimination and injustice as would precipitate unending race riots if he were not more tolerant, more patient, and more law-abiding than his white neighbors. He must suffer incessantly and . . . if he were to rise in rebellion . . . he would be shot down like a dog, and I fear that vast numbers of "liberty-loving Americans" would say that it served him right: that he should take what he gets and be thankful for it: that he should know his place and be content with it.

The temperature reading of some of the listeners to this talk rose to fever point, and station after station below the Mason-Dixon line cut the talk midway through the program. A lot of chamber music was played over the air that day all over Dixie—at least while James Gillis was broadcasting from New York.

This talk caused a sensation, which in the Gillis idiom meant that he had tagged an issue again and in so doing ruffled a lot of feathers, fine and not so fine. A reprint of the sermon appeared in a mission magazine with the explanation that his radio address gave rise to some adverse criticism. The reprinting was made despite the circumstances because the talk was considered a straightforward and forceful presentation of Catholic doctrine.

The phrases of the speech struck chords in more quarters than a mission review. Dorothy Day used it to bulwark an editorial in the *Catholic Worker*, and the Negro newspaper, the *New York Age*, prominently featured the sermon in double-column headings on its front page.

The Negro cause was not sidetracked after the stirring and much-quoted sermon of 1932. Articles on Blessed Martin De Porres, comments on Negro "types" in the theater, lectures and forums on Negro conditions and problems, a biting denunciation of the justice meted out in the Scottsboro case—these and other ways and means were used to advance the Negro cause so that full justice would be given the race.

The world's swift trend to war, America's internal political situation, and a host of other enthusiasms fought for a share of Father Gillis's attention.

Despite all the pressure, he found time to champion not only the plight of the Negro but the intolerance accorded the Jews. In fact, the first talk of the 1924 Sunday-evening series at St. Paul's was on injustices perpetrated against the Jews. This was the same series in which he dealt with the Negro question. True, the more sensational response was made over this latter subject, but points made by Father Gillis on the Jewish issue were no less important or stirring.

The Ku Klux Klan was the butt of his attack as he said:

I read recently a charge by the Ku Klux Klan that the Jews are too clannish. Not only are the Klansmen without sense but apparently without humor. . . .

Hostility to the Jews is based on the fact that they refuse to abandon their religion, claimed Father Gillis, and he noted:

A great many 100 per cent Americans want not only an American flag, country and Constitution, but an American God.

If the time ever comes when persecution shall blaze forth in this country as it has in Europe, I pray God that not one Catholic hand shall ever be raised against any Jew, and I hope and pray that should such a persecution begin, 19,000,000 Catholics will leap to the defense of the Jews.

The *Sunday Independent*, a newspaper in Dublin, picked up a news release on the talk and quoted it with the recommendation that the utterance was worthy of being cabled to the ends of the earth. No indications exist that the sermon was flashed to the borders of the world, but some small note was made of it in a few papers. The *Jewish Daily News*, the *Jewish Daily Bulletin*, and the New York *Times* carried references to the sermon and hailed Father Gillis as defender and warm friend of the Jews.

It was the Hitlerian pronouncements on Aryanism and the dictator's persecution of the Jews that brought from Father Gillis some of the strongest editorials and sermons he ever composed. He had been studying, and not liking, the semimaniacal posturings and mouthings of the leader of German National Socialism. The inflammatory nature of the Hitler speeches and the dictator's hostile asides about the Jews in Germany were obvious.

Father Gillis, as so often, anticipated the possibility that sparks from such wildfires as Adolf had kindled could leap an ocean. He felt that a drop of prevention was worth a gallon of water should the blaze spread. One month before the Fuehrer

rose to head the Reich, Father Gillis delivered a nationwide
radio address on the need of promoting good feelings between
Gentile and Jew.

No one naïvely argues that this quickly settled any conflict
between Gentiles and Jews in America. The point is not what
was settled but what a Catholic priest was doing. He was a
vanguard for both Jewish leaders and Christian leaders to imitate—not ignore while they sat to moan or cluck or whine over
this crisis or any crisis. James Gillis's example *then* found application that can be transferred to any place, time, or group
that faces parlous moments.

The Paulist editor moved out to the front of the battle
as soon as Hitler came to power in 1933. He lectured before
Knights of Columbus, church groups, and social organizations.
With his series of 1932 completed on NBC, Father Gillis
jumped to the microphones of the struggling Paulist station
WLWL, lampooning and lambasting the stupidities of Hitlerian propaganda releases.

One Gillis talk on WLWL gathered attention and received a
response perhaps never accorded any other sermon preached in
this country. Speaking on WLWL on November 23, 1933,
against Hitler and the Nazi attempt to do away with the Old
Testament, Father Gillis stated:

> We have and can have no sympathy and no agreement
> with those who try to de-Judaize Chrisianity. To elimi-
> nate the Jewish element from our faith would be to tear up
> and throw away the roots of the Christian religion.

The *whole* sermon—not the quotation alone—was printed,
double-page spread, in *Variety*, one of the papers dealing with
show business news, on January 2, 1934. The legend at the
bottom of the spread reads: "Printed in memory of my dear
friend, Sime Silverman." The tribute to Mr. Silverman, founder
of *Variety*, is not half so impressive as the accolade such a display gave Father Gillis.

Publicity for his outspokenness was not a concern of James Gillis. As with the Negro question, the priest was not preaching for headlines, he was preaching for justice—for common, decent fair play. Whether all the world or only one person in it listened to him, James Gillis pointed out injustice wherever he saw it.

Here is the resolution of all the work of these twenty-six years that were so stormy for Father Gillis. Analyze and study, compare and weigh the work, the effort, the suffering of this quarter of a century; when the search is ended, the spur to the life of James Gillis will prove to be justice.

The Paulist spares us the travail of tracking down the reason behind his zealousness for causes. In the May 1928 issue of *The Catholic World,* James Gillis introduces an editorial with words that could be the preamble to his life:

> When I was studying early church history at the Catholic University, our professor (Dr. Shahan, most enthusiastic and inspiring of teachers) called our attention to the all-including zeal and universal sympathy of Pope Gregory the Great. "If ever there was a man . . . who hungered and thirsted for justice, it was Gregory. Truly he fitted his name 'Gregory, the watchful one.' Wherever there was injustice, his voice was heard, and his assistance felt. . . . His letters and his messengers were sent to every corner of the world where there was unhappiness and oppression. He was the outspoken, courageous, unrelenting foe of all that was wrong in public or in private life." We young priests who sat at the feet of the enthusiastic professor caught some of his admiration for the pope who would not remain "silent in the presence of sin."
>
> I have never since lost the conviction that one indispensable quality of any one in authority, political or ecclesiastical, is to rebuke injustice. . . .
>
> Silence may be at times a virtue, but silence in the presence of sin and crime may be itself a sin and a crime.

James Gillis's timely talking was not always appreciated. This is indicated by the many critical letters that told the Paulist he was out of his element. These letters were and always would be twice-told tales as far as Father Gillis was concerned. He had received hundreds of such missives long before he became an international figure; he received thousands and thousands of them in the years of fighting President Roosevelt, the war, the United Nations, Mussolini—all the combatants against whom he squared off.

These letters would lead one to believe that all his life James Gillis was out of his element. Like installments in a continued and repetitious story, they go on and on abusing him for meddling. The color of the paper or ink may vary, this note may be ignorantly scrawled, that elegantly typed, one writer may damn him vulgarly, another may argue respectfully, but all got to one point— "Mind your own business!"

That was precisely what Father Gillis was doing, and he never swerved from that conviction as long as he lived. James Gillis argued heatedly and strongly, but never wildly or loosely, that a priest's business was exactly in the fields and among the issues which he tackled. He did not agree that there were areas of moral values that a priest forgot about when such values involved political, social, or economic matters.

He was not unaware of the dangers, the labels and tags, the disrepute that could attach to his activities. James Gillis was fully cognizant of the conflicts that whirled about the head of Father Charles Coughlin of Royal Oak, Michigan. He knew he was not immune to the same kind of controversy.

The Paulist had determined policies about his right to speak on world and national affairs. These policies he announced clearly and vigorously on the Paulist station WLWL in 1934, the year after his *Catholic Hour* sermon on the Negroes brought heavy criticism.

These principles, though dealing with politics, are the basic promptings behind all of James Gillis's controversial speaking and writing:

As for the right of a clergyman to discuss such matters, if my critic is not only a Catholic, but a well-read Catholic, he will know that every great theologian in the history of Catholic thought has discussed politics in the higher and nobler sense—St. Thomas Aquinas, Suarez and Robert Bellarmine.

Aristotle and Aquinas would have considered it impossible, fatal, to divorce politics from the other sciences. They didn't believe a man really educated unless he had a fairly good grasp of all the sciences there were. He was accounted badly educated if he had unco-ordinated knowledge.

What we need is a closer relationship, a closer association of religion and ethics with politics and . . . a liason officer to combine the two.

That in my opinion may well be one of the duties of the clergyman—to fight against the divorce of ethics from politics. I believe that the alienation of politics from religion—consequently from ethics—is the cause of most of our political troubles.

Here is where I come into the picture. . . . It is my business to deal with morals and there is an ethics governing nations as well as an ethics governing individuals . . . with which a clergyman has a perfect right, as a matter of fact, a duty to deal. . . . He must as a teacher of morals concern himself with ethics.

The point I have taken again and again is that it is unethical and hence immoral, unwise, unjust, unchristian . . . to persecute a man because of his race or religion. . . . It is wrong for czars to punish the Poles . . . the white man to penalize the black . . . the fascists or any others to penalize the Jews. . . .

You have no right to tie the tongue of a priest any more than of any other public speaker. Part of a priest's vocation is to teach public as well as private morals.

Such an extensive quotation is fully justified when we realize that in it lies the motivation of one of the most outspoken priests in the history of the Catholic Church in America. A lifetime of hectic debate, damning attack, and lonely vigilance for justice's sake was suffered because of this platform. Fifty years of hungering and thirsting deserve a fair chance to state completely the reasons behind so assiduous a practice of the eighth Beatitude.

PRIVATE VIEW
OF A PUBLIC LIFE

chapter IX

There is a private view which gives perspective to the public life of James Gillis during 1921–47. The sources are off the record. The material was not kept by secretaries but remembered by family and friends—and sometimes enemies. It embraces anecdotes, news comments or interviews, personal correspondence, and, finally, sporadic diary jottings by Father Gillis himself.

As in previous matters, the foremost Boswellian aid to these years is Monsignor Gibbons of Providence. The revelation James Gillis had made that he needed Joseph Gibbons is easily substantiated by the fact that he spent nearly all of his vacations for fifty years with the Monsignor; any free time not given to a visit home was spent invariably at Providence or in travel with the Rhode Island pastor; each editorial crisis of the harrowing pre- and post-war years was decided with Monsignor Gibbons; every major illness of the Paulist was endured and overcome in the companionship of this chosen friend.

The word *chosen* is well taken because it describes exactly what James Gillis did in making this friendship at St. Charles College in 1896. He had decided on Joe Gibbons then as the friend of a lifetime. It was Jim Gillis who was the aggressor in the relationship to the point where he cut out other earlier companions of Joe Gibbons. He arranged school games, hikes, and vacations so that they could share the time together.

Monsignor Gibbons says that the early attention paid him by Jim Gillis had surprised him. He had admired the aloof, slightly grave and withdrawn boy from Boston but he had not thought him the type for deep friendship with anyone. He looked, spoke, acted as one apart or above the rest. Monsignor said he learned the reason behind this later. Jim Gillis was not a snob— if anything, his problem was shyness and extreme fear. The shyness prevented him from openly demonstrating affection; the fear plagued him that, should he try to make friends, they'd ultimately disappoint him.

Once convinced that Joe Gibbons was a sincere, loyal, and trustworthy person, Jim Gillis lost his fear of being hurt or ridiculed in his feelings of friendliness. He took the offensive in making the companionship deep and enduring, and the years showed he succeeded admirably well. The friendship became the greatest human bond he forged in a life that was crammed and jammed with people and things. Not even in his own Community did James Gillis find so real a tie as the one begun as a boy at college.

The summary of this friendship between Monsignor Gibbons and James Gillis is given in a brief note written by the latter after he had recovered from a serious illness. When he'd returned from the hospital, Father Gillis wrote to Monsignor Gibbons:

> I have sent a note of thanks to everybody who was so wonderful and who helped me so much in my illness. I've saved you for the end and thanking you seems to be out of place. I mean by that that it is impossible to really thank your own flesh and blood.

The knowledge of this friendship is no surprise to anyone who knew James Gillis. The surprise is in the fact that the

Gillis of the well-contained manner and mien could be embarrassingly affectionate about the association.

Monsignor Gibbons tells of occasions when this was true: "Jim Gillis was very warm-hearted—more so than I. I used to amuse my mother by telling her of my meetings with Jim in New York. He'd be at the train and when I'd come in he'd take my bag and put his arm in my arm and off we'd go up the crowded streets. That was the way Jim was. He couldn't do enough for me."

Monsignor Gibbons doesn't add that whatever was done for him was repaid handsomely in the years of their friendship. He was a patient, tolerant, always-willing buffer, companion, nurse, and confidant to Jim Gillis.

Joseph Gibbons had a staunch, unswerving faithfulness to all that Father Gillis upheld, but he was not blind or gullibly loyal. An independent thinker, sought for counsel by bishop after bishop in his area, an unusually outspoken and frank critic of even his closest associates, Monsignor Gibbons truly appreciated James Gillis. He knew the foibles of his popular friend and did not minimize their presence. He estimated that the greatness of James Gillis far outweighed the weaknesses.

Because of Monsignor Gibbons' closeness to Father Gillis and yet his sound balance in judging him, these active years of the great Paulist can be viewed in a most personal and revealing fashion. The human Gillis stands forth to be known—the flesh-and-blood Gillis can be grasped beyond the learned line and thunderous speeches we have seen.

One of the first calls on the talents and the time of James Gillis was the call made by his Community in 1919. He was elected by the Paulist Fathers in their General Chapter of that year as a member of the Council whose work it is to supervise the activities of the Paulist order. Father Gillis had some misgivings about his ability and his temperamental adjustment to

such a job. It is known that at the time of his election he wondered if he should accept the office or bow out in favor of another man who might be better adapted to the work. Father
McSorley, a lifelong friend of James Gillis in the Community
and at that time an associate on the General Council, begged
him to try the job.

James Gillis served for six years—one term—as second consultor with Father McSorley and three others elected to the
Council. His experience in the job had convinced him that he
did not belong on the Council. He found that it was almost impossible to keep his mind on the many business discussions, the
many business transactions, and the problems arising out of
business that constantly beset the General and his consultors.
Father Gillis's thoughts were over at *The Catholic World*
office. All his interest, all his energy pushed toward a life that
was free from the trammels of business details that absorbed so
much time of each consultive meeting. When in 1924 he was
re-elected for a second term he knew that he must make a
break with the office.

His first decision was to ask Father McSorley, who had been
elected Superior General on that occasion, to relieve him of the
duty and appoint another man. Father McSorley again prevailed upon him to continue in the office, agreeing, however,
that if the work became absolutely onerous, then he would see
his way to allowing James Gillis to resign. After a few months
the editor was back at the Superior General's door petitioning
that he be allowed to drop out of the Council. Reluctantly
Father McSorley accepted the formal resignation of Father
Gillis and freed him from the necessity of putting his energies
into a work for which the editor did not feel he had any particular ability or inclination.

His reasons behind tending his resignation are given on a
sheet of paper that he had pasted in the pages of his preaching

diary. The typewritten sheet, which seems to indicate a desire to register his opinion for future Paulists to read, states:

> . . . I explained that my wish to resign is due to the fact that a very large percentage of the work that comes before the Board of Consultors has to do with financial projects: the building of schools, the building of houses, the disposal of the property on Sixth Avenue, etc. etc. As a result of five years experience in the Consultorship, I have come to the conclusion that I am very greatly lacking in acumen on financial matters. I have not a good business head, and I have thought it better that somebody with a good business head should be in my place.

The letter and the matter of resignation bring up an interesting question. Did Father Gillis really know himself when he stated the reason behind his resignation? That he felt he had no head for business is very probably a legitimate enough statement and conclusion upon which he could act in bowing out of the job on the Council. But was there also a possible rationalization of his position? Was he merely finding a good reason for resigning the Consultor responsibility? Was there some other work he preferred but did not want to admit as his main attraction?

An interesting speculation on this point occurs as we consider an issue that arose within a couple of years of his resignation from the Counsultorship. James Gillis was told to consider the possibility of quitting his speaking engagements if he felt he was being overworked. His answer to this suggestion states flatly:

> I suppose one might say that if I feel overworked I could eliminate public speaking. But I cannot. What I would gain in time would be lost because of the tediousness and weariness of incessant desk work. Public speaking gives me an outlet for nervous energy as well as a certain satisfaction in doing some work that is directly apostolic.

There is a good enough suspicion that the tediousness and weariness which James Gillis complained of in regard to incessant desk work would be factors in driving him from his position on the Paulist Council. It is apparent that the Consultorship was a boring chore for the pent-up energies of the lecturer and writer. Throughout his life and especially at this time, his travels and talks, his jammed engagement book reveal that he had to be on the move and among people.

Monsignor Gibbons says, concerning this trait in James Gillis, "He had to have company. I knew that I could often be alone. I could go apart, but he couldn't. Jim would make a retreat by himself and be serious about it and want no company or distraction, but apart from these occasions he moved constantly among people. I can remember how I would come to New York, get off the train, and after being at Fifty-ninth Street for a few minutes Jim would say, 'Joe, we're going out to supper tonight.'

" 'Look Jim,' I'd reply, 'I just want to sit in my room and read. I'm tired.'

"Then he would wave his arms and, speaking enthusiastically, would tell me of all the people—the important people—who would be there. He'd say, 'We're going to have dinner with the editor of the *Wall Street Journal* and Anne O'Hare McCormick will be there and George Sokolsky and Father Talbot of *America*.' So we'd have a little dinner together and chat on through the evening until the late hours.

"But that was Jim Gillis's life, and a person has to understand that about Jim. He was a writer and a speaker, and all these men and all the occasions, the wit and the stories, all of their experiences—these were grist for an editor's mill. I know occasion after occasion where things that occurred in Jim's presence or interesting incidents that were told eventually appeared in his writings. He stored those things, thought them over, and gradually worked them into some point his own work was trying to make. People were important to him because they fed him ideas."

This is probably a fair-sized part of the complete explanation behind the incessant activity of James Gillis in his twenty-six years of public prominence. Another part of the explanation must be James Gillis's own statement that public speaking gave him some direct feeling of doing apostolic work. Yet these two factors cannot be adduced as the entire drive behind the incessant and crowded moving and turning and traveling and shifting of position that Father Gillis engaged in for a quarter of a century.

By the oddest of quirks it is perhaps just as true that nervous energy (which he himself admitted) was as much a driving force behind his constant travels as any other thing that can be considered. Interestingly enough, he suffered in these years most seriously from the nervous disease already described. It was in the late years, when a certain mellowness had crept into his manner and mood, that his psoriasis began to disappear. When nature finally forced him to settle down and quit the activity to which he had pressed himself, the affliction dwindled to a small rash on the side of his head.

The total explanation must include many more views. Knowing the writings of Father Gillis and reviewing the causes that he championed, we must admit that he was driven on by a high sense of integrity, a warm drive for humanity's rights, a fierce claim that justice be given all men—and these things tell us that not all, not even the great part, of James Gillis's activity was due to mere self-interest or purely natural emotional causes.

There is a story that Monsignor Gibbons tells which brings out very explicitly a facet of this need of people that James Gillis showed. Monsignor describes a vacation in Florida with Father Gillis at the time the Paulist had suffered a serious physical and nervous breakdown.

"For the first couple of days he would repeat over and over, 'Joe, this is too expensive, too expensive. You've got to get me out of here.' I would remonstrate with him and explain that we had planned for the rest and it had been seriously advised for him and he should relax and enjoy it. His answer would always be that it was too expensive and we couldn't afford it.

"Actually Jim was too sick and too weak to enjoy anything, and I do not think he was as much bothered by the expense as his repetitions of that fact indicated. He was restless and moody and upset in mind and body. He could find no simple, easy way of settling back and letting cares go hang. Finally I agreed that we would leave if he really insisted and I told him I would be willing to arrange tickets for our departure.

"The evening that I had promised him that we would try to make some plans for getting out of Florida we went down in the hotel dining room. I left him at the door of the room and told him I wanted to see the headwaiter about a table near the door so that if he felt too weak to finish the meal downstairs he could leave unnoticed and hurry back to the room. As I was coming across the floor to return to Jim, a man stood up from one of the tables and touched my arm. 'Is that Father Gillis, the famous Father Gillis, standing over there?' he asked. 'Yes,' I replied. The man said, 'Would it be all right to go over and speak to him? I would feel highly honored to shake his hand.' I said I thought it would be most acceptable to Father Gillis and I brought the man with me.

"The fellow was actually thrilled to meet Jim. He pumped his hand and told him in terms of high praise how he had listened to Jim on the radio year after year and had collected all of the radio talks. Jim thanked him very much, and I noticed that there was a little sparkle in his voice as he spoke to the man. It was apparent that the old war horse was beginning to smell the scent of the battles he'd been in and, at the knowledge that someone shared the memories of his side of the battles, his spirits began to rise.

"Well, the best of it was yet to happen. While we were standing there chatting with the man, a lady who was proceeding into the dining room overheard the name of James Gillis. Immediately she turned and said without any by-your-leave, 'Father, I would be honored greatly if I might shake hands with you too. I have read everything that you've written.' When she finished, she pulled someone else over and introduced the person to Jim and they shook hands.

"He lasted all through the meal and felt none of the weakness that had plagued him on the trip down and during the days we had spent in Florida up to that time. When we returned to the room and I said I would go out to make arrangements for leaving, I had to laugh when he told me that perhaps Florida would not be so bad after all. He felt a little stronger, having made the trial of going downstairs and moving out of the room for a change.

"You see, the incident of the evening had given him spirit. He had been picked up by the recognition and the warm and sincere adulation of the people who had come to him. I think in the human order that Jim needed that. He needed to be told every so often that a thing he had done was good. But I think that is a human trait and nothing against the greatness of the soul he possessed or the depth of the character that he formed.

"Remember, in 1944 Jim was to all intents and purposes a rejected man. With all the work he had done through his years as an editor and all his radio talks and the good for souls that he had poured into the Church, he was at the point of life where people knew he had been shunted from the *Catholic Hour*. With some of that causing him doubts about his work or its effectiveness and with the heavy sickness, it is not too much to expect that he would like to be told by a few fine, sincere souls that his years in the priesthood had been of great benefit and pleasure to them. That's a pretty human sort of want."

On this sojourn in Florida at the height of this mental and physical anguish, Father Gillis was struck with a great sorrow. His sister Katherine had been ailing through the years of the forties. When he left for Florida she was seriously ill, but he was advised to make the trip despite the gravity of her condition. The doctors believed that she would linger and not worsen during the time that he was away resting.

Without any warning that Katherine's strength had sharply declined, James Gillis received a telegram that she had died suddenly. He was crushed by the blow and, in his condition, almost too stunned to move. Monsignor Gibbons roused him and told him that he must throw off the shock and put on a firm face to meet the family that was suffering at home. It would not help matters at all for the family to have to be unduly anxious over him while stricken with grief over Katherine.

It is evident that Father Gillis's favorite was Katherine. The early notes that he made as a young priest list his concern over the drudging housework that his sister had to do. James Gillis was ever depressed by the fact that Katherine was sacrificing herself as she cared for the home. He believed that with her disposition and personality she could make a splendid family life for herself with some fine man.

There was a manner about Katherine that made her attractive beyond the mere external appearances of looks and feature. Perhaps because she was the baby—even to this day Mary Gillis refers to Katherine as "our baby sister"—perhaps because James Gillis felt she deserved so much more from life than the meager portion allotted to her in tending the home, perhaps because of the indefinable grace or charm that Katherine had—whatever the reason, James Gillis had a deep and warm, almost sentimental, remembrance and recollection of this sister. Even at his last public appearance James Gillis referred to his younger sister and mentioned her endearingly.

These sudden shocks along with the perduring illnesses that afflicted Father Gillis cannot be stressed too much as we take up a phase of his life that is known best by those who lived close to him. Temperamentally James Gillis was not an easy man for anyone to adjust to in the years of prominence. A typical story of this temperament is the one that concerns him and Monsignor Gibbons when they were vacationing at Atlantic City. Monsignor Gibbons describes how they woke one morning after they had been at Atlantic City for a day or so and Father Gillis was very cross.

"Jim was as cross as cross could be. 'Joe,' he said seriously, 'I coughed half the night.' 'Jim,' I replied, 'I heard you. You've got a bad cold there.' 'Well,' he said, 'I can't have a cold. I've got a lecture for every night next week. I can't have this cold.'

" 'Well,' I said, 'you've got it. What is there to do about it?' He said, 'There's one man who can cure me—he's Dr. Kelly up in New York. He can cure me.'

" 'What are we waiting for?' I asked. 'You know and I know, if you want Dr. Kelly, there is only one thing to do. We'll go up to New York and you see Dr. Kelly.' 'It will spoil the trip,' he said. 'Nonsense,' I answered, 'it will not spoil my trip. I'm out of my parish—letting the burdens take care of themselves for a while. What difference does it make if I relax at Atlantic City or at the North Pole? You want to go and that's all right with me. Get shaved and we'll go down, have breakfast, and while breakfasting I'll make reservations on the train.'

"Jim couldn't get over it. 'You mean you really don't mind?' he asked two or three times during breakfast. 'No,' I said, 'why should I mind? You go up to the city and see the doctor and I can sit in my room at the Paulist house and at the end of the week I'll go home.' But he couldn't believe that anyone could act like that or move so suddenly and change their plans."

If James Gillis did not believe that someone could act this way at his behest, he still accepted whatever attention or consideration was given his demands. People fell into his way of doing things—at least those people who were very close to him. To a certain extent he relied upon their fitting the pattern of his expectations, and his line of life shows a man who had some inclination to accept being waited on.

Another scene bearing out some of this pattern is one that is told of his days of activity at *The Catholic World*. He would be busy at the desk, writing feverishly at some column or speech or working over a point to fill out his editorial. Suddenly he would reach for a book on the desk. He would not look up but merely grasp for the book which he expected to be at hand. If it was not in place there would be a roaring growl that it was supposed to be there.

When the noise had caught the attention of one of the members of the staff he would ask imperiously, "How many times must I tell you that each of these books is to be in its special place? I must be able to find each volume without looking for it," he'd cry. "I have no time to be hunting and searching to find what should be at hand."

Whatever criticism is to be made on the temperament of James Gillis, the criticism cannot be too honestly drawn unless time and again the overwhelming tonnage of pain is placed on the scale that weighs him. Only then can the stories or incidents of his sharpness or irascibility that crop up throughout this quarter of a century be estimated fairly.

The pain factor was physical, mental, social, economic. James Gillis was cursed with bodily ills of a highly irritating nature. These he carried about daily. In the tense years of his editorship these constant drains on his good nature were flicks of pain compared to the serious physical breakdowns that marked the first steps toward the ultimate collapse that overtook his whole being.

His mental suffering was acute because of disparate factors. James Gillis was a sensitive person, easily wounded by rebuff or outright rejection. The years of controversy built for him some armor plating, but he never developed fully the ability to shrug off unpopularity. Yet his sense of justice forced him repeatedly to support unpopular causes and make unpopular speeches. This meant anguish to a heart and mind that liked to be liked.

Along with the political wrangling and abuse that he endured, James Gillis suffered worries over his family, over the financial rockiness of *The Catholic World*, over his public life that challenged the harmony between his Community and ecclesiastical authority, over his publicized but unexplained tussle with the *Catholic Hour* people, over the diminishing health and strength that affected his mental acumen and endurance.

Each separate suffering was often involved in the sum total of disturbances that plagued Father Gillis. The social and economic problems can be discerned running in and out of his physical and mental concerns. As an instance, take the matter of his diminishing health. James Gillis was highly conscious that *The Catholic World* had been a financial drain on the Paulist Fathers for all the years he'd been at the helm. He knew that in the mind of his critics he was the incarnation of the constant annual red-ink entry made on the Community books opposite the words *The Catholic World*.

Whenever these illnesses struck him, he would become desolate at the knowledge that his hospitalization was adding more red ink to the ledger. No one could tell him that the black side of the book showed an incalculable deposit of credit in his name. The Paulists never underestimated the prestige, fame, good will, and hard work he had poured into his priesthood, and they told him so. James Gillis brushed this advice aside. He saw only bills, expenses, costs and—himself responsible. He became conscious of his actual dollar-and-cents contribution to the Community. He seemed to think that he could prove in earnings that he more than carried his load.

In his preaching-assignment book you can almost read his mind as it thinks out this problem. The first twenty years of his priesthood, with mission after mission, lecture after lecture noted, no stipend or offering is listed as received for the work. He received stipends but he never found their total any argument proving he was doing his job. As he moved deeper into the work on *The Catholic World* the entries on stipends begin. The years show an increase of marginal bookkeeping. He begins noting doctor and medical bills as against his income, as though to assure himself that he was no added expense to the Fathers.

In the late years, when his illness incapacitated him and his hospital expenses soared with the cost of living, the folly of his earlier anxieties struck home. With private nurses at the house, the best of doctors on regular call, and his simplest or greatest need fulfilled, James Gillis realized he had let his sensitivity betray him. His fears about shouldering his share of the burden had been foolish vanities.

He had proved nothing by his well-kept stipend total. If it was meant to indicate he had been doing his job, it was a useless *Q.E.D.* The Community's care, attention, and concern demonstrated that the Paulists had recognized James Gillis's well-done job no matter what he had figured out as his credit rating.

So the twenty-six years went by, filled with these kinds of annoyances and frets that were no help toward softening a demanding disposition. James Gillis's wrath or scorn could be withering under normal situations without the need of prodding from constant sufferings.

The intolerance and impatience that showed in his column and editorials were not things that Father Gillis turned on and off—neither was his apodictic, take-it-or-leave-it manner of discussing things. These qualities were with him always, and they were not found to be particularly endearing ones by those who might be his victims when he was angered or argumentative.

Those who liked him deeply forgave the outbursts or checked them off to some category like "allowance made for an important man." Those who respected him but were not absolutely enamored of the Gillisan viewpoint walked away or decided he was behind the times or just plain spoiled by his satellites.

The early Gillis—the Gillis of the nineteen-twenties and thirties—was far less attractive a personality than the mellowing man of the late forties and the years up to his death. The younger Gillis had become accustomed to audiences; he met little contradiction among his friends, who gave him adulation undiluted by even the simplest of disloyalties. As a quip summarized it: "When Jim Gillis talked to his intimate fans they wouldn't even look away from him lest it be interpreted as disagreement with him."

Father Gillis was not unaware of his own unquestioned top rank as the authority, the mind, and the voice of millions of American Catholics. He was not naïve or falsely humble about his being an important priest. He had enough letters and cards from bishops, priests, and lay people, from Protestants and Jews as well as Catholics, which told him repeatedly that he was an important man on the world scene as well as on the national and local level.

James Gillis couldn't help feeling his strength among men. He was being consulted, quoted, reprinted in all parts of the world. He was marked explicitly as an important enemy of Mussolini, put on the Red Russian purge list, battered by friends of the New Deal—it is heady stuff to have your position measured by world leaders! No wonder you could demand attention and not brook challenges to what you did or said.

Unfortunately the prophet is not always the most honored and listened-to speaker in his own bailiwick or at his Community breakfast table. Especially is this true if the house holds a few men of highly individualistic natures and talents in their own right.

Some of James Gillis's greatest struggles were over the bare but well-polished tables in the Motherhouse refectory. As he admits in his editorial work, not all the Paulists agreed with him. In the typical American spirit of the Community, the men who disagreed told Father Gillis so.

Actually most of the intramural contests were not on points of politics or on what James Gillis had said in his last speech or editorial. The contention was more a struggle to control the conversation. Not all the household wanted to munch its meal and sit rapt in admiration at some sonorous harangue about racketeers or isolationism or Hitler or Father Gillis's ever-lasting punching bag, Franklin Delano Roosevelt. Some of the Fathers wanted to talk about anything but politics; in some cases they got to the point of just wanting to talk to each other rather than make up an audience on which Father Gillis might try out a new speech.

Another element belongs in this résumé of table talk and what it signifies about James Gillis in his relationship to the men with whom he lived. To those already described, there must be added a group best denoted as the teasers. These are kissing kin to what are known as "leg-pullers."

James Gillis was fair game (in late years he himself came to know and learned to enjoy this fact) for any joker who flaunted the red cloth of controversy just to create a stir. The point could be outlandish, but if it touched on a nerve end of Gillisan interest, it could produce a long and anguished tirade. With the greatest pretense of seriousness a man might remark that he had been reading Eleanor Roosevelt's column and had found in it a host of points for meditation. From there on he could heatedly defend the viewpoint and Father Gillis would be lambasting every defense, never for a moment tumbling to the ruse until the string was played out.

James Gillis had a keen sense of humor which persisted despite troubles or pressures or tensions. It was a saving sense of humor that popped out in his writings and speeches and gave him a release from the grave issues he was treating.

That this humorous strain was not of an ordinary brand is easily confirmed by Father Gillis's friends. Yet to call it odd or strange would be unfair. His sense of humor was offbeat, but not in the vein of the buffoon or zany. He was not a bright, glib comic, but rather a refined raconteur whose stories had a flavor of fun or an ironic twist about them.

Today the Gillis type of humorist is deader than vaudeville. It does not go with the modern times that will accept nothing but the trip-hammer delivery of the gabby, snappy-patter wit or the slam-bang idiocy of the seltzer-squirting clown. The Gillis taste ran to the mordant side, with the satiric flavor getting his preference. Sid Caesar, not Milton Berle, was his favorite modern comedian, which is some resolution of the question of what kind of fun the priest liked.

Any breakdown of so mercurial a quality as a man's sense of humor is bound to reveal inconsistencies. He can be found on one side laughing his head off at T. S. Eliot's fragilely funny *Cocktail Party* and, on the other, splitting his sides at Jackie Gleason's rambunctious *Honeymooners*. So it was with Father Gillis. Having listed him as preferring the upper reaches of satire, we find he had a predilection for puns and word-play jokes that could cripple the gayest of spirits. These, fortunately, were not constant practice of his, but they presented a temptation to which he succumbed easily.

In the late years, with the influx of younger assistants and missionaries to the staff at the Motherhouse, James Gillis was beginning to assimilate some of the roisterous nature of their joking and fooling. He was not entirely sympathetic to their noisy give-and-take that shattered his breakfast calm, but unless he was seriously indisposed he enjoyed occasionally getting into the banter and taking on the young lions.

If the rioters carried their noise up to the fifth floor, that was a different story! There Father Gillis wanted peace and quiet to read or chat or write. He was known to walk unannounced into a neighbor's room, stride to the radio that played too loudly for his taste, snap it off, and march majestically out without a by-your-leave.

What Father Gillis felt was *too* loud was just about audible to the man sitting in the room. But small noises or insistent sounds are like the roar of Niagara to a tensely sick man. Irritating pain was often the culprit that provoked such a summary action on the part of James Gillis.

Ordinarily he bore these incidents with a good spirit and found some humor in the situation. One of his corridor companions who attests to this is Father Francis Ryan, the former head of the New York Mission Band. Father Ryan enjoyed listening to his record collection on the rare opportunities when the mission schedule gave him a breather. As with all hi-fi enthusiasts, the young priest believed that the perfection of the recordings could be appreciated only with the volume control all the way up.

Father Gillis appreciated concert-hall power and clarity, but he preferred it over at Carnegie Hall on West Fifty-seventh Street. He did not relish the whole symphony orchestra playing Beethoven's Ninth right on his doorstep. Yet he realized from his own early days on the road that a missionary has very little life with the Community because the pressure of the mission schedule keeps him away from home. He was reluctant to spoil the few days Father Ryan had with the Community by lecturing him about noise. The older man's ready sense of humor came to his aid. Quickly he sat down and composed the following jingle:

> *I've a big, noisy neighbor named Ryan*
> *His conduct is sometimes quite tryin'.*
> *He plays records galore*
> *With a blare and a roar.*
> *I could moider da guy—I ain't lyin'!*

He slipped the paper under the missionary's door and waited developments back in his room.

They were not long in coming. Father Ryan had spied the limerick and let out a roar in his best missionary tone. The clamor may have shaken a few days off Father Gillis's life, but it was worth it. The young priest got the hint and turned down the volume.

James Gillis was not as cocky, positive, and filled with confidence behind the scenes as his external appearance led one to believe. He lived all his years in one mortal dread—that he might dissipate his priesthood through foolishness, pride, or obduracy in some error or cause that ensnared him.

He was considered an attractive man by his associates, possessed of a dynamic presence that could have led to many temptations. Flattery, praise, attention, sympathy for his viewpoints —these came his way in a constant flow from men and women. Yet he shuddered interiorly that he might be beguiled by any of these to desert his priesthood for an instant of unfaithfulness or disloyalty.

The description given of Father Gillis, who ranked in his mature years as one of the outstanding priests in America, is that "he was fearful of himself." Monsignor Gibbons relates that the Paulist editor used this expression in speaking of his busy life.

"I knew him to go down on his knees and say an Act of

Contrition. He'd fall there beside his desk and beg God to keep him and preserve him in all humility. He had that saving grace that helped him know his danger, and he lived afraid."

Reading the sermons and lectures, thumbing the editorials of these years, one feels that Father Gillis himself was the only person of whom he was afraid. He certainly was willing to step up in any weight division and pull on the gloves with its top contenders.

The boxing metaphor brings to mind a story that deserves telling at this time. Father Gillis was a strong and vehement opponent of prize fighting. He supported the theologians who alleged the immorality of the sport.

Often in late years when he'd be sitting with the priests watching television, one of them would get up and switch to a channel presenting a fight. The maneuver was made half in interest at the fight, half in intention to flush out Father Gillis.

One or two punches were all that the anti-pugilistic Gillis needed. He'd groan in disgust at the spectacle, shake his head in hopelessness, and squirm about to determine how truly interested anyone was in this exhibition. Sometimes he'd launch into a growling attack on the evils of the sport, not caring whether his companions answered him or not. Ultimately he'd rise majestically from his chair, stand there in the semi-darkness for all to witness his protesting action, and stalk mutteringly from the room.

Any of the priests could always tempt him into a verbal fight over fighting. If they raved about some contest and described in enthusiastic terms the goriness and savagery of the bout, Father Gillis would be ready with a sharp, well-turned comment about such goings-on and the people who supported them. He never tired of such battles over boxing and he never tumbled to the fact that most of these bloody atrocities were exaggerated jocosely just to stir his ire.

The amazing sequel to all this still leaves the Fathers wondering if they were fooling him or were themselves being fooled gloriously. About three of four years before James Gillis died he was deeply interested in a boys' camp under the supervision of Father Ronald Burt, one of the young Paulists. The older man wanted to do something for the camp and promised to send a gift to aid the youngsters.

A large package arrived one day at camp. It was Father Gillis's gift to the boys—several sets of boxing gloves! No one has yet analyzed the switch—if there was one on the part of James Gillis. Whatever the twist, it is a neat one and a perfect example of the argument that James Gillis was himself capable of a little teasing now and then.

INTEREST—EVERYTHING; ADDRESS—ANYWHERE

chapter x

Frequently in his life James Gillis would express the idea that he longed to go off to a monastery and spend the time in contemplation and prayer, thinking over the problems of his life and of the world. No one doubted the sincerity of that statement or the yearning it expressed, but there was some doubt as to the accuracy of the remark. He may never have resolved what the yearning or want in the depth of his heart really was, but the facts of his life do not bear witness to the point that the unplumbed or unfound focus of life was in cenobitic meditation.

His constant traveling and journeying are frank indicators that James Gillis was not exactly the solitary sort. He gave no hint at any time that all of this moving about ever became a burdensome duty. Everything in Father Gillis's life points to travel as being one of his keenest pleasures, and it would seem that he wanted monastic solitude about as much as a mountain climber hankers after a sudden rock slide.

His many short trips—jaunts outside New York City to nearby New Jersey, Pennsylvania, or New England spots—are in the thousands. His longer trips, while not as numerous, make up in distance what they lack in frequency. Outstanding are the journeys Father Gillis made to speak at various Eucharistic Congresses all over the world.

The first of these Congresses he attended in 1926, two years after he had resigned his Paulist Consultorship. He traveled to Chicago for the first International Eucharistic Congress ever held in the United States.

James Gillis was a reporter at this Congress. His editorial on the magnificent spectacle and its side lights is a flowing piece from his pen. All his pride of faith, his feeling and sensitivity for great moments, his deep concern for the Church in America are in this report of the American Church's finest hour. He states:

> At Chicago we came—so to speak—out of our holes and corners, out of our catacombs into a blinding light. We became the cynosure of the eyes of America, and of the world, and even according to the judgment of our most exacting critics, we conducted ourselves as those "to the manner born."

Eleven years later James Gillis would be more than a reporter. His ascending star, which shot up into the heavens through the days of the twenties after "False Prophets," would reach a zenith in Manila at the International Eucharistic Congress.

Before the eleven years passed, each year of the period would be filled with its own special event or problem. Ever present would be his own physical frailty. The pressure of the five years as editor and lecturer had caused the need of emergency treatment for his skin disease. Doctors suggested rest, sun, quitting his arduous job entirely, going to some place to take mineral-water baths. James Gillis decided on following all the advice. He'd get the rest, have the sun, leave his job for a short while, and take the baths. He embarked on the *Leviathan* in May 1928 and journeyed to Karlsbad in Germany.

The days at sea, the healing waters at the springs alleviated his trouble and refreshed him for a return to the busy life he had quit. But his return was not to a situation that was calculated to keep his quieted nerves very quiet. Alfred E. Smith had been nominated in the summer that Father Gillis had been abroad. In the nerve-racking days that followed, James Gillis must have wondered why he hadn't thought to bottle some of those Karlsbad waters when he'd been splashing about in them.

The Smith versus Hoover campaign must have caused James Gillis a special rash all its own. He knew from the inception of the contest that things would not get better, but very much worse for Mr. Smith and the Catholics who daydreamed about his chances in an election. Father Gillis warned his readers shortly after Smith's nomination:

> From now on until election day we Catholics must be prepared to hear all manner of accusations—from the most plausible to the most ridiculous—against ourselves and our Church. Every day the newspapers speak of the "whispering campaign" against the Catholic candidate. . . . Many of these whispers are too obscene for publication.

Preparedness was a grand word but a futile shield for Father Gillis or the Catholics who suffered through those nightmarish days. The Paulist editor was riven by the campaign. His earnest hope was the possibility that Governor Smith, Al of Fulton Street fame, the gravel-voiced, hard-hitting, honest boy who captivated New York, could win the country.

Father Gillis was crushed when he saw where Al was going to wind up once the smearers and slimers got through with him. The priest was so right but so unhappy that he had been right in his guess. Al Smith was a badly and bitterly beaten candidate. The first Catholic ever to try for the presidency on a major party ticket had proved only that Father Gillis's fears were correct—in a showdown in America the Catholic was a second-class citizen. He lamented:

> Only one religion, or at the most two, are made reasons for discrimination; one is the Catholic, the other the Jewish. All Protestants, as well as all infidels, are immune.

When the election was over, the sad truth sank in that being a Catholic meant political martyrdom for a presidential aspirant. The editorial that James Gillis wrote congratulated Mr. Smith on having earned his martyr's palm nobly. Then he turned his words to the readers:

> Naturally, we Catholics are pained to see one of our number rejected principally or even partially because of his religion. But we can survive that slap in the face. We belong to a Church that . . . can "take it" . . . We shall not wither up and blow away now that we have been told —with such unnecessary and brutal over-emphasis—that no Catholic can occupy the White House.

Such words were a surprisingly calm, almost anticlimactic ending to the Al Smith story. Being told that they can take it was small comfort for the Catholics who had hoped for so much. At that time some of the Gillis readers must have clamored for loud, shocking, reverberating protestations. He alludes to this fact when he remarks:

> Perhaps most of the faithful readers of these rambunctious editorials may have expected that my first and most violent reaction to the recent disastrous election would concern religion.

He disappointed and apparently intended to disappoint that expectation. The campaign had sickened him and he wanted to fly from it. His discouragement at so flagrant an abuse of the much-publicized American sense of fair play was overwhelming. Father Gillis felt the campaign was over—he'd had all he could stand of it.

Father Gillis might have longed at the end of the Smith defeat to be able to indulge in some of the travel that he loved so much. His schedule, however, did not call for any extended trips, and most of his journeys were of a local nature or at most to the Midwest and back to New York. Within a year the heart that had been wounded by the personal sense of defeat that had accompanied the election of 1928 was now completely smitten in the social cataclysm that descended on America in the stock market crash of 1929.

Father Gillis had pointed out at the time of the Smith campaign the danger—without investigation, without careful study —of the constant cry: "Prosperity, Prosperity, Prosperity." In an editorial of December 1928 commenting on the Smith defeat, he took particular issue with the paeans of praise that had been sent up by the Republican party over their contribution to the prosperity of the country. His attack was on the fact that such talk was basically motivated by a greed and a worship of nothing but money rather than prosperity.

His words, brief and concise, were a condemnation of all that had been engendered by the consuming greed and concentration on money and more money and better and softer living that had affected America. He was striking out at the whole decade of the twenties, striking out at Mr. Coolidge and his preachments that America would continue on this prosperity binge; he was whacking at the greed and the crime and the vice that flourished in a society that was learning to compromise with the abuses that prohibition had brought as long as money was there to make up for the compromise; he was pounding against the philosophies and attitudes of the Menckens and Fitzgeralds and against the newspapers and the movies and the novels and periodicals of the era which seemed to be inciting people to lose their grip on reason and decency and integrity. Father Gillis felt that avarice was behind all of the giddy, the semi-hysterical, the openly uncontrolled attitudes that were afflicting the nation in that period.

His reaction to the stock market crash is not surprising when we look back to this editorial of the year previous. On October 31, 1929, speaking over WLWL, two days after the Black

Tuesday that saw the market plunge to its worse level, Father Gillis said:

> Our atmosphere is filled with post-mortems on the crash in Wall Street and almost everybody is having his say—so I presume that there can be no valid objection for a priest's venturing to make a few remarks *apropos* of the financial debacle. . . . I am not going to moralize on the stock market business nor do I intend to offer any advice, since I am such a rank outsider to such transactions. But if any man cannot draw his own moral from the events of the last few days, he must be a moron. The pity is that people didn't learn wisdom before the fact rather than after.
>
> I have just heard a story of a man who was asked, "Is your son dabbling in stock?" "Yes," said the man. "Is he a bull?" "No," answered the man. "A bear?" "No," answered the man. "Well, what is he?" asked the inquirer. "Just a plain damn fool," said the man. To me that is the situation in a nutshell.

The talk was strangely intolerant of the people who had lost money in the stock market crash. James Gillis harkened back to the warnings that should have been evident in the false claims of the Republican party that "prosperity could do nothing but get more prosperous." The point of his intolerance, of his almost contemptuous attitude over the moans and wails of the losers in Wall Street, is explained by the fact that he demanded they admit they were gambling. He indicated that the innocent who entered the stock market were not warned by the professionals in the market that buying stocks on margin was strictly a gamble. He concluded this very unsympathetic talk with the words:

> I have not much confidence that these warnings will be heeded. I have given them a thousand times in private and I have been laughed at. Human nature is fond of gambling — Well, if you must gamble, at least don't fool yourself— don't speak of investments when you mean gambling.

If James Gillis cared little about the machinations and the manipulations of finance on the market that had caused it to shudder and crack, he did not have the same reaction to a new and different problem confronting the people.

Within the year after Black Tuedsay of 1929 the employment crisis moved deeper and deeper into the everyday lives of the people. Whole neighborhoods, whole industries, whole cities were affected. Men lined up, futilely hoping, begging for any kind of work at all to support their families. The famous apple sellers of the thirties began to appear in the business sections of metropolitan cities. The gloom that had been sudden and sharp, like a shock, when the market crashed now had fanned far out and had sunk deeper and deeper into the American spirit.

Within a very short time James Gillis recognized the enormity of the problem that confronted the nation. The people wanted answers to the questions concerning their lives, their futures, and the world that lay ahead for their children. Unschooled in economics, not caring for the fine points of how money is scarce or plentiful, how jobs come and go, how inflation or retrenchment must be managed in the economic spirals and phases that fall upon a nation, the people were getting to the point where they wanted the answers fast.

A kind of terror was sweeping the country as the banks, their assets paralyzed because of the mortgages they had carried, began to fold and close and wipe out the savings of millions of Americans. This atmosphere was the kind that bred revolution, and revolution in turn could bring another kind of terror that history warned about all too well.

Conscious of the ominous possibilities if something constructive was not offered, Father Gillis pushed himself to give answers to the people as best he could and to the extent of his influence. Whenever the opportunity presented itself he turned his sermons and lectures toward some aspect of the unemployment crisis. In October of 1930 he spoke about the problem over WLWL; within two weeks of that talk, on November 13, again on the radio, he considered the matter of unemployment as a precursor of a change of our system; within seven weeks, at St. Paul's Church, as the new year of 1931 began, he preached on "Unemployment, Economic Distress and Religion"; and in that year, again at St. Paul's, he discoursed on the "Moral Aspects of the Unemployment Crisis."

Father Gillis was convinced that there must be a change in the economic system America had had for all these years. He sensed that a change was in the air and he knew that if it was not acceded to it would be forced into effect by the people in their need, in their poverty, in their hunger.

He preached and wrote and prayed that America would see the great desire for change that moved in the world. He tried to lay bare the root of the problem and get at the evils that would cause the change if people did not heed the warning of the times. James Gillis dreaded the possibility that the change would be even the smallest share of the godless ideas that had caused a revolution in Russia.

In 1933, remembering the scenes of unemployment and depression that he had seen in his travels around the country, he wrote in an editorial:

If the stand-pat, die-hard advocates of an immutable capitalism care to learn why communism threatens, it may be not altogether futile to explain to them that it is not because of the laborious and incomprehensible economic philosophy of Karl Marx, not because of the success, such as it is, of Russian Sovietism, not because of an academic theory, or of violent propaganda, or of a combination of the two, but because of the hideous, ghastly inconsistencies of a system under which a few men make millions a year and millions of men make nothing or next to nothing a year. At bottom all questions, even economic questions, are simple. The Pope, for example, solved the problem of the depression, supposedly so intricate, with one word—greed.

As a priest who was determined to preach at every opportunity the doctrine of Christ against the dangerous doctrines that were looming on the horizon, Father Gillis developed a two-edged sword. Taking a lead from some of the Pope's statements, he added to his criticism of communism the new and stronger idea of preaching social justice. From now on and all through the late thirties and through the forties he studied and read and preached his convictions of the need for social justice, for its techniques and philosophy as the means to solving so many of the danger points in the American way of life.

In the fall of 1934 Father Gillis devoted the whole series of *Catholic Hour* talks to social justice problems. The note of dedication in the front of this collection of talks is truly the summary of the whole social situation as Father Gillis saw it. Whether or not he felt the people would accept it or the average person was ready to practice it is not known to us. His dedication is not a new statement or a different statement from the point he had discussed in a sermon at St. Paul's Church. The dedication page reads: "With infinite reverence to the poor man of Galilee Whose life and Whose gospel are the only solution of the social problem."

If Father Gillis was not preaching an idea different from the earlier sermon that he had delivered, he was now preaching a different solution for the evils of the day. He was trying to explode among the members of the Church a new concept of practicing Christianity in the changing order of the twentieth century. He wanted to bring home forcefully, to what he felt was a complacent Catholicism, the need for a strong and vigorous and violent kind of Christian action. He said in one of his radio sermons:

The Communists are stealing our thunder. Barring their atheism, their vicious method of arraying class against class, their denial of the right of private ownership and their other incidental lunacies, the Communists have got hold of a big idea and a great enthusiasm, the idea of social justice and the enthusiasm for suffering mankind.

What James Gillis wanted of the Catholic people he stated in an almost tempestuous conclusion to one of his talks:

> I believe there is, or there was, on the stage in New York a play called *A Sleeping Clergyman*. What it is about, I confess I don't know, and I am not sufficiently interested to inquire. But the title strikes, irritates me, stimulates me. Too many of us are sleeping clergymen, and too many of the laity are likewise in a trance. Who was it that said lately that there is a church militant but there should be no church dormant? It does seem to me that what we need is not warnings to "pipe down" but commands to "cry out"; not taps but reveille—not soothing syrup, laudanum, the hashish of contentment with a system that has again and again eventuated in vast and even universal economic demoralization, not a sense of satisfaction with the sins and crimes of the existing social and industrial order, but a prod, a goad, a stick of moral dynamite, an ounce or two of mental nitro-glycerine out of the Gospels, the Fathers, and the papal encyclicals.

James Gillis believed that what was needed most was some form of action that would be dynamic and have the Church meet the Communist on his own level or with his own tools or techniques. At one time in a talk he suggested that we should stop denouncing communism from the pulpit but should rather open a hundred and fifty or two hundred centers of operation in slum sections of the city. To these centers we should appoint delegations which would carry on the fight for winning back to Christianity the people who had been disaffected and had fallen prey to Communist activities in unions and in labor disputes and strikes.

Some answer must be given to a very simple and natural question that arises after hearing the advice reported in the last paragraphs. When someone says we should rent cheap halls and serve coffee and bread and offer a bit of warmth and conversation about the faith, who wouldn't ask, "And what about the man who recommended these things?" The normal response is to expect the suggester of such a technique to be the leader in putting that technique into effect.

As far as we know, James Gillis did not regularly serve buns and coffee in any of the gathering places for the homeless and down-and-outers. He is not known to have been consistently an apostle to those of faded hopes or jaded pasts; he has no reputation of having been endearingly called "Padre" by the flophouse-fraternity set. That he worried over the poor or shared his meager purse with the unfortunate or anguished over the horrible effects of poverty on people is undeniable, but that he went about in rags or brewed some soup kitchen's daily broth or each evening tucked in the sheets for some scraggly, indigent has-been is not part of the James Gillis story.

Was he then himself doing "all his fighting with his mouth"? Time and again we see his recommendations for solutions to problem after problem in the life of the American Church. Yet there is no time taken out for effecting the solution in the sphere where the problem has occurred. In James Gillis's life one cause succeeds another, one enthusiasm follows quickly upon enthusiasm, one practice, one suggestion, one way of doing things is scarcely uttered when another cause, a new practice, a new technique, a new way of doing things is offered. The response to such a man is that he is merely doctrinaire, a theorizer; and, as with all theorizers, there comes the suspicion that while it is so easy to suggest these things it is so difficult to stick with them until they are carried out.

Monsignor Gibbons, in frankly assaying this kind of criticism which he admitted had been leveled at James Gillis throughout his life, claimed that Father Gillis's vocation was to be a publicist of ideas rather than a man actively involved in putting ideas into effect. He said that it was a very natural thing with James Gillis to see and grasp and become involved and enthusiastic about some condition or circumstance of life. He would take it as a cause, plead it, and never actually get down to the business of putting the enthusiasm to a practical test.

"It was not necessary for Jim to be putting every idea he had to the test," commented the Monsignor. "James Gillis was a popularizer. He brought forth ideas and tried to publicize them and get them down to the people. When any important idea came to him on a current situation, he would seize on it with earnestness and push it to the point where he wanted everyone to know and see what he knew and saw about the situation. That he could be criticized as impractical for this is very easy but not very logical.

"I myself would tease him about such a fault on occasion. For example, I remember one night when we were walking along the Common and he was filled with this notion of politicians being perfectly frank and honest with the people. He was all disturbed with the idea and seemed to think that if people talked bluntly and openly about issues there could be no problems in life.

"I let him go on for a while and finally I stopped him and said, 'Now, Jim, that's all very good, but let's take a practical example. Look at this woman coming along the street. That's a crazy hat she's got on and her dress is crazier still and to boot she's a homely jigger. Now you stop and tell her—be frank, be honest, be direct—tell her about that hat and the dress and her looks.' Well, he threw up his hands in disgust and stormed away from me along the street.

"Actually, I was wrong in demanding that he put his ideas into effect. I knew what he was getting at and I perverted the idea to a situation that could do no one any good. I might tease him that way but I must admit ideas were his forte. It was his nature to have ideas and see circumstances and issues that needed remedies and to suggest the remedies. It was no more necessary for Jim to put those ideas into effect than it is necessary for a surgeon with a new operating technique to climb up on the table and start slashing himself.

"Leaders in the world of ideas are few and far between, and it is ridiculous to expect that they are to be involved so greatly, so heavily, so deeply in effecting their ideas that they are to be bogged down with details and small operations of carrying out an idea. It is a little bit like asking the man who designs an automobile to get into the factory and turn out all of the parts, when actually his idea is a benefit to the thousands and thousands who can be employed because of the one idea."

Monsignor Gibbons' analysis leads to another thought. If James Gillis had stopped at one idea and placed himself to the task of completely effecting it, he could not have given as much of his time and talents and health as he did to the career of ideas that he followed. It is interesting to note that he predicted, knowingly or not, the kind of career that he would have. An early series of talks, far back in 1936 when speaking on the Paulist radio station, was delivered under the title, "A Parade of Ideas."

The more we press the criticism that Father Gillis was something of an armchair general moving the pins and pieces on the battlefield map but never entering into the battle, we learn that wherever possible he did make some practical application of his theories and ideas. It was not quite possible for him to become unemployed and stand in a bread line or sell apples along Wall Street, but where he could meet and talk or listen to those in unfortunate circumstances he did so.

It was not possible for James Gillis to give away a fortune, because he had no fortune. His own life was lived in simplicity and poverty, his room was not ornately decorated, nor did he surround himself with gimmicks and gadgets and things that could provide for his comfort.

He could not change his color or his race and become a Negro or a Jew and thus shoulder the burden of intolerance toward them which he fought against in his sermons, but he could and did enter into any organizations or any associations that legitimately advanced the cause of toleration for these peoples.

Whatever the critics of this man's practicality expected him to do would be hard to say. Perhaps their expectation was that Father Gillis should have leaped along the streets ready to embrace the first vagrant he might meet; perhaps they expected him to be in his shirt sleeves, making coffee or serving the doughnuts in the settlement houses that he advocated; perhaps any one of a hundred suggestions of practicality would be forthcoming from the critics. As can usually be discerned, the very practical critics do *none* of these things themselves and, what is more to the point, they do not even *have ideas* about doing them. Their practicality seems to be that they sit around criticizing all the impractical men they can find—men like Father Gillis.

If James Gillis was not chief cook and bottle washer at settlement houses or was not down in the financial district peddling bright red apples, he was still very busy about the appointed work of being a missionary priest.

Checking the year 1931 in only the period of Lent, we find that Father Gillis was giving in that season three separate Lenten series in three different cities on three different evenings of the week! On Monday evenings he was in Providence, Rhode Island, giving one of the Lenten talks; he would leave and speak in Jersey City, New Jersey, on Wednesday evenings; and on the Sunday following, he was preaching at St. Paul the Apostle Church in New York City. The three series listed in his preaching diary show that in each of the cities he was delivering a different talk on the successive occasions. For example, the opening talk in Providence was on the soul, two nights later in Jersey City the initial sermon was on happiness and sorrow, and on the next Sunday opening in New York he spoke on Leo the Great and Attila the Hun, the first in a series under the title "Dramatic Episodes in the Lives of the Saints."

This triple series was carried on for six straight weeks, which meant that in this array of talks alone he was delivering eighteen different sermons. He concluded by speaking at the Good Friday broadcast over WEAF in New York City on "The Man of Sorrows"—the nineteenth different talk in one Lent! With such a schedule, just how practical can a man get?

With the work at *The Catholic World*, the "Sursum Corda" column—and the talks coming as frequently as this triple Lenten series indicates—with the worries of home, with the high nervous energy that churned up inside of him, Father Gillis suffered a minor breakdown. In 1933 he was hospitalized for six weeks. Recovery was slow, and it was decided in that year that when spring came he would be wise if he took some time off for his health. His illness had occurred early in the spring, and to facilitate his recovery he was given a trip as chaplain for a group of pilgrims going to Europe for the 1933 Holy Year.

Beyond the intense spiritual feelings that Father Gillis experienced in this trip was to be the thrill of being a member of a rather historic broadcast from the Italian liner *Rex* as it steamed into the Mediterranean and moved toward Rome. On April 7 the newspapers reported that there would be an attempt to pick up the broadcast by the American pilgrims and transmit it over the NBC network at six in the evening.

The next day's papers reported that the music and talks were startlingly clear in the pickup and the network was able to carry the full program across the country. Rosa Ponselle, the Metropolitan Opera soprano, sang Schubert's "Ave Maria,"

and the *Rex's* orchestra played Handel's "Largo." Both Father
Gillis and Michael Williams, the editor of *Commonweal*, spoke
and made a common plea that all Christians in Europe and
America unite against the common foes of religion.

James Gillis had looked forward to this trip, not only because of his health or because of the implications of visiting
Rome in the Holy Year, but also because he wanted to learn
firsthand the truth of the words and criticisms that he had been
leveling against Mussolini. As we have seen, it was from this
trip that his pessimism deepened concerning the possibilities
of avoiding war in the years ahead.

Father Gillis's reputation had flourished and become world-
wide. His popularity made him the ideal choice to deliver one
of the principal addresses at the International Eucharistic Congress to be held at Manila in 1937. Early in January of that year
he crossed Canada and embarked for Manila on the *Empress of
Japan.*

The oriental trip was an exciting one for Father Gillis, though
he himself indicates little of this fact. What information there
is comes from letters written by Minna Berger, one of his
close friends in San Francisco. Miss Berger describes aspects
of the voyage and tells of the splendid sermons Father Gillis
gave.

He had been asked originally to speak at the sectional meeting
for the American group at the Congress. While en route to
Manila the Paulist received a radio message asking if he would
add to the sectional talk another sermon that would be delivered
at the international meeting of all the delegates.

Of these sermons Minna Berger's letter states: "Father's talk
last night was inspiring and commanding. Without any question, in my opinion, the best speaker out here. His talk at the
Ataneo was most inspiring. I liked that best—it was on the
Mass."

James Gillis's success at the 1937 International Congress in Manila was to be followed by an invitation to speak at the 1938 Congress, which was to be held in Budapest. Attendance at the Budapest Congress had deep implications in 1938 for James Gillis. He had scheduled the first part of the trip through that section of Europe which was controlled by the Nazis. This could lead to difficulties for the outspoken critic of Adolf Hitler.

Father Gillis and a priest-companion were to travel through Germany to arrive at Budapest. The friend was not too happy about the fact that they would be asked at the German border to present passports. The name James Gillis on a passport might mean the internment of the Paulist editor—and friend. The man pleaded that they go by another route. The indomitable editor said he was going across Germany into Budapest or he was not going at all. The companion, figuring detour was the better part of valor, begged leave to go around Germany and enter Budapest by the longer southern route. Father Gillis bade him good-by, boarded the train, and passed through Germany without incident.

The great appeal of the Budapest visit was the opportunity to meet the priests and peoples of all nations and get the flavor of their opinions of world conditions. It was a stimulating time for the inquisitive and acquisitive mind of James Gillis. He stored the knowledge that he received and used all of it in the writings and lectures of the decade that followed his journey.

The traits that we have spoken of previously—Father Gillis's affectionate nature, his need of people, his warmheartedness despite the seeming aloofness of his manner—are highlighted when we study these trips he made. Many priests going on tour as spiritual directors often find that the work becomes a hard and annoying chore when they are at the behest of the people who are traveling with them. With Father Gillis it was exactly the reverse; he enjoyed the trips because of the com-

panions in his group. Records and reports show that he contributed immeasurably to the happiness of the people who were
with him.

Even with the voyage over, James Gillis maintained contact
with many of the people who had been in the parties he had
led. There are records of arrangements made for reunions or
get-together dinners of a group called Father Gillis's Pilgrims.
One of these dinners shows that there was a complete enter-
tainment list made out for the evening of the reunion. Each
member of the group was expected to perform some little act
or some little situation that would retell a part of the trip that
had been taken. The leader in encouraging these entertainments
was Father Gillis himself. Apparently he was most active in
keeping the evening alive by directing or managing the program so that all went off swiftly and humorously.

Quickly upon the completion of the second great Eucharistic
Congress which Father Gillis attended came the war in 1939.
All the hopes and prayers of the pilgrims to Budapest had to be
turned now to beg God for a sure and immediate peace. Father Gillis on the home front was traveling as much as ever,
working for his causes, becoming involved in all of the activities
we have considered previously.

In the years that followed these travels there were to come
the end of the *Catholic Hour* series, the Roosevelt controversy,
the haggling over isolationism, peace treaties, and the U.N.
Then, from the strains and tensions, came the little ills, the
recoveries, and ultimately the relapse to the major breakdown
that Monsignor Gibbons described.

Little by little all the signs were pointing to the fact that a
great man of the American Catholic Church was not as strong,
not as vigorous, not as powerful as he had been before. The
activities through the twenties and thirties and into the forties
—the torrid pace, the nerve-racking ordeals, the facing of public

issues that brought evident unpopularity—all of "the slings and arrows of outrageous fortune" were beginning to wear him down.

Much like a shooting star whose greatest burst of light is at the point when it reaches the zenith and from there on plunges downward to darkness, James Gillis's bursting light of activity and fame had reached its zenith and was now on the way down. He would be active through 1944 and '45, '46, and '47, but the activity would be crippled by a new disease that racked his body. In those years arthritis crept into his fingers and arms and legs and began to check the swift pace of James Gillis.

He would come to the table in the morning, after having said Mass, and where once he had been ready for conflict, argument, debate with his fellow Paulists on some issue, now he would seek a chair at the edge of the table and slowly sip his coffee or juice and not become involved. As he explained it, his mind did not work too nimbly until later on in the day, perhaps ten or eleven o'clock; then, with the blood flowing more freely, charging the cells of the brain, he would begin to sparkle. He would be ready to take on his correspondence or his "Sursum Corda" column or begin work on another article.

The slowing down that others saw and talked about was not something that James Gillis did not know himself. He was aware from the talks he had with his doctors, from the very feeling of the diminishing forces in his body, that there would not be many years for him to go.

With that good sense that he had manifested throughout his life, he decided that if he could not do the work and carry on the job of editing *The Catholic World* as it should be edited, then he must get out. In 1947, after he had returned from the National Eucharistic Congress in Buffalo, he asked that he be given an assistant. The Paulist Superiors appointed Father John Sheerin, who had been on the Paulist Mission Band and a professor at St. Paul's College, to understudy James Gillis until the older man should want to retire.

The old man wanted out in 1948. He knew that it was impossible and unnecessary for him to continue at *The Catholic World*. Twenty-six glorious years had been in his hands and he had not one regret for any of the things he had made or fashioned in those years. It was time to retire and he did so.

James Gillis continued the "Sursum Corda" column through the next seven years because, much as he might have wanted to lay down the editorializing pen and quit it all, he still was not able to let go completely. The sense of challenge and that great spirit and burning zeal for righting all the wrongs of the day— these compelled him to continue. Soon even this became an impossibility, and in 1955 he begged leave to drop the "Sursum Corda" column.

In a strange way he was getting ready to die. Much as a man takes stock of his life and counts the things he has done and decides to put his house in order, James Gillis was cutting away all the entanglements and ties that could bind him to earth. He was stripping himself of many of the exciting and eventful things he loved so dearly that he might come closer to God.

In the last years James Gillis turned to writings of a spiritual tone. He had doted on publishing these spiritual essays and was overjoyed when finally they appeared in book form. Almost like a sign that he knew he was loosing the bonds and slipping the ties of earth, he called his book *So Near Is God*. It would be two years later, in 1957, that God would be so near to James Gillis that he would see Him.

ACCENT ON AN IDEAL

---

chapter XI

On December 16, 1951, James Gillis was feted on the approaching occasion of his fiftieth year in the Catholic priesthood. The Paulist Superiors spared no effort to make the occasion one of the memorable moments in the life of the jubilarian. High point of the day was the bestowal of an honorary degree of Doctor of Sacred Theology from the Angelicum, the Dominican university in Rome. The Very Reverend Emanuele Suarez, Master General of the Dominicans, awarded the honor to Father Gillis in the presence of Francis Cardinal Spellman at St. Paul's Church in New York.

On the anniversary of his ordination, December 21, guests gathered for dinner in the great refectory of the Paulist Motherhouse. Father Gillis was prevailed upon to talk after the other speakers had had their say. He rose to address the silent, admiring group of friends who had paid him such fond and high tribute on this day.

The usually immobile countenance, the customarily stern-looking eyes, the stiffly straight back, and the strong voice were not as predominant in the mien of Father Gillis as he stood by the table. He was deeply touched by the words and the presence of these men. In the softness of his very soft heart there was nothing but the desire to cry out his thanks. He was grateful beyond thanks for the meaning these friends had given to this day.

In his heart, too, was the wonder if he had been worthy, not just of this present attention that had been paid to him, but of the priesthood in which he had labored. None of the tributes that had extolled his fifty years of service could convince him that he was as important or as great or as outstanding as these men had said.

A little story bringing out this fact is the byplay that took place between Bishop Fulton J. Sheen and Father Gillis on this occasion. Bishop Sheen told of the invitation extended to him by the Paulist Fathers to speak in the great Church of St. Paul at Fifty-ninth Street. He confessed that he had been fearful at the thought of stepping into one of the most hallowed pulpits in America. The Bishop ran off the names of the great Paulists who had preceded him. He concluded with the thought that even if none of these had made him tremble, certainly the realization that he was stepping into the pulpit hallowed by James Gillis caused him concern.

When Father Gillis replied to this story he said: "It was not at all as the Bishop recounts it." The jubilarian explained that the Bishop had not ended the story as any good storyteller should. He had failed to tell that though he had been afraid and had had misgivings about following any Paulist, let alone James Gillis, into the pulpit, the young Father Sheen had stepped up and made the people forget many of the Paulists and certainly James Gillis as preacher.

This Alphonse and Gaston routine drew a hearty laugh from the priests gathered in the dining room. Yet even as he bantered about his being forgotten Father Gillis admitted a grave doubt that he had written any lasting record. He laid no claim to having achieved any mark in the priesthood that could not be equaled or outdistanced by the zealous priests and bishops around the table. In fifty years of the priesthood, the humility that he had prayed for, the sense of littleness, and the fear of losing God—these stood him in good stead as he spoke.

When the jubilee day closed, Father Gillis's feelings were much the same as they had been on other occasions when something flattering was written or spoken about him. Once when he had come upon a complimentary piece about himself penned by one of the Paulist students he wrote to the young man, "I feel like the Irish bull—sure half the lies they tell about me aren't true. I feel that half the sweet things they say about me aren't true. But when a man manages to stumble through fifty years of the priesthood without falling into the hands of the police, I suppose compliments are inevitable."

The compliments of the fiftieth anniversary dinner celebration were unanimously the same despite Father Gillis's explanation of their inevitability. Constantly and unvaryingly as the speakers talked came the simple but stirring praise: "Gillis is a priest's priest" . . . "Father Gillis is a great priest" . . . "James Gillis is all priest" . . . "This is a priestly priest."

The tributes all carried that one stamp: whatever James Gillis was—an editor, a lecturer, a political or a non-political writer, a logician, an author, a preacher, a theorizer, a practical man— any one of a dozen labels—the one steady light that shone in his life was his priestliness. He was all priest.

The importance of those last four words is hardly indicated by their monosyllabic succinctness. A lifetime of prayer, sacrifice, study, and work can be spent trying to grasp one small measure of the import of what it means to be a priest. The sacrament of Holy Orders confers upon a candidate the priesthood. To possess the power of the priest, to be charged to say Mass and hear confessions and dispose people to receive the grace of God—these things are conferred by virtue of ordination. But to comprehend the priesthood and the meaning of being a part

of its gloriousness is something that can escape a man for all
his days after that ordination.

Father Gillis from his earliest years fought desperately to
understand the fullest implication of what it meant to be a
priest. One set apart from men for the things of God, a mediator
between God and men, another Christ, a bridge across which
men might walk to God—unraveling the mystery of all of these
and pin-pointing the essence of each one so that the priesthood
would be a reality—this was the thing that Father Gillis fought
to know and fought to hold and fought to live by.

If we return as far back as 1902 in the priesthood of Father
Gillis we find the demand upon himself to search out the meaning of his vocation. On August 21, 1902, James Gillis scribbled
in the front page of a retreat book these words: "My first retreat after ordination to the holy priesthood. Hence a chance to
recall my dispositions, my promises, my aspirations of the beginning of my life as a priest—a chance to nip in the bud whatever unpriestly vices may have begun to show themselves. . . .

"Perhaps during this period of thought and retirement I may,
please God it shall be so, learn something about prayer. I have
been reading not a little on the matter. I hardly dare say my
aspirations for progress in prayer have grown stronger—but I
do now pray God . . . that I may now at last begin to understand and to practice a better prayer than has been mine.

"As for the particular aims of this retreat . . . I think they
ought to be these—my efforts, all—all ought to aim at this, that
(1) I may better offer the all-Holy Sacrifice. (2) I may come to
a working plan with regard to mortification . . . (3) To arrive
at better grounded convictions of the nature of the priestly
office. My relations with God and with God's people depend
on my character as a priest."

That retreat from August 21 until August 28 of that year
moved through a series of conferences that sounded one theme
—the ramifications of the priestly vocation and the need to

possess the priestly virtues to the greatest extent. The resolution of all this thinking and meditating is found in a fervent passage that Father Gillis writes as he makes notes on one of his prayer periods: "I cannot believe that a priest can go through the course of his training and be ordained and exercise his ministry for any length of time without having had call after call to live not a respectable life but a holy life, not to be a man of work alone, but a man of prayer, to aim after perfection. There it is in black and white—to aim after perfection—he cannot have been without this call and he knows what it means—it means prayer, and the stricter, vigorous, searching fidelity to conscience and to God that prayer demands."

Twenty years later Father Gillis was asking of himself the fulfillment of the same demands to which his first retreat in the priesthood had inclined him. In 1922, making a retreat at Westhampton on Long Island, he writes more on the priesthood. Though the writing is not as copious as twenty years before, the lines are as great and majestic as the earlier lines in their command of his efforts to perfection.

In one of his meditations of this 1922 retreat he writes: "A priest ought to be in no place where his Master would not go and likewise do nothing that his Master would not do. . . . This means that a priest must be a saint—he cannot serve two Masters—to the priest 'One is your Master.' " Writing further in this meditation Father Gillis advances this statement: "Only the highest standard is possible—only the highest standard is permissible—always the priest, never a man of the world."

If we jump ahead about twenty more years, to the year of 1943, the consistent pattern of James Gillis's high regard for the priesthood and the need of sanctity in the priesthood is found in the funeral sermon he delivered over Father John F. Fenlon, the Provincial of the Sulpician Fathers. In the opening remarks of that sermon Father Gillis poses the question of what Father Fenlon would wish at this moment. The eulogist answers the question by saying that he knows very well what Father Fenlon's wish was concerning a sermon at his funeral. "Whatever you do," Father Gillis said Father Fenlon told him, "beware of eulogy; reserve panegyrics for the saints; you may take occasion of my demise to praise the things that I loved best, the Faith, the welfare of the Church; you may dilate upon the supernatural dignity of the priesthood and the consequent obligation of priests to be saintly."

Father Gillis then adds one parenthetical thought which indicates his feeling about his own death. He begs that when the time comes his eulogist will follow what he has proposed for Father Fenlon. "I would agree with him," says Father Gillis, "since indeed I desire similar treatment when someone else shall mount the pulpit and look down not upon his but upon my mortal remains."

This pattern which has been traced over twenty-year periods did not change in the remaining years of Father Gillis's life. Up to the end he carried the great thought that his concern and his vocation were to understand this supernatural dignity of the priesthood and the obligation of priests to be saints.

At one time one of his friends said to Father Gillis, "Why don't you give more retreats to priests?" Father Gillis answered, "I have given some, but in late years I have not been doing much of that work." "With these ideas," insisted the friend, "you should be giving priests' retreats." Father Gillis laughed and said, "With these ideas, I would be afraid to give priests' retreats—I think if I said some of my hard things to some of the men, I'd be stoned."

The statement was, naturally, an exaggeration. James Gillis would have been welcome on any priests' retreat because of the admiration the priests had for him and because of the priestliness in his character. He could not have helped transferring this quality into his conferences and manifesting it in his spiritual counsel.

If there was any situation in giving priests retreats for which James Gillis could have been stoned, it was not in the challenging things he might say or the severe critical attitude he might take. The one problem of his retreats was pointed up some years before his death when he conducted a retreat for the Paulist Fathers themselves at their summer home near Lake George in upper New York State.

Father Gillis opened the retreat in a very auspicious manner. He had promised to speak of the priesthood and in particular of the priesthood in relationship to the Paulist vocation. In the first talk an old Gillisan habit began to manifest itself and irk some of the priests. Anyone familiar with Father Gillis's writing or speaking would recognize the habit immediately: he was quoting short phrases, using Latin or Greek or French—whatever the particular language of the original—and he was translating the brief references for the benefit of the retreatants.

Many of the men sitting before him were Doctors of Theology, Doctors of Philosophy, instructors in the classics at the Paulist college. At least all the men had a seminary background and education equal to that of Father Gillis. As the opening day moved on, the conferences that succeeded the first one carried more instances of this little mannerism of James Gillis.

Some of the men, highly conscious of this habit, became restless, nodding toward each other each time Father Gillis indulged it. At the end of the last conference on that first day one man threatened: "If this keeps up, I am changing my retreat place."

By the next day the news of the threat had gone around among the priests and there was great anticipation as Father Gillis began the first talk. The opening paragraphs had no little foreign phrases and accompanying translations. Peace reigned supreme. Then, to illustrate a point and to underline the confirmation of a statement that he had made, Father Gillis re-

marked: "As Garrigou-Lagrange says, '*Mon Dieu.*' " A hush
fell on the chapel as the retreat master paused after that expression; then in a sonorous voice, unmindful of the threat
that had been made, Father Gillis translated the simple French
phrase, "My God."

Reporters say it was not audible but was quite evident that
the man who had become impatient with the irritating translations whispered his own "My God," and his facial expression
was not as reverent as the retreat master's.

On the next day after Mass a solitary figure, the threatener,
was seen going down the road to take a bus into the town where
he might entrain for another retreat stop. Rumor has it that ten
other men stood at the upper-floor windows and watched the
figure depart, envying him the courage of his conviction.

No Paulist was unaware of the deep perception that Father
Gillis had developed on his vocation to Sacred Orders. All the
men of the house realized that he was a match for even the
youngest in the fervor and devotion with which he approached
the Holy Sacrifice of the Mass. Often it was remarked that there
was little difference between the James Gillis who said his last
Mass and the James Gillis who offered his First Mass. Father
Gillis would approach the altar—his favorite altar at Fifty-ninth
Street being the altar of the Annunciation—with the same
measured step and sense of importance of his action as when he
had approached the altar in his home parish in 1901.

Mary and John Gillis had stressed the same characteristic.
James Gillis had never changed in the manner of offering Mass
from the time he was a young priest. Even in his last months
when he returned to Boston for the dedication of the center that
bears his name, his sister Mary said that "though Jim offered
Mass sitting down because of his illness, he was still precise and
careful and reverent to the point of awe."

There were many traits by which the Paulist Fathers recog-

nized the priestliness of their Father Gillis, but one of the outstanding characteristics was a very subtle clue that only a
family of priests can recognize and appreciate. Father Gillis had
an absorbing interest in the young priests stationed with him at
St. Paul's, and the counterpart of this clue is that the young
priests of the house had a deep and familial affection and admiration for the older man. His company was a delight, his
humor was always engaging and challenging, and his interest
was highly flattering to the junior members of the staff.

Father Gillis would take every opportunity that presented
itself at table or in common recreation to discover the interests
or the enthusiasms of the young men. He was not overbearing
in his advice to any of them but always judged carefully how
well the advice would be taken. Wary of offending, he was
ready to stimulate greater progress in priestly development
only if the young man responded to his attentions. On no occasion did he force the issue or act as the monitor of anyone's
life. If the priest showed reluctance or did not respond, Father
Gillis was quick to know it and sensitive enough to avoid giving
counsel in the future.

Father John Sheerin revealed that once James Gillis retired
from *The Catholic World* and stepped out of the office he
never criticized or interfered or meddled in magazine matters.
The new editor was on his own in his managing of the office and
staff which had been schooled under Father Gillis. At the same
time the older man was not unaware of what was going on, admitted Father Sheerin. Where and when help was needed,
help would come. The present editor of the magazine said that
on one occasion when a particularly annoying problem had
arisen, Father Gillis was among the first to offer his recommendations. He jotted a note to Father Sheerin suggesting how the
crisis could be handled. The letter closed with encouragement
to take the whole thing in stride as part of the business of growing old with a magazine.

One of the great assistances Father Gillis made to the young men was the aid he gave to those who were hopeful aspirants to the preaching and writing ministry. He must have recalled his own early days as a priest when he had repined over the lack of criticism and comment that could help him develop in his desire to be a missionary. Mindful of this handicap, he made the preaching of the young priests a particular interest of his. Those who showed even a slight enthusiasm or zeal for a mission career and a flair for preaching were sure to get a major share of Father Gillis's attention.

Customarily he would appear at the High Mass on Sundays when some one of the junior members of the house staff had been assigned to preach. He would listen carefully to the sermon, noting the matter and the delivery and the possibilities inherent in the young man. Deliberately he would take time out to give his opinion or his encouragement to the priest. In more than one case, when he found that the young Paulist was eager to be put on the Mission Band, Father Gillis went to the Superiors and petitioned them for the aspirant. He would repeat his petition until the priest was assigned to the missions for a trial at the work.

What Father Gillis did not do by direct word to assist the young priests to a better grasp of their vocation, he did by his example in the house. He had a great sense of Community spirit—not merely a pride in the Paulist Fathers but a sense of wanting to be with them in what they did and in the lives they lived.

Among the most entertaining recreations were the ones at which James Gillis participated when health allowed. He could be teased into launching forth on an argument, as we have seen, or, more to the enjoyment of the other priests, he could be coaxed into playing a game of pool. These games were turned into real contests when the side-line jockeys would rail scornfully at his lack of skill or his chances to win a game.

James Gillis would leave recreation as jubilant over winning a pool game as he might be over gaining a point in an argument. None of the triumphs he had enjoyed during his long active career exceeded in spirit the triumphs that he achieved over his younger challengers in a simple game of billiards.

The games typified every bit of the life of Father Gillis that was pointed out by Monsignor Gibbons from the time they met at St. Charles. The boy who had hated to lose the prize when he was in his first year of college was still to be seen flashing through these moments of Community recreation. The burning desire to be good and to excel came out in him over the simple execution of a maneuver in the game. He would be as chagrined over a bad shot and as articulately crestfallen over a poor position on the table as he could have been had he heard that Mussolini or Hitler had returned from the dead to head a government.

It reminds us of the excellence that had to be his playing handball, baseball, or football in the seminary; that excellence that had to be his writing an editorial or delivering a sermon; that excellence that drove him to do extra work, to be superior, to be a little better, to be the top in whatever he was doing.

This was not a matter of pride or vanity; it was not a childish and empty desire to be the best of the game so that superiority could be flaunted in the face of others. James Gillis was too spiritual a man to be lost in this kind of childish or petty vanity.

The question of being good in all the parts of his life started and ended with the notion of being good not for personal satisfaction but for the sake of God. This cry for perfection is seen in the resolutions and statements he formed about wanting excellence in the matter of mental prayer or contemplation.

Father Dunstan Dobbins, the Minister Provincial of the English Capuchin Fathers, writing at the time of Father Gillis's death, made this observation:

> God was very near to Father Gillis. He has always been in my mind when I have tried, however feebly, to deal with the problem of prayer, even with the problem of the mysterious Prayer of Quiet. For this man who was identified with an absorbing activity that would quite worthily have filled the lives of three can only be explained in the light of his cultivation of prayer.

The twenty-year periods we have used to sketch the idea of priestliness are much the same series that would be used to frame this argument of Father Gillis's prayerful life. One of the most important resolutions that James Gillis felt he had ever made was the one formed at the end of his seminary career when he commanded himself to practice fidelity to prayer. He believed firmly that the priest who avoided prayer was avoiding Christ and to a certain extent avoiding a check or a survey on his life. James Gillis maintained that there was something in such a man's life that was not particularly pleasing to him and that he would prefer not to face in the presence of his Master.

The intensity of James Gillis's fidelity to prayer can be known from the first half of his priesthood. Over twenty handwritten books deal with the daily meditations he had made. The meditations are written out quite completely. The resolutions of each meditation were set down dutifully so that there would be some practical application of the points on which he had prayed.

How faithful—almost scrupulous—Father Gillis was concerning this regular daily practice is gathered from looking at some of the copybooks where there are odd pieces of paper pasted in at certain points. Apparently for that day Father Gillis was either away from the house or engaged in some activity that did not permit him to attend the regular Community prayer time. The meditation itself, however, was not missed. These papers pasted in the notebook show that he must have made the prayer at some other time or in some other place, scribbled the gist of it on whatever paper was handy, and added it later to the book of meditations he was keeping.

Assiduousness to mental prayer and the demand that it be kept up were fostered by his constant reference to the need for mortification. With each resolution on prayer that he made he repeated the notion that there could be no progress in prayer and no union with Christ if there was attachment to bodily comfort or to material things.

His retreat journals show that he specified little mortifications for himself to be made at the table or in the pursuit of the common life. Beyond this there are the resolutions that he asked of himself to maintain a simplicity in his furnishings and in the effects he had for use in his room. The admirable part of these obligations is that they were made despite the fact that his body was scourged by a succession of ills that weakened his resources and caused him to need hospitalization, operations, and constant medical treatment.

In line with these ideas about James Gillis's presence at meditation, we might add this note concerning the years of his retirement.

There was no missing the fact that Father Gillis was present for prayer. In the last years of his life his voice had become very husky, and he had a great deal of trouble clearing his throat. You could always tell when Father Gillis was coming down the corridor or moving along the hall or entering the sacristy or the dining room. You heard this great clearing of the magnificent throat that was almost like a bark or the sounding of a horn for battle.

One of the places where the condition seemed most acute was in the chapel at prayer time. In the silence, with the lights turned down after the points of meditation had been read, the

Fathers would be startled into rigidity. This great roar would rise from his throat as he tried to clear it of its obstruction. This might be done once, twice, three times during the first half of meditation. It might be repeated three or four times in the second fifteen minutes of prayer time. Anyone with the slightest tendency to doze or the slightest desire to permit himself a drift into distractions would be brought sharply to attention as Father Gillis coughed and growled until he had cleared his throat.

The action annoyed many of the Fathers, and the annoyance is understandable. When one is trying to pray it can be a major distraction to have someone with the powerful lungs and throat of Father Gillis hacking and harrumphing as if he were strangling to death in the chapel darkness. But a point in favor of Father Gillis should be considered. He knew that his ailment was irritating to some of the Fathers and he was keenly sensitive to the fact that it was a distraction. It was as distressing for him to be so afflicted as it was irritating to the other priests to have him afflicted so. But Father Gillis knew he was to be at prayer, and when the bell rang for the observance, he would present himself morning and evening at the chapel. Throat closed or open, he would continue what he had always considered the great practice of his priesthood—to be a man of prayer.

Adherence to prayer must have been a struggle for Father Gillis. It is not an easy thing for anyone to place himself in the presence of God and to pray when his life is filled with distractions and activities, with crises and controversies. Father Gillis, as was remarked by Father Dunstan, crammed enough activity into his life to fill that of three people. This was certainly a handicap to making a consistent practice of prayer, but Father Gillis did fight the handicap that his life placed on him.

A sign of how some of the time away was spent in regard to prayer can be seen in a letter that was written by one of the voyagers on the trip Father Gillis made to Manila. The letter tells that each evening during the voyage Father Gillis would gather with some of the travelers and would preach a few points on a special subject and pause for a period of recollection. When the period was done he would offer another point of meditation and continue this until at least half an hour had been spent in making this daily prayer.

Another handicap James Gillis must have battled as he sought union with God was his warm nature that attracted him to people. He liked gatherings of friends; he liked formal dinners and the conversation and companionship of celebrated people—his was an outgoing nature. Such extrovertic tendencies present obstacles that are often insurmountable no matter how great the desire to be prayerful.

Yet there was no wrench in Father Gillis's character as he balanced his natural drift and his supernatural drive. James Gillis fought to have a life of prayer despite the affections and energies that tugged him in the opposite direction. The valorous accolade of his life is that he never quit the battle to overcome nature. To add insurance to his victory, he chose to join a religious Community and imposed upon his nature a rule of life that would channel his nature.

True, he was not bottled or contained by his Superiors. Father Gillis, in the years that we have discussed as the tempestuous twenty-six, was his own boss. It could be (and was often) said that he wrote his own ticket. This can be alleged as a severe criticism of James Gillis. He traveled the world; he met thousands of important people; his time, his schedule, his friends, his whole life were his own to determine and to decide.

The history of many such men is the story of tragedy—tragedy of indiscretions, tragedy of pride, tragedy of obstinacy when checked, tragedy of ultimate delinquency from duty. James Gillis portrayed none of these tragedies at the time he closed his career. The important tribute to James Gillis is the fact that with unlimited freedom, unchecked by Superiors, un-supervised, and allowed free reign, he might have written his own ticket—written it selfishly and badly—but he did not.

Though James Gillis did fairly much as he pleased, it never did please him to violate any of the serious obligations of his life in the Paulist Community. As a public figure there were no occasions when he was careless or indiscreet or foolish in using his position to foster personal ambition. In every year of the twenty-six he was a respected and highly regarded priest of the Church, and American Catholics give a multitude of testimonies that his life was a credit to the ranks of their priesthood.

The judgment on James Gillis in these years is better based on what he could have done and what he could have become had he been a man of less sterling character. We must face the fact that, when the days of activity were over, this was a good and exemplary and noble priest who had settled down to live the close life of the Community. If he had learned bad habits in his extrovertic-activist days, there was no evidence of these in the sense of poverty, the depth of chastity, and the grasp of obedi-ence that he possessed and demonstrated as an example to all—particularly the young men of the Community house.

One last aspect of James Gillis's ideal is left for consideration: how faithful was he to the Paulist facet of his life? The peculiar note of his Community's vocation is convert work. How did he live it?

From the first days of his mission life it was obvious that he adhered as closely as he could to the ideal set for him in the seminary. His mission sermons and instructions, his interest in the Question Box, his work with converts were all part of focusing on the great goal of the Paulists—Make America Catholic. The records of the twenty years of mission life show the pattern of consistency in staying with this ideal. When he moved to *The Catholic World* as editor, there seems to have developed a shift in the focus of his vocation.

The word *seems* is used because this last analysis maintains there was not a shift in the Gillis focus. He kept his sights on his Paulist ideal of convert work. His adjustment was in his field of vision, not in the vision itself.

Trained to the Paulist apostolate, the conversion of America, Father Gillis had instructed his converts, had baptized them, checked and watched to see that they persevered in the Faith. Moving out of situations where he could deal directly with converts, he must have been conscious that he was not engaged in the basic ministry of the Paulist Fathers, the making of converts.

Granted, this was something beyond his control because the work of editing *The Catholic World* made instruction and convert work almost prohibitive. James Gillis sought to adapt his new position to the apostolate of his Community. By chance he came to the reading of an article in which the author mentioned the fact that in the present day the non-Catholic was concerned not so much with distinctly Catholic dogmas as he was with the moral or religious implications of secular affairs.

The idea captured Father Gillis's imagination, and whether he argued himself into acceptance or forced his arguments a little bit to make the theory completely acceptable, he determined to use this method in reaching non-Catholics. In his own explanation (which he gave to one of the Paulists who was dealing with a non-Catholic problem and had asked Father Gillis to write on it) he admitted his preoccupation with matters that were regarded by many as secular. But having read of this new approach, he had determined to give a great deal of attention to secular matters because he felt that this was where he could reach the non-Catholics swiftly; in answering their immediate religious and moral problems he could prepare them to be receptive to the basic theological teachings of the Church.

It was something of a vestibule approach, a dealing with people who are not inclined to move inside the Church and see the glories within. Naturally, those seeing the man working always in the vestibule of the Church or constantly remaining to deal with people who were not in the Church would have a sharp reaction to such methods. Unless his reasons were known—that his activities were an attempt to lead others inside or to lead others to an appreciation of what was inside—then the natural criticism would be that he himself was more entertained and fascinated by being involved with interests only remotely connected with the Church.

This activity of James Gillis, wherein he dealt with the ethical or moral aspects of secular questions or issues, must have had its effect for good when it could be written at the end of his life by Father Manton that he was a priest "who did perhaps more good for the Church in the United States than any other priest in the last quarter century."

These words reaffirm the volumes of letters that are stacked high in James Gillis's files from people outside the Catholic Church. When he wrote on the Jewish question, Jewish leaders from all over the country commended him on the work he was doing. They spoke of the benefits that accrued to the Church by his manifesting the signs of charity and love for the cause of more toleration for the Jewish people. When he wrote on the Negro question and involved himself in controversies over injustices to Negroes, the leaders of that race matched the Jewish leaders in enthusiasm and gratitude for the positions he took to foster toleration for the Negro.

There is no record that any of these letter writers became Catholic. To measure in numbers the effectiveness of the good will and the goodheartedness that was developed by James Gillis in handling these issues is impossible and, to some extent, foolish. Father Gillis felt that the apostolate for the conversion of America depended upon many factors, and if he was preparing the way and others later reaped the harvest, then he did the part of the job that was assigned to him.

Father Gillis himself would have looked for more telling results had he remained in work that was connected directly and specifically with the apostolate of conversion. His opening remarks in 1950 at a speech in Syracuse to the Confraternity of Christian Doctrine prove this:

> The danger to Catholics is not that they snatch the lead from the clergy and the hierarchy, but that they don't follow when the hierarchy leads. Invited to take part in some great movement—to be specific, the conversion of America to the Faith—they hold back and say, "Let the priests and the bishops attend to it; we are only the laity." It is like saying that the Mystical Body of Christ could exist and thrive, half dead and half alive. That Body which is the Church must be alive from the core of its heart to the tips of its fingers. Otherwise, whatever work the Church has to do, for example, the conquest of Communism, or the almost equally difficult job which concerns us here and now, the job of persuading our separated brethren of the truth of Catholicism, will not be done. The conversion of America is not a merely ecclesiastical project.

In the March 1954 issue of the Paulist paper, *Techniques for Convert Makers*, Father Gillis is reprinted on much the same theme. In an article taken from *The Thomist* magazine, in which he deals with the sacrament of Confirmation, James Gillis says, speaking of the coming of the Holy Ghost:

> There were none of the faithful who escaped the fiery tongues, none who escaped this power from on high, none who avoided the obligation consequent upon this gift— the apostolate. This was the birthday of the Church, and it was marked by the mobilization of the infant Church to battle.

In his own Community Father Gillis was considered a leader in convert work. His early life shows the constant attempt on missions to insert non-Catholic topics. His reputation will always stand as one of the first who tried the great non-Catholic missions in New York City. With Father Conway he had that spirit of adventure which tried evangelism in New York City long before techniques had been developed to popularize evangelism—and that spirit never quit him.

Any new idea that was offered by younger Paulists was earnestly considered and discussed by Father Gillis. When the ideas were not forthcoming, he himself would propound possible plans of action so that convert work could flourish on a greater and more impressive scale. One of his dreams was to hire a huge auditorium, much like the Garden in Boston or New York, advertise the mission throughout the city, bring in five or six of the top preachers in the country, and conduct a city-wide mission for Catholics. Though the plan was never tried and the scheme never really picked up enough force to get off the ground, the wisdom of the plan was vindicated a season or so back when one leading evangelist did hire the New York Garden and for week upon week was able to draw hundreds of thousands of people to hear his message.

Father Gillis himself during the years of his traveling and lecturing and editorial work was not involved heavily in the instruction of converts. To search the baptismal book, one would wonder, seeing the few times that Father Gillis's name appears, whether or not he was truly interested in converts despite all of his preachment and encouragement on the situation.

Father Gillis was interested but could not possibly handle the calls that came to him requesting instruction. Rather than stall the work and hamper the people in their desire to learn and embrace the Faith, James Gillis would turn the inquirer over to one of the priests set aside for that specific task. He took none of the credit, he asked none of the recognition, he was pleased in the sense that the work was going on much in keeping with the words of St. Paul: "I have planted, Apollos watered, but God has given the growth."

The summation of Father Gillis's interest in convert activity and convert work even up to the last years of his life is perhaps best found in the statement of Father John A. O'Brien, himself a great convert worker in the past decades.

Father O'Brien conducts a weekly syndicated column on the winning of converts. At the time that James Gillis retired from his "Sursum Corda" column, Father O'Brien devoted his whole column to the convert-making life of the Paulist. Father O'Brien explained that, though the column was usually some story about conversion, he felt it necessary to make exception in this instance and give the column to Father Gillis.

His argument was that in any column on the winning of converts the story of Father Gillis belonged absolutely. He indicated how the whole life of the Paulist priest had been spent in gaining souls for Christ. Like all the members of the Paulist Community, Father Gillis had been filled with the Community zeal to bring the truths of Jesus Christ to the churchless millions of America.

SO NEAR IS GOD

---

chapter XII

Father Gillis retired from *The Catholic World* in 1948 to write. The sentence makes a strange impression after we have considered twenty-six years of writing for a monthly magazine and more than thirteen hundred "Sursum Corda" columns, adding to that the incidental (hardly a correct choice of word since *incidental* does not describe the *extra* writing that Father Gillis did) articles and pieces and reviews and criticisms that came from his ready pen. We have, as James Gillis's files indicate, mountains of written material that seem to make a mockery of his retirement to write.

Yet the desire and the will to write were the explicitly stated reasons behind James Gillis's resignation. In the opening paragraph of his last editorial for *The Catholic World* he says:

> Perhaps I owe the regular readers of these editorial columns a statement of my reasons for resigning. I need not, thank God, allege ill health. Nor do I feel—though perhaps I deceive myself—that my mental vitality has so notably declined as to make me unfit to continue. But for some years past I have desired time to devote to a different type of work. Just as every "ham" actor hopes not to die until he has played Hamlet, I suppose every writer, no matter how amateurish, cherishes the ambition to be the author of a book. I mean a real book, not a compilation of editorial

comments or of platform speeches upon evanescent happenings, but something substantial on a subject of lasting importance. If the writer is a priest, he desires above all to produce something on religion or theology. . . . In other words he would like to write what Catholics call a "spiritual book." Such—may it please those who have been patient enough over the years to be faithful readers of these editorials and kind enough to say that in general they enjoyed the reading—such and nothing else whatever is the reason I give up this kind of writing and pray to be spared to take up another.

There was little doubt in the years and the months prior to the moment of retirement that Father Gillis eagerly looked forward to the writing of this book. Frequently he would chat about the prospect and explain each time that his great urge through all the last years had been to get at a work of this sort. Part of his feeling, and evident as he expressed it, was the sense of chagrin that he had waited until his seventies before getting down to what he truly believed was an important bit of writing.

On many occasions he fervently exhorted younger Paulists who were interested in writing, "Don't wait until you are too old to write your book. Write it now while you are alert and vigorous and have the ability to keep at the hard work that is necessary to finish a book."

Father Gillis was truly dissatisfied with most of the writing he had produced up to this point—dissatisfied in the sense that it did not meet the standard he set for achieving a real spiritual book in his life. His editorial comments in the quotation above indicate that he was aware of the limitations of the books he had published through the years of his priesthood.

His most popular book, *False Prophets*, did not satisfy him because it was more philosophical than spiritual. Two large volumes of collected editorials under the title, *This Our Day*, were no better in Father Gillis's eyes than *False Prophets*. All these writings were clear, incisive, powerful, and set in the classic Gillis style. All of them bore the marks of thoroughness and erudition that so distinguished the Paulist's composition. Very few men of the past fifty years were as well equipped as James Gillis to deal with the issues of the day, spiritual or political or social.

The simplest indication of how much resource Father Gillis could draw on is seen in a story that Monsignor Gibbons tells about his being with Father Gillis at the time he was to give an important talk. He came into James Gillis's room just as his friend was to leave for church. He watched the Paulist busily picking up paper after paper that had been spread across the desk. Father Gillis leafed the collected pages together and touched them to the desk rapidly to square the edges.

Monsignor Gibbons was surprised at the number of papers. "Is that your speech, Jim?" he asked.

Father Gillis smiled and said, "No. If it were, it would take me a couple of days to deliver it. These are simply notes I've made on background material. I must have it at my fingertips before I would dare to give this talk. I will be plagued with questions and inquiries once this is over. People will ask where I got this fact or how I found this information or what is my authority for this or that statement I make. I want all the answers on this subject because I'll be bothered by many of the questions that come up concerning it." When Father Gillis prepared a sermon or a lecture—he was thoroughly prepared.

The material he had gathered was not something discarded. The things Father Gillis absorbed from his preparations were retained in his mind and flashed forth in his writings on occasion after occasion. The matter of preparation and the depth of resource can be seen if we pick up one of his editorials at random and check the variety of background references that Father Gillis makes on just one subject.

Take for example an editorial of September 1941. Skimming through the piece is worth the exercise for anyone interested in realizing how well Father Gillis was grounded in the information he was using in this editorial.

The title of the September piece is "Propaganda: Latest Style." In the second paragraph there is a quotation from President Wilson, a recommendation to read Sir Philip Gibbs's *Now It Can Be Told* and *More That Must Be Told*, and also a recommendation to read Ponsonby's *Falsehood in War-Time*.

The next page carries a reference to a newspaper interview with Cardinal Mercier; this is followed by a quotation from James Bryce; then later on a reference to Walter Lippmann; a follow-up with a quotation from Senator Walsh of Massachusetts; after this an extended quotation from Anne O'Hare McCormick; beyond her words are the remarks of Mr. Churchill.

The editorial continues, and there is a reference from Shakespeare; in the paragraph following there is a statement out of St. Thomas Aquinas; this is followed by a remark from Justice Oliver Wendell Holmes; then a comment on an editorial of the New York *World-Telegram*; after this an analysis of the Hutchins poll which concerned our involvement in war; and the next reference is to Etienne Gilson's *Christianity and Philosophy*.

Moving down to the end of the piece, there is a statement of Benjamin De Casseres; this remark is followed by a quotation from the *Herald Tribune*; this is followed by remarks from the New York *Times*; and in conclusion a quotation from the book *Christianity and Crisis!*

Remember this list is not an indication of quotations being sprinkled about to impress the readers. Father Gillis's editorial ran somewhere around five thousand words, and these quotations are woven skillfully into his own argument throughout the whole composition.

Father Gillis's own ideas and his own thoughts were the basic frame of his writings. He could and did use the ideas of others to bolster or advance a point he was making in his own debate. The number of names and articles and books indicated above was a common occurrence in any of the writings or speeches of James Gillis. They are a partial reference file of the voluminous reading and note-taking that he practiced all his writing life.

But erudite and thorough as all his works might have been, James Gillis could not be satisfied until he sat down to write that one spiritual book he had dreamed of all his life. The completing of this book was not to be an easy task. Father Gillis had been used to the active life. Total retirement to write was not achieved with the cutting of the strands that bound him to *The Catholic World*. His preaching diary shows that he had signed up for lectures and talks and retreats covering almost sixteen months beyond his retirement. All these engagements must be fulfilled before he could settle down and give his full attention to the writing of his book.

Five years passed before *So Near Is God* appeared. Many of the reviewers—and the book was widely reviewed—approached the volume with some misgiving. The remarks in some reviews indicated a predisposition not to accept the writing of Father Gillis and an intention not to let him share any thoughts with the reviewers. As one man phrased it: "Not sharing Father Gillis's political inclinations, I confess that I approached his latest book with something less than enthusiasm." This reviewer and the others who had not reached for the book with great interest or enthusiasm were forced at the end of their reading to admit that this was a Gillis they had never dreamed existed.

The summation of all the reviews was that this book would be most rewarding to the reader. The commentary was universally on the plus side. There was a tone of admiration at the greatness of life manifested in the book. Many expressed delight that James Gillis had taken the time out to record his ideas on man's relationship to God and his need of unity with Him, and with few exceptions the critics heartily recommended *So Near Is God* for its content and form and praised it as one more witness to the contribution that James Gillis had made to American Catholicism.

Father Gillis was interested in the reviews and the way the book would be accepted; but it was evident that, whether accepted or not, he had a sense of having achieved something that gave him a great satisfaction in the late years of his life. His reaction to comments about the book were accepted with the readiness and eagerness of a man who was turning out his first, not close to his last, piece of copy.

The publication of the book gave Father Gillis that sense of accomplishment that he had lamented when writing his final editorial for *The Catholic World*. When you talked to him and spoke about the book and its sale, you caught the impression that he was really saying behind his answers: "I have done it— I have finally done it. Sales or no sales, I have written the one book that all my life I yearned to get into print."

Yet, pleasant as was the experience of having the book in print, Father Gillis was not content that this should be the last of his spiritual works. Even while he had been waiting for *So Near Is God* to come off the press, he had already begun jotting down ideas for another book, which appeared in 1957 under the title *This Mysterious Human Nature*.

Despite the years of writing and the editorials and columns that James Gillis had turned out, he was best known as preacher and as a Paulist missionary. This is something that cannot be fathomed and cannot be analyzed and cannot be categorized. If the popular imagination retains an impression of James Gillis as a speaker, that must be admitted as the impact that he made on the people. It is the memory that they retain and pass down to the younger generation. It is no mean impact to have made. James Gillis would rest contented in the knowledge that he would be described as a great missionary even though he might be flattered by the thought that he would be remembered as a great spiritual writer.

Anyone who knew Father Gillis realizes that he was, first and foremost, a preacher—he was a personality that had to be seen and heard to be appreciated fully. Even when you read his editorials or his columns you can hear behind the paragraphs and sentences the orotund phrasings of the speaker. You catch, as if in echo, the sharp, clear call of his voice to follow God; you feel the deliberate, sure, and measured movement of his preaching.

In the best sense of the word, Father Gillis was more the player than the playwright. He was born to move down an aisle and strike a pose and lift his head and look out in silence on an audience until the coughing and the hacking had stopped and quiet expectancy gripped a congregation. He was meant to talk, and the gift of the great voice—which he himself said had never been trained—was as good a sign as anything else that God intended him to be a preacher.

A further analysis that has been given as to why James Gillis is remembered as a preacher says: "In his preaching he was identified with spiritual values while in his writing he was identified with political issues." He himself would have been the first to recognize that his political work, even directed to moral values, was a transient and temporary thing, meeting only the need of the moment, something which in the quick tempo of our times could be outmoded with the coming of the next decade. In his preaching he worked with the eternal, unchanging truths. Their glowing brilliance captured his own soul and carried across in his message—his preaching partook of the enduring memorableness of the truth itself.

There is every good reason to believe that had *So Near Is God* been poorly received James Gillis would have gone on undaunted. He had never sought recognition in any of his works. In a human way he liked interest, he liked comment, and he liked compliment and admiration. But in the serious sense he was a big enough priest and a great enough Paulist to know before God that the work of the Paulist Fathers had to go on whether James Gillis was recognized or not.

Yet recognition came to him a hundredfold from the people who had read him or heard him and from the honors and awards that had been bestowed on him through the years in his work. He had been cited on hundreds of occasions by authorities in every field in which he had dealt. He was given untold recognition in the requests for him to address or grace dinners, meetings, convocations, and congresses.

There was almost no phase of his life, no enterprise in which he had engaged, that had not selected him for its greatest tribute. In June 1955, the Catholic Institute of the Press, of which he was a vigorous member, presented him with a scroll that carried their words and their belief on what his activities had meant to them. The commendation he received reads in glowing terms:

> As an editor, author, and columnist he has exerted a blessed influence for a more extended time over more persons than any other religious journalist of his generation.
>
> As an Apostle of all channels of communication, he has been a modern St. Paul, unwavering in principle, resolute against injustice, wise in counsel, and, amid the tragedy of our times, communicating to his readers and auditors that serenity of soul that flows from his Christlike charity.

In February 1955, upon his retirement from the "Sursum Corda" column he was honored by the men with whom he had been associated in his more than quarter century of press activities. At that time Mr. Patrick Scanlon, managing editor of the famous *Tablet*, the Brooklyn diocesan newspaper, testified to the great popularity of Father Gillis among readers of his paper. He said that there would not be a successor to James Gillis in this generation.

He was accorded the same degree of tribute and honor by the Knights of Columbus. From his early missionary days James Gillis had a warm feeling for the Knights. They had been among the first to rally to his and Father Conway's aid when the missionaries were presenting their non-Catholic services in New York City. Much of the leg work, much of the financial interest had come from the Knights, and Father Gillis never forgot this encouragement.

He was always interested in the Knights' activities, always eager to be a part of their meetings, ready to attend and to take part in their forums, willing on any occasion to foster the great work the Knights did for the advancement of the Catholic Church in America. In return for his untiring fidelity to the organization of which he was a Fourth Degree member, James Gillis was given by the Knights a solid-gold card on which was inscribed the perpetual membership they wished him to enjoy in the organization.

In the matter of recognition, perhaps the most significant words on whether James Gillis wanted it or not were uttered by Father Gillis himself in 1955, two years before his death. At that time, when he was writing the last "Sursum Corda" column, he put down these words:

> It has often been rougher. Time was when hostile criticism of this column outweighed approbation. But for the last few years, and especially in recent months, the bouquets have outnumbered the brickbats by a hundred to one. Indeed of late the commendations of my point of view in regard to national and international affairs have been so laudatory as to be embarrassing. In fact many persons have written in to say that to them this column has become indispensable. Of course it isn't. All writers and speakers are expendable.

Father Gillis was well aware that approbation had not always been his and was not entirely his even at the time that he was writing this final column. His quotation reveals that he had opponents who disagreed with him heatedly on many issues. He had critics among the clergy and among the lay people, even to the last of his days.

The critics were strong and they were sharp and, in some cases, they carried a justifiable rightness and correctness for their opinion. On some issues where James Gillis was apodictic and intransigent, he had no right to be. Some of the issues concerning world politics—the United Nations, the question of American isolation—on these things James Gillis was unmovable and unyieldingly antagonistic, and on these he was criticized seriously for being outmoded.

This last criticism was a little bit of the truth—or, as the strongest opponents of James Gillis saw it, a lot of the truth. There were many who thought that the parade had slipped ahead of Father Gillis for the first time in his life as he came to these final years.

This matter of being outdated was noticeable also in his preaching, which hewed to a style and length that had gradually fallen by the wayside. He was still as vigorous, still as strong, still as firm and dynamic in the pulpit or on the platform as he had ever been. Unfortunately he was still as long as he had ever been, and the time consumed in his speeches was more than the generation of the fifties could take.

Perhaps this, more than his ideas and philosophy on world politics, was the thing that caused some of the critics to say that James Gillis was behind the times. On many issues he still kept abreast of the times and on many issues he was still in the forefront of the parade—still able to fathom the situation and to point out things which others persisted in not seeing or not wanting to see.

In spiritual matters—in his retreats or in his sermons—he was

certainly not outmoded. He was long and he was criticized
for being long, but he was in demand even until 1956. During
the years after his retirement from *The Catholic World* he continued the preaching pace that he had maintained in his most
vital periods. His book of preaching assignments and engagements shows a constant series of dates, listings on where he
traveled, and the subjects on which he spoke. Spiritual topics
predominate, and the book shows more engagements for retreats and special-occasion sermons. Notably during these years
there is an increase of his speaking at forums and discussions
concerning problems in the matter of modern living and the
Christian life.

A few of the forums retained the old issues on political ideas
or philosophies, problems of the world's being confronted by
communism. The notations on them, however, do not seem to
have the fervor, the stress, or the intensity of those of twenty
or more years back.

This relaxing of that driving restlessness to set right the
whole world is understandable when we consider that during
these late years of the forties into the fifties, James Gillis was
passing through his seventy-first to his eightieth birthday. He
was settling back to look over his life, to consider the things
that must be righted in himself before the end would come, and
he did not fool himself that he had years upon years in which to
work out all of the desires of his soul.

In 1945 the Paulist Fathers had asked James Gillis to take
upon himself a begging mission. Thinking of new foundations,
they asked him if he would go to Boston and petition Archbishop Richard Cushing to accept the Paulist Fathers and their
work in his diocese.

Archbishop Cushing was eager to have the Paulists and told
Father Gillis that they were very welcome. He was enthusiastic about the possibilities of bringing the Community to Bos-

ton and expanding the convert apostolate in the archdiocese. Three buildings were purchased on historic Park Street opposite the Boston Common, and the Paulist Center became a reality.

Convert work progressed at the Center to such a degree that expansion became a mounting necessity. Archbishop Cushing agreed to the need of enlarging the scope of the Paulist work, but he had his own ideas on the matter.

The Archbishop had been moved deeply when Father James Gillis retired from writing his "Sursum Corda" articles. The prelate was determined that as the valiant Paulist moved into that shadowland where he would no longer be a prominent speaker and writer, he would not be forgotten. In January 1955, while broadcasting at a Boston radio station, WMEX, the Archbishop announced a new and surprising plan. He expressed the hope that the new project of the Paulist Fathers on Park Street would become a completed dream in 1958, when the Paulists would celebrate the hundredth year of their existence as a Community. Then came his great surprise—His Excellency requested that in view of the distinguished service to the Catholic Church that James Gillis had rendered for over fifty years, he wanted the new center to be called the Father Gillis Catholic Center.

Father Gillis was overwhelmed and pleased by this announcement of the Archbishop. He was grateful beyond expression for the tribute, but he hoped that the center would be known as the Paulist Center or the Catholic Information Center. Father Gillis did not guard jealously the hope that it would be the Father Gillis Center.

It did not seem that he would ever see the completion of the center that would bear his name. Through all of the forties and fifties his health had become a very delicate thing. Arthritis had gripped him strongly—so badly one year that it had been impossible for him to return home for Christmas in 1948, a practice which he had tried to keep up since his parents' death.

The year after this the arthritis was so severe that he was forced to the hospital for seventeen weeks and managed no activity except the continuance of his "Sursum Corda" column. With all his will he tried desperately to make a recovery. Progress was slow and incomplete. Still suffering, he finally quit the hospital and went back to his work of preaching and writing his articles.

The ill health that had plagued him all his life was a strong enemy of the man who had known always activity and more activity. He spoke or he wrote in these years, pain a frequent irritating companion. Days would go by when he would have to permit himself complete rest before he could return to accepting engagements for talks in the cities all over the country where he was in demand. He managed to carry on through the early fifties. Suddenly, in 1956, he was struck down and incapacitated more seriously than he had ever been before.

No one knows how hard, how difficult this time was for James Gillis. All his life he had dreaded an illness that would deprive him of his faculties. Now God asked him to accept a cross that was as bad and as serious as any he had ever dreaded he might be expected to carry. The stroke had impaired his speech and his alertness. It had left him weak and unable to move about without a cane. And this was the saddest to watch: James Gillis, heavy-tongued, slow-thinking, reduced to a cane, moving haltingly behind a world for which he had set the tempo.

Even the interior fires that had burned brightly and kindled interest after interest seemed now to have come down to nothing but dead ash. When Father Gillis returned from the hospital after this illness and was placed in the infirmary section of the Paulist house, he appeared to have no care for any of the things that had made his life so vibrant. The sixty-odd years of history that had coursed through his mind and had quickened his blood seemed to mean nothing to him.

Monsignor Gibbons came to New York at this time to be of some assistance, if he could, to the great companion of his own priesthood. He shuddered to see the brilliance and glow of this man reduced to nothing but a shadow. Aided by Father McSorley, he demanded that James Gillis get paper and pencils, that he get books and put them in his room and sit down and work. The two old friends were determined that James Gillis shake off this pall of lethargy and disinterest which seemed to have caught him and seemed to be suffocating the very life of the man who had been so vital.

The determination worked. James Gillis did snap back into some of his own manner and some of his own style. To everyone's delight, he returned with a certain gusto to the feelings and interests that had been his before. He began work on another series of spiritual reflections.

The fond hope of all Father Gillis's friends was realized when his doctor agreed that he was strong enough to make the journey to Boston. Their one last wish was that he would be able to say a few words. They knew that he had returned from grave illness to a likeness of the vigor that was once his, but they were not unmindful that a talk could be far beyond his strength. It would be no easy task to stand up on a platform outdoors and speak to the great crowd that would be massed for the dedication of the center.

He entrained for Boston accompanied by Father Vincent Holden, one of the younger Paulists. Father Gillis was still feeble enough to need all the assistance afforded him.

At the time of the dedication Monsignor Hickey gave the benediction, and then James Gillis was announced. Everyone watched the old, shrunken man leaning on his cane snap to attention as the introduction was made. A thrill went through the priests and the people as the erectness and the stiffness, the military bearing that had been James Gillis's came to play as he stood before the crowd. As Monsignor Gibbons would have expressed it, the old war horse smelled the scent of battle and was ready.

James Gillis was ready—but for no more at that time than a fond expression of gratitude to the Archbishop for his kindness to himself and to the Paulist Fathers. And then he thanked his family. There was a sense that though his brother and sister were present and he was mentioning them, he was looking off beyond their presence to the mother and father to whom he had lived as if in debt. Emotionally and reverently he expressed thanks for the gifts of life and the opportunity for the priesthood they had made to him.

The speech was very short, perhaps the shortest that Father Gillis had delivered in many a year, but it was intensely filled with all that he felt at that moment. The speech he made at the dedication of the center that would bear his name was not about kings or presidents, it was not about politics or politicians, it was not about wars or rumors of wars, it was not about issues or crises; it was a few paragraphs of thanks—the expression of gratitude from a heart that was bursting with the sense of what was owed to all those who had made his priesthood possible.

The talk had meant much to Father Gillis, but the only note that indicates he had a sense of being the missionary or lecturer of the old days—the only note that showed his remembrance of the days when he had stood before thousands in Europe, in America, in the Philippines, before armies in battle camp, before bishops and before the humblest of people—was his remark at the end of the ceremony that he thought he had detected a little of the old timbre in his voice. What more permissible vanity could there be than this? Of all the things he might cherish at the end, how fitting that it should be that great voice by which he had served his church and his God so zealously.

Father Gillis came back to New York and seemed to be in better spirits and in better health than he had ever been before. The interests that he had always had were now alive. The opinions, the ideas, the fixed notions about the world and all of its politics and all of its prospects and future—these things absorbed him for a little bit.

Suddenly, in the early part of 1957, he was taken sick and brought to the hospital. He had a bad siege, seemed to weather it, and had recovered sufficiently to be considered out of danger. Then, without warning, on March 14, a little after noon, he relapsed critically and died.

The end, which had been expected for some time and which all knew could not be postponed much longer, still came as a shock to the Paulist Community, to the bishops, priests, and people who loved James Gillis. It came as a shock even to those who, if they had not loved him, had come to admire him.

Telegrams, letters, telephone calls poured in to the Paulist Fathers. All were in tribute to James Gillis. Columns and editorials of the Catholic papers—and a few secular ones—added their praise to the eulogies.

The tributes, brief or extended, all resolved to one awareness: a true American, a great churchman, an apostolic Paulist had left us—and he would be missed. He had been a giant in his time—and the death of a giant leaves a large place to be filled.